THE CHILDREN
OF DICKENS

DAVID COPPERFIELD AND PEGGOTTY BY THE PARLOUR FIRE

THE CHILDREN OF DICKENS

Samuel McChord Crothers

Illustrations by
Jessie Willcox Smith

Published by arrangement with
Charles Scribner's Sons

Academy Chicago Publishers

Published in 1999 by
Academy Chicago Publishers
363 West Erie Street
Chicago, Illinois 60610

By arrangement with Charles Scribner's Sons.

The section on Pip has been edited by Anita Miller.

Printed and bound in the U.S.A.

Library of Congress Cataloging-in-Publication Data

Crothers, Samuel McChord, 1857-1927.
    The children of Dickens / Samuel McChord Crothers ; illustrations
by Jessie Willcox Smith.
        p. cm.
    Summary: Retellings of portions of books by Charles Dickens,
featuring such memorable characters as David Copperfield, Oliver
Twist, and the Jellyby family. Includes background information on
the novels.
    ISBN 0-89733-475-2
    [1. England—Fiction.] I. Dickens, Charles, 1812-1870.
    II. Smith, Jessie Willcox, 1893-1935, ill. III. Title.

PZ7.C883 Ch 1999   99-010244

CONTENTS

LIST OF ILLUSTRATIONS

DICKENS HIMSELF

I

DICKENS HIMSELF

I once sat with several thousand people on one summer evening to watch an historical pageant at Warwick in England. Back of us were the walls of the great Norman castle, around us were the old trees that had been there for centuries, and through the trees we could see the little River Avon. Then the townspeople acted out for us the romantic scenes that had taken place on that very spot. First we saw the Druids building their altars; then the Romans came; and after them the Saxons. After a while we saw Norman knights riding under the greenwood trees. Warwick the king-maker rode up to his castle. Then there was a stir on the river, and we saw Queen Elizabeth in her barge. When she had been received in state, the officers of the neighboring towns were presented to her. Among them was Mr. Shakespeare from Stratford, who brought with him his young son, William. Then came Cromwell's soldiers and the men who have made history since Queen Elizabeth's day.

It was all very picturesque, and we felt that we were really watching the events that had taken place on that spot through the centuries of English history. But when the Druids and the Saxons and the Normans and the great personages of every degree had passed out of our sight, there was only one person left. It was the little boy from Stratford. He stood there all alone, thinking it all over. Then he walked away.

Now the thing that made the most impression upon us was this boy who had the gift of seeing all we saw and more in his imagination. For, after all, the great thing about the River Avon is that this boy once played upon its banks. And the pleasant Warwickshire country has for its chief charm the fact that William Shakespeare knew it and loved it.

Now and then a person is born who has the gift not only of seeing things more clearly than we do, but of making us see them more vividly than we could without his help. Such a person we call a genius. He gives us the use of his mind. When such a person writes a book, it is as if he had created an interesting country and filled it with all sorts of things for our amusement. He invites us to visit him and make ourselves at home. And the best of it is that we are not invited for a particular day. The invitation is open to us for a lifetime. Whenever we feel inclined, we may visit Shakespeare's country and meet all the Shakespearian people and listen to their talk. And the more often we go on such visits, the more enjoyment we find.

Now it is the same with Dickens. To be sure, his hospitality is not on so grand a scale as Shakespeare's. He does not show us kings, or knights in armor, or vast parks and lordly castles. But he opens to us a world of imagination that is his own. It is filled with common people, but they are uncommonly amusing. We see not only what they are doing, but also what they think they are doing, which is often absurdly different. We see their "tricks and their manners" as they cannot possibly see them. That is where we have the advantage of them. Some of them strut about as if they owned the earth, while some that wear poor clothes and endure hard knocks turn out to be the real heroes. Dickens is not like some writers who pride themselves on not telling what they think of their characters. He has his likes and his dislikes, and he doesn't care who knows it. He hates a bully, whether he is a man or boy, and he loves the people who knock the bully down. That is because he suffered so much from bullies when he was a boy.

THE CHILDREN OF DICKENS

When he was twelve years old, his father lost his money and was thrown into a debtors' prison. It was a queer way they had then of treating a person who couldn't pay his debts. They shut him up where he couldn't earn anything. Charles had to visit pawn-shops to try to borrow money for the family. Then he was put to work in a big, gloomy establishment where they made blacking for shoes. His work was to sit all day on a bench pasting labels on the boxes. Then he would have to find ways of keeping alive on a few pennies he got each day.

But though he had a very hard time for a year or two, he spent his time greatly to his own and our advantage. Before he was thirteen, he had accumulated a great deal of experience. He had kept his eyes open and had seen a side of life at most people never see at all.

Dickens sees so much more in his characters than other persons would who did not have his advantages. He does not look down on his characters. He meets them on their own level, because he has been there. And so he makes us see them.

He learned very early that, no matter where a person is, he is always the centre of his little world. He always has something that he is afraid of and always has something that he hopes for. And he learned to sympathize not only with the big hopes and fears but with the little hopes and fears. They are the things which wise people often overlook, but they are really very important, for there are so many of them.

Dickens did not write children's stories—that is, stories about children who stayed as children. Of course there are children in his novels just as there are in the London streets—plenty of them. But they are all mixed up with the older people. And then they are all the time growing up just as they do in real life. You get acquainted with a small boy in one chapter; and the next time you meet him he is at boarding school, and before the end of the book he is out walking with children of his own.

This is the reason why it would not be worthwhile to try to tell the stories of the children in the novels of Dickens. The moment you got to the most exciting part of the story you would find that they weren't children at all. They are quite grown up.

When we sit down by the fire on a winter evening, someone says: "What shall we read? We haven't time to read a book through—only a chapter." Now the chances are that we choose a chapter from Dickens. And it's very likely that we will choose some scene which we all are most familiar with.

THE CHILDREN OF DICKENS

We come into an inn. The coach has just arrived, and there is a cheerful bustle. We hear the blowing of the horns and the cracking of the whips, and if Mr. Weller happens to be driver, or if Mr. Pickwick and his friends happen to be on board, we are sure that we will be left in a state of great good humor.

Or we drop into a shabby little house, and climb the stairs till we come to a room where some of our friends are having a little dinner. They are making speeches to one another, and acting in a most extraordinary manner. It's their way of having a good time, and we are glad that they can enjoy themselves over so little.

We hear people quarrelling and crying and laughing, and we are curious to know what it is all about. The best of it is that Dickens always tells us. If a man is a villain, we see it at once; and if he is a good-hearted person, we give him credit for it. We do not have to read the book through to get the flavor of it. We go at once to the scenes that please us best.

The scenes that are selected for this book are those in which children appear, and we want to see them as Dickens did.

PIP

II

PIP

As I have said, almost all the Dickens people lived in London or went up to it sometimes. But all were not born there, and many of them, as children, lived in little villages. When they got to be seventeen or eighteen, they went to the great city to seek their fortunes.

There was Pip. I don't care so much for him after he grew up. When he got to London he became very much like other folks. I like him best when he was a small boy in the country.

His name was Philip Pirrip. This was hard to pronounce, and puckered up the lips like "Peter Piper picked a peck of peppers." The best he could make of it was Pip, and so everybody called him that for short.

His father and mother had died, and he was brought up by his older sister, who had married Joe

Gargery, the blacksmith. She was twenty years older than Pip and had forgotten how she felt when she was his age. This made trouble for them both.

Pip had a hard time with Mrs. Gargery, and so had Joe, and so they became great chums. Joe was a big man, and his arms were strong, as all blacksmiths' are, but he had never learned to read and write, though he knew some of the letters of the alphabet and was very proud over that.

The house where the Gargerys lived was in the marsh country near a river. One could look out on a dark flat country with little ditches running through it in every direction. It was a place where one could easily get lost, and where robbers could hide. There was a prison ship down near the mouth of the river, and now and then some of the prisoners would escape and get into the marsh.

* * * * *

Once, Pip tells us, he was down in the churchyard visiting the graves of his parents when . . .

I heard a terrible voice say "Hold your noise!" as a man started up from among the graves at the side of the church porch. "Keep still, you little devil, or I'll cut your throat!"

PIP AND JOE GARGERY

A fearful man, all in coarse grey, with a great iron on his leg. A man with no hat, and with broken shoes, and with an old rag tied round his head. A man who had been soaked in water, and smothered in mud, and lamed by stones, and cut by flints, and stung by nettles, and torn by briars; who limed, and shivered, and glared and growled; and whose teeth chattered in his head as he seized me by the chin.

"O! Don't cut my throat, sir," I pleaded in terror. "Pray don't do it, sir."

"Tell us your name!" said the man. "Quick!"

"Pip, sir."

"Once more," said the man, staring at me. "Give it mouth!"

"Pip. Pip, sir."

"Show us where you live," said the man. "Pint out the place!"

I pointed to where our village lay, on the flat in-shore among the alder-trees and pollards, a mile or more from the church.

The man, after looking at me for a moment, turned me upside down, and emptied my pockets. There was nothing in them but a piece of bread. When the church came to itself—for he was so sudden and strong that he made it go head over heels before me, and I saw the steeple under my feet—when the church came to itself, I say, I was seated on a high tombstone, trembling while he ate the bread ravenously.

"Now lookee here!" said the man. "Where's your mother?"

"There, sir!" said I.

He started, made a short run, and stopped and looked over his shoulder.

"There, sir!" I timidly explained, pointing to the graves. "Also Georgianna. That's my mother."

"Oh!" said he, coming back. "And is that your father alonger your mother?"

"Yes, sir," said I; "him too; late of this parish."

"Ha!" he muttered then, considering. "Who d'ye live with—supposin' you're kindly let to live, which I han't made up my mind about?"

"My sister, sir—Mrs. Joe Gargery—wife of Joe Gargery, the blacksmith, sir."

"Blacksmith, eh?" said he. And looked down at his leg.

After darkly looking at his leg and at me several times, he came closer to my tombstone, took me by both arms, and tilted me back as far as he could hold me; so that his eyes looked most powerfully down into mine, and mine looked most helplessly up into his.

"Now lookee here," he said, "the question being whether you're to be let to live. You know what a file is?"

"Yes, sir."

"And you know what wittles is?"

"Yes, sir."

After each question he tilted me over a little more, so as to give me a greater sense of helplessness and danger.

"You get me a file." He tilted me again. "And you get me wittles." He tilted me again. "You bring 'em both to me." He tilted me again. "Or I'll have your heart and liver out." He tilted me again.

I was dreadfully frightened, and so giddy that I clung to him with both hands, and said, "If you would kindly please to let me keep upright, sir, perhaps I shouldn't be sick, and perhaps I could attend more."

He gave me a most tremendous dip and roll, so that the church jumped over its own weather-cock. Then, he held me by the arms in an upright position on the top of the stone, and went on in these fearful terms:

"You bring me, tomorrow morning early, that file and them wittles. You bring the lot to me, at that old Battery over yonder. You do it, and you never dare to say a word or dare to make a sign concerning your having seen such a person as me, or any person sumever, and you shall be let to live. You fail, or you go from my words in any partickler, no matter how small it is, and your heart and your liver shall be tore out, roasted and ate. Now, I ain't alone, as you may think I am. There's a young man hid with me, in comparison with which young man I am an Angel. That young man hears the words I speak. That young man has a secret way pecooliar to himself, of getting at a boy, and at his heart, and at his liver. It is in wain for a boy to attempt to hide himself from that young man. A boy may lock his door, may be warm in bed, may tuck himself up, may draw the clothes over his head, may think himself comfortable and safe, but that young man will softly creep and creep his way to him and tear him open. I am keeping that young man from harming of you at the present moment, with great difficulty. I find it wery hard to hold that young man off of your inside. Now, what do you say?"

I said that I would get him the file, and I would get him what broken bits of food I could, and I would come to him at the Battery, early in the morning.

"Say, Lord strike you dead if you don't!" said the man.

I said so, and he took me down.

"Now," he pursued, "you remember what you've undertook, and you remember that young man, and you get home!"

"Goo-good-night, sir," I faltered.

"Much of that!" said he, glancing about him over the cold wet flat. "I wish I was a frog. Or a eel!"

At the same time, he hugged his shuddering body in both his arms—clasping himself, as if to hold himself together—and limped towards the low church wall. As I saw him go, picking his way among the nettles, and among the brambles that bound the green mounds, he looked in my young eyes as if he were eluding the hands of the dead people, stretching up cautiously out of their graves, to get a twist upon his ankle and pull him in.

I looked all round for the horrible young man, and could see no signs of him. But now I was frightened again, and ran home without stopping.

It was Christmas Eve, and I had to stir the pudding for next day, with a copper stick, from seven to eight by the Dutch clock.

"Hark!" said I, when I had done my stirring, and was taking a final warm in the chimney-corner before being sent up to bed; "was that great guns, Joe?"

"There was a conwict off last night," said Joe, "after sunset gun. And they fired warning of him. And now it appears they're firing warning of another."

I was afraid to sleep, even if I had been inclined, for I knew that at the first faint dawn of morning I must rob the pantry.

As soon as the great black velvet pall outside my little window was shot with grey, I got up and went downstairs; every board upon the way, and every crack in every board, calling after me, "Stop thief!" and "Get up, Mrs. Joe!" I stole some bread, some rind of cheese, about half a jar of mincemeat, some brandy from a stone bottle, a meat bone with very little on it, and a beautiful round compact pork pie. I was nearly going away without the pie, but I was tempted to mount upon a shelf, to look what it was that was put away so carefully in a covered earthenware dish in a corner, and I found it was the pie, and I took it, in the hope that it was not intended for early use, and would not be missed for some time.

There was a door in the kitchen communicating with the forge; I unlocked and unbolted that door, and got a file from among Joe's tools. Then I put the fastening as I had found them, opened the door at which I had entered when I ran home last night, shut it, and ran for the misty marshes.

DAVID COPPERFIELD

III

DAVID COPPERFIELD

Dickens makes David Copperfield tell the story of his life. He begins at the beginning and tells everything that happened to him as a boy, the places where he lived, and the people whom he met. There are few persons whom we can know as thoroughly as David Copperfield. It is all the more lifelike because many of the scenes are taken from the life of Dickens himself.

David's father had died and his mother had married again. His stepfather, Mr. Murdstone, a gentleman with very black hair and whiskers, was all that a stepfather ought not to be, so that David was happiest when he was away from home.

Happily he had a nurse, who was big and good-natured and really loved David. Her name was Clara Peggotty, but they always called her Peggotty. Her home was in a town by the sea. Mr. Peggotty and his nephew Ham and a despondent old lady named Mrs.

Gummidge lived in a houseboat on the shore. David was about seven years old when he went with Clara on a carrier's cart to visit the Peggottys.

Ham met them as they got off the cart. He was a great big fellow, six feet tall, and he carried David's box under his arm, while Peggotty trudged along through the sand at his side. There was a fishy smell about everything. There were boats and fishermen's nets scattered about, and an air of pleasant disorder. Everybody seemed to have all the time there was in the world, and nobody was hurried. Evidently Yarmouth was a very pleasant place for a boy on his vacation. There was plenty of room to play in, and no Mr. Murdstone to make him afraid.

"Yon's our house, Master Davy," said Ham.

David looked out and saw a barge high and dry on the beach, with a snug little house built upon it. There was a stovepipe with smoke was coming out of it. When they came up, they found everything was as pleasant as could be. There was a door on one side and tiny little windows. On the mantelpiece was a Dutch clock, and the table had all the tea-things on it.

Peggotty opened a door to show David his bedroom. It was in the stern of the boat where the rudder used to be. There was a little window and a little look-

LITTLE EM'LY

ing-glass framed with oyster-shells and a tiny bed, and there was a blue mug filled with fresh seaweed.

Pretty soon Mr. Peggotty, Peggotty's older brother and the master of the house, came in. "Glad to see you, sir," said Mr. Peggotty. "How's your ma? Did you leave her pretty jolly?"

David gave him to understand that she was as jolly as could be wished.

"Well," said Mr. Peggotty, "if you can make out here for a fortnut, 'long with her," pointing to his sister, "and Ham, and little Em'ly, we shall be proud of your company."

When I spoke of the people who lived on the old boat, I had forgotten to mention little Em'ly, who turned out to be the most important member of the family in David's eyes. She was a very pretty little girl, who wore a necklace of blue beads, and thought that she would like to be a lady and marry a prince, or even an earl.

"If I was ever a lady," said Em'ly, "I'd give Uncle Dan," that was Mr. Peggotty, "a sky-blue coat with diamond buttons, nankeen trousers, a red velvet waistcoat, a cocked hat, a large gold watch, a silver pipe, and a box of money."

David thought that was very fine, though it was easier for him to think of Em'ly as dressed like a princess in the fairy books than it was to think of big Mr. Peggotty walking about in a red velvet waistcoat and a cocked hat. As for little Em'ly marrying a prince, that seemed all right if David could be the prince.

All of the Peggotty family were so healthy and cheerful that even Mrs. Gummidge, who lived with them, could not make them unhappy. Mrs. Gummidge was a person who felt that it was necessary to have someone to pity, and as she couldn't pity the Peggottys she got into the habit of pitying herself. She would sit by the fire, and take out an old black handkerchief, and wipe her eyes, and tell her troubles, and then tell how wrong it was in her to tell them.

Mr. Peggotty had just come in from his work, having stopped a few moments at the public house, which was called The Willing Mind. Mrs. Gummidge was wiping her eyes.

"What's amiss, dame?" said Mr. Peggotty.

"Nothing," returned Mrs. Gummidge. "You've come from The Willing Mind, Dan'l?"

"Why yes, I've took a short spell at The Willing Mind to-night," said Mr. Peggotty.

"I'm sorry I should have drove you there."

"Drive! I don't want no driving," returned Mr. Peggotty. "I only go too ready."

"Very ready," said Mrs. Gummidge. "I am sorry that it should be along of me that you're so ready."

"Along of you! It ain't along of you! Don't you believe a bit of it."

"Yes, it is," cried Mrs. Gummidge. "I know what I am. I know I'm a lone lorn creetur, and not only that everythink goes contrairy with me, but that I go contrairy with everybody. Yes, I feel more than other people do, and I know it more. It's my misfortune. I feel my troubles, and they make me contrairy. I wish I didn't feel 'em, but I do. I wish I could be hardened to 'em, but I ain't. I make the house uncomfortable. I don't wonder at it. It's far from right. It ain't a fit return. I'm a lone lorn creetur, I'd better not make myself contrairy here. If things must go contrairy with me, and I must go contrairy with myself, let me go away."

But Mrs. Gummidge had no idea of going away to the poorhouse, as she always threatened; and the Peggottys had no idea of letting her leave their cheerful little home. It was Mrs. Gummidge's way of carrying on conversation, and they had got used to it.

The delightful visit to Yarmouth came to an end, and after a time Mr. Murdstone sent David to a school near London. We can see the shy little boy starting off for his first journey alone in the big world.

DAVID COPPERFIELD

It was in the inn at Yarmouth that David fell in with a jolly waiter who ate up his dinner for him. David was very much afraid of doing something which he ought not to do. Everything seemed so big and strange.

THE LITTLE BOY AND THE HUNGRY WAITER

The waiter brought me some chops, and vegetables, and took the covers off in such a bouncing manner that I was afraid I must have given him some offence. But he greatly relieved my mind by putting a chair for me at the table, and saying, very affably, "Now six-foot! come on!"

I thanked him, and took my seat at the board; but found it extremely difficult to handle my knife and fork with anything like dexterity, or to avoid splashing myself with the gravy, while he was standing opposite, staring so hard, and making me blush in the most dreadful manner every time I caught his eye. After watching me into the second chop, he said: "There's half a pint of ale for you. Will you have it now?"

I thanked him and said "Yes." Upon which he poured it out of a jug into a large tumbler, and held it up against the light, and made it look beautiful.

"My eye!" he said. "It seems a good deal, don't it?"

"It does seem a good deal," I answered with a smile. For it was quite delightful to me to find him so pleasant. He was a twinkling-eyed, pimple-faced man, with his hair standing upright all over his head; and as he stood with one arm akimbo, holding up the glass to the light with the other hand, he looked quite friendly.

"There was a gentleman here, yesterday," he said, "a stout gentleman, by the name of Topsawyer—perhaps you know him!"

"No," I said, "I don't think—"

"In breeches and gaiters, broad-brimmed hat, gray coat, speckled choker," said the waiter.

"No," I said bashfully, "I haven't the pleasure—"

"He came in here," said the waiter, looking at the light through the tumbler, "ordered a glass of this ale—*would* order it—I told him not—drank it, and fell dead. It was too old for him. It oughtn't to be drawn; that's the fact."

I was very much shocked to hear of this melancholy accident, and said I thought I had better have some water.

"Why, you see," said the waiter, still looking at the light through the tumbler, with one of his eyes shut up, "our people don't like things being ordered and left. It offends 'em. But *I'll* drink it, if you like. I'm used to it, and use is everything. I don't think it'll hurt me, if I throw my head back, and take it off quick. Shall I?"

I replied that he would much oblige me by drinking it, if he thought he could do it safely, but by no means otherwise. When he did throw his head back, and take it off quickly, I had a horrible fear, I confess, of seeing him meet the fate of the lamented Mr. Topsawyer, and fall lifeless on the carpet. But it didn't hurt him. On the contrary, I thought he seemed the fresher for it.

"What have we got here?" he said, putting a fork into my dish. "Not chops?"

"Chops," I said.

"Lord bless my soul!" he exclaimed. "I didn't know they were chops. Why, a chop's the very thing to take off the bad effects of that beer! Ain't it lucky?"

So he took a chop by the bone in one hand, and a potato in the other, and ate away with a very good appetite, to my extreme satisfaction. He afterwards took another chop, and another potato; and after that another chop and another potato. When he had done, he brought me a pudding, and having set it before me, seemed to ruminate, and to become absent in his mind for some moments.

"How's the pie?" he said, rousing himself.

"It's a pudding," I made answer.

"Pudding!" he exclaimed. "Why, bless me, so it is! What!" looking at it nearer. "You don't mean to say it's a batter-pudding!"

"Yes, it is indeed."

"Why, a batter-pudding," he said, taking up a table spoon, "is my favorite pudding! Ain't that lucky? Come on, little 'un, and let's see who'll get most."

The waiter certainly got most. He entreated me more than once to come in and win, but what with his tablespoon to my teaspoon, his despatch to my despatch, and his appetite to my appetite, I was left far behind at the first mouthful, and had no chance with him. I never saw anyone enjoy a pudding so much, I think; and he laughed, when it was all gone, as if his enjoyment of it lasted still.

Finding him so very friendly and companionable, it was then that I asked for the pen and ink and paper to write to Peggotty. He not only brought it immediately, but was good enough to look over me while I wrote the letter. When I had finished it, he asked me where I was going to school.

I said, "Near London," which was all I knew.

"Oh! my eye!" he said, looking very low-spirited. "I am sorry for that."

"Why?" I asked him.

"Oh, Lord!" he said, shaking his head, "that's the school where they broke the boy's ribs—two ribs—a little boy he was. I should say he was—let me see—how old are you, about?"

I told him between eight and nine.

"That's just his age," he said. "He was eight years and six months old when they broke his first rib; eight years and eight months old when they broke his second, and did for him."

I could not disguise from myself, or from the waiter, that this was an uncomfortable coincidence, and inquired how it was done. His answer was not cheering to my spirits, for it consisted of two dismal words: "With whopping."

The blowing of the coach horn in the yard was a seasonable diversion, which made me get up and hesitatingly inquire, in the mingled pride and diffidence of having a purse (which I took out of my pocket), if there were anything to pay.

"There's a sheet of letter-paper," he returned. "Did you ever buy a sheet of letter-paper?"

I could not remember that I ever had.

"It's dear," he said, "on account of the duty. Three pence. That's the way we're taxed in this country. There's nothing else, except the waiter. Never mind the ink. I lose by that."

"What should you—what should I—how much ought I to—what would it be right to pay the waiter, if you please?" I stammered, blushing.

"If I hadn't a family, and that family hadn't the cow pock," said the waiter, "I wouldn't take a six-pence. If I didn't support an aged pairint and a lovely sister,"—here the waiter was greatly agitated—"I wouldn't take a farthing. If I had a good place, and was treated well here, I should beg acceptance of a trifle, instead of taking it. But I live on broken wittles—and I sleep on the coals"—here the waiter burst into tears.

I was very much concerned for his misfortunes, and felt that any recognition short of ninepence would be mere brutality and hardness of heart. Therefore I gave him one of my three bright shillings, which he received with much humility and veneration, and spun up with his thumb, directly afterwards, to try the good-ness of.

OLIVER TWIST

IV

OLIVER TWIST

Oliver Twist was born in a poorhouse, where his mother died. The superintendent, Mr. Bumble, was a detestable man, who did all that he could to make the paupers in his institution even more unhappy than they were. He fed the boys on very thin gruel and gave them very little of that. One day when he was particularly hungry, Oliver said: "Please, sir, I want some more."

Every one was horrified, and poor Oliver was beaten and shut up in a little room where he could meditate on his sin. Soon after, he was given into the hands of Mr. Sowerberry who was as cruel as Mr. Bumble himself. The upshot of it was that Oliver put a crust of bread, a shirt and two pairs of stockings in a bundle, and ran away. Of course, there was only one place to run away to, and that was London.

Oliver had been six days on the London road when he limped into the little town of Barnet. There he met a boy of his own age, who was the queerest-looking creature he had ever seen. His name was Jack Dawkins, but he was known by all the people who knew him as the Artful Dodger. He was a snub-nosed boy with a dirty face. His hat was on one side of his head and was always about to fall off. He wore a ragged coat which was too large for him, and had turned the coat-sleeves back half-way up his arms.

"Hullo, what's the row?" said the Artful Dodger.

"I am very hungry and tired. I have walked a long way. I have been walking seven days."

"Walking for sivin days! Come, you want grub, and you shall have it."

He took Oliver into a little shop and bought some ham and bread, which was quietly devoured.

"Going to London?" said the strange boy.

"Yes."

"Got any lodgings?"

"No."

"Money?"

"No."

The strange boy whistled; and put his hands into his pockets, as far as the big coat-sleeves would let them go.

"Do you live in London?" inquired Oliver.

OLIVER'S FIRST MEETING WITH THE ARTFUL DODGER

"Yes, I do, when I'm at home," replied the boy. "I suppose you want some place to sleep in to-night, don't you?"

"Yes, I do," answered Oliver. "I have not slept under a roof since I left the country."

"Don't fret your eyelids on that score," said the boy. "I've got to be in London to-night; and I know a 'spectable old genelman as lives there, wot'll give you lodgings for nothink, and never ask for the change; that is, if any genelman he knows interduces you. And don't he know me? Oh, no! Not in the least! By no means. Certainly not!"

So Oliver Twist went with the Artful Dodger through the narrowest and crookedest streets in London till he came to the house of old Fagin, who kept a school for pickpockets. Every day the boys would be sent out on the streets and would come home at night with pocket-handkerchiefs and purses which they had snatched from people in the crowds.

Five or six boys were in the room, and Fagin was cooking sausages in a frying-pan.

"This is him, Fagin," said the Artful Dodger; "my friend Oliver Twist."

Fagin grinned, and shook hands. "We are glad to see you, Oliver. Dodger, take off the sausages and draw a tub near the fire for Oliver. Ah, you're a-staring at the pocket handkerchiefs! eh, my dear? We've just looked 'em out, ready for the wash; that's all, Oliver; that's all."

Oliver wondered very much why they had so many handkerchiefs. Fagin employed him in picking out the marks in them, and that kept him busy for several days. One day he went out with the Artful Dodger and his friend Charley Bates. Dickens tells the story of their adventure:

*　　*　　*　　*　　*

The three boys sallied out; the Dodger with his coat sleeves tucked up, and his hat cocked, as usual; Master Bates sauntering along with his hands in his pockets; and Oliver between them: wondering where they were going: and what branch of manufacture he would be instructed in, first.

The pace at which they went, was such a very lazy, ill looking saunter, that Oliver soon began to think his companions were going to deceive the old gentleman, by not going to work at all. The Dodger had a vicious propensity, too, of pulling the caps from the heads of small boys and tossing them down areas; while Charley Bates exhibited some very loose notions concerning the rights of property, by pilfering divers apples and onions from the stalls at the kennel sides, and thrusting them into pockets which were so surprisingly capacious, that they seemed to undermine his whole suit of clothes in every direction. These things looked so bad, that Oliver was on the point of declaring his intention of seeking his way back, in the best way he could; when his thoughts were suddenly directed into another channel, by a very mysterious change of behavior on the part of the Dodger.

They were just emerging from a narrow court not far from the open square in Clerkenwell, which is yet called, by some strange perversion of terms, "The Green," when the Dodger made a sudden stop and, laying his finger on his lip, drew his companions back again, with the greatest caution and circumspection.

"What's the matter?" demanded Oliver.

"Hush!" replied the Dodger. "Do you see that old cove at the book-stall?"

"The old gentleman over the way?" said Oliver. "Yes, I see him."

"He'll do," said the Dodger.

"A prime plant," observed Master Charley Bates.

Oliver looked from one to the other, with the greatest surprise; but he was not permitted to make any inquiries; for the two boys walked stealthily across the road, and slunk close behind the old gentleman towards whom his attention had been directed. Oliver walked a few paces after them; and, not knowing whether to advance or retire, stood looking on in silent amazement.

The old gentleman was a very respectable-looking personage, with a powdered head and gold spectacles. He was dressed in a bottle-green coat with a black velvet collar; wore white trousers; and carried a smart bamboo cane under his arm. He had taken up a book from the stall, and there he stood, reading away, as hard as if he were in his elbow-chair, in his own study. It is very possible that he fancied himself there, indeed; for it was plain, from his utter abstraction, that he saw not the book-stall, nor the street, nor the boys, nor, in short, anything but the book itself; which he was reading straight through; turning over the leaf when he got to the bottom of a page, beginning at the top line of the next one, and going regularly on, with the greatest interest and eagerness.

What was Oliver's horror and alarm as he stood a few paces off, looking on with his eyelids as wide open as they would possibly go, to see the Dodger plunge his hand into the old gentleman's pocket and draw from thence a handkerchief! To see him hand the same to Charley Bates; and finally to behold them, both, running away around the corner at full speed!

In an instant the whole mystery of the handkerchiefs, and the watches, and the jewels, rushed upon the boy's mind. He stood, for a moment, with the blood so tingling through all his veins from terror, that he felt as if he were in a burning fire; then, confused and frightened, he took to his heels and, not knowing what he did, made off as fast as he could lay his feet to the ground.

This was all done in a minute's space. In the very instant when Oliver began to run, the old gentleman, putting his hand to his pocket, and missing his handkerchief, turned sharp round. Seeing the boy scudding away at such a rapid pace, he very naturally concluded him to be the depredator; and, shouting "Stop thief!" with all his might made off after him, book in hand.

But the old gentleman was not the only person who raised the hue-and-cry. The Dodger and Master Bates, unwilling to attract public attention by running down the open street, had merely retired into the very first doorway round the corner. They no sooner heard the cry, and saw Oliver running, than, guessing exactly how the matter stood, they issued forth with great promptitude and, shouting "Stop thief!" too, joined in the pursuit like good citizens.

Although Oliver had been brought up by philosophers, he was not theoretically acquainted with the beautiful axiom that self-preservation is the first law of nature. If he had been, perhaps he would have been prepared for this. Not being prepared, however, it alarmed him the more; so away he went like the wind, with the old gentleman and the two boys roaring and shouting behind him.

"Stop thief! Stop thief!" There is a magic in the sound. The tradesman leaves his counter, and the carman his wagon; the butcher throws down his tray; the baker his basket; the milkman his pail; the errand-boy his parcels; the schoolboy his marbles; the pavior his pickaxe; the child his battledore. Away they run, pell-mell, helter-skelter, slap-dash: tearing, yelling, and screaming: knocking down the passengers as they turn the corners, rousing up the dogs, and astonishing the fowls: and streets, squares, and courts re-echo with the sound.

"Stop thief! Stop thief!" The cry is taken up by a hundred voices, and the crowd accumulates at every turning. Away they fly, splashing through the mud, and rattling along the pavements: up go the windows, out run the people, onward bear the mob, a whole audience desert Punch in the very thickest of the plot, and, joining the rushing throng, swell the shout, and lend fresh vigor to the cry, "Stop thief! Stop thief!"

"Stop thief! Stop thief!" There is a passion *for hunting something* deeply implanted in the human breast. One wretched breathless child, panting with exhaustion; terror in his looks; agony in his eyes; large drops of perspiration streaming down his face; strains every nerve to make head upon his pursuers; and as they follow on his track, and gain upon him every instant, they hail his decreasing strength with still louder shouts, and whoop and scream with joy. "Stop thief!" Ay, stop him for God's sake, were it only in mercy!

Stopped at last. A clever blow. He is down upon the pavement; and the crowd eagerly gather round him: each newcomer, jostling and struggling with the others to catch a glimpse.

"Stand aside!"

"Give him a little air!"

"Nonsense! he don't deserve it."

"Where's the gentleman?"

"Here he is, coming down the street."

"Make room there for the gentleman!"

"Is this the boy, sir!"

"Yes."

Oliver lay, covered with mud and dust, and bleeding from the mouth, looking wildly round upon the heap of faces that surrounded him, when the old gentleman was officiously dragged and pushed into the circle by the foremost of the pursuers.

"Yes," said the gentleman, "I am afraid it is."

"Afraid!" murmured the crowd. "That's a good 'un."

"Poor fellow!" said the gentleman, "he has hurt himself."

"*I* did that, sir," said a great lubberly fellow, stepping forward; "and preciously I cut my knuckle agin his mouth. *I* stopped him, sir."

The fellow touched his hat with a grin, expecting something for his pains; but the old gentleman, eyeing him with an expression of dislike, looked anxiously round, as if he contemplated running away himself: which it is very possible he might have attempted to do, and thus afforded another chase, had not a police officer (who is generally the last person to arrive in such cases) at that moment made his way through the crowd, and seized Oliver by the collar.

"Come, get up," said the man, roughly.

"It wasn't me indeed, sir. Indeed, indeed, it was two other boys," said Oliver, clasping his hands passionately, and looking round. "They are here somewhere."

"Oh no, they ain't," said the officer. He meant this to be ironical, but it was true besides; for the Dodger and Charley Bates had filed off down the first convenient court they came to. "Come, get up!"

"Don't hurt him," said the old gentleman, compassionately.

"Oh no, I won't hurt him," replied the officer, tearing his jacket half off his back, in proof thereof. "Come, I know you; it won't do. Will you stand upon your legs, you young devil?"

Oliver, who could hardly stand, made a shift to raise himself on his feet, and was at once lugged along the streets by the jacket-collar, at a rapid pace. The gentleman walked on with them by the officer's side; and as many of the crowd as could achieve the feat, got a little ahead, and stared back at Oliver from time to time. The boys shouted in triumph; and on they went.

OLIVER TWIST

*   *   *   *   *

Fortunately this time things turned out for the best for Oliver. The old gentleman, whose name was Brownlow, believed his story and took him to his own home, where he treated him as if he were his own son. They lived in a pleasant house on a quiet street, and Mrs. Brownlow was as kind as her husband.

This was only one of the adventures of Oliver Twist. He always seemed to be falling in with unusually bad people, and then being rescued by unusually kind people, who lost no time in receiving him as one of the family. The changes in his fortune were as sudden as those in the *Arabian Nights*. But then everything came out right in the end.

THE JELLYBY CHILDREN

V

THE JELLYBY CHILDREN

To know the Jellyby children you must know their mother. Mrs. Jellyby had a very kind heart and wanted to do good. Unfortunately the people she wanted to do good to lived a long way off. This was very inconvenient, as it was very difficult to get at them, especially as she didn't know their names or what they looked like. The people she was particularly interested in lived in Borrioboola-Gha, on the left bank of the Niger, in Africa. Mrs. Jellyby had to write a great many letters to all sorts of people about the state of things in Borrioboola-Gha, and this took up the time she might otherwise have given to her children.

What Mrs. Jellyby would have done if she had lived in Africa, we do not know. But in London she didn't find much to interest her: everything was too near. So the little Jellybys were left to grow up as best they could. There was no one whose business it was to see that they were properly fed or clothed or taught how to behave. Mrs. Jellyby couldn't look after them, because she was too busy making plans for the Africans. And Mr. Jellyby couldn't do it, for he had to listen to Mrs. Jellyby and do errands for her. So nobody did it, and the little Jellybys got on as best they could, which was not very well.

In *Bleak House,* Dickens makes Miss Summerson tell of her visit to Mrs. Jellyby.

*   *   *   *   *

We were to pass the night, Mr. Kenge told us, at Mrs. Jellyby's; and then he turned to me, and said that he took it for granted that I knew who Mrs. Jellyby was.

"I really don't, sir," I returned.

"In-deed! Mrs. Jellyby is a lady of great strength of character. She devotes herself entirely to the public."

"And Mr. Jellyby, sir?"

"Ah! Mr. Jellyby," said Mr. Kenge, "I do not know that I can describe Mr. Jellyby better than by saying he is the husband of Mrs. Jellyby."

We arrived at our destination and found a crowd of people, mostly children, about the house at which we stopped, which had a tarnished brass plate on the door, with the inscription, JELLYBY:

"Don't be frightened!" said Mr. Guppy, looking in at the coach-window. "One of the young Jellybys been and got his head through the area railings!"

"Oh, poor child," said I, "let me out, if you please!"

"Pray be careful of yourself, miss. The young Jellybys are always up to something," said Mr. Guppy.

I made my way to the poor child, who was one of the dirtiest little unfortunates I ever saw, and found him very hot and frightened, and crying loudly, fixed by the neck between two iron railings, while a milk-man and a beadle, with the kindest intentions possible, were endeavoring to drag him back by the legs, under a general impression that his skull was compressible by those means. As I found (after pacifying him) that he was a little boy, with a naturally large head, I thought that, perhaps, where his head could go, his body could follow, and mentioned that the best mode of extrication might be to push him forward. This was so favorably received by the milk-man and beadle, that he would immediately have been pushed into the area, if I had not held his pinafore, while Richard and Mr. Guppy ran down through the kitchen, to catch him when he should be released. At last he was happily got down without any accident, and then he began to beat Mr. Guppy with a hoop-stick in quite a frantic manner.

Nobody had appeared belonging to the house, except a person in pattens, who had been poking at the child from below with a broom; I don't know with what object, and I don't think she did. I therefore supposed that Mrs. Jellyby was not at home; and was quite surprised when the person appeared in the passage without the pattens, and going up to the back room on the first floor, before Ada and me, announced us as, "Them two young ladies, Missis Jellyby!" We passed several more children on the way up, whom it was difficult to avoid treading on in the dark; and as we came into Mrs. Jellyby's presence, one of the poor little things fell down-stairs—down a whole flight (as it sounded to me), with a great noise.

Mrs. Jellyby, whose face reflected none of the uneasiness which we could not help showing in our own faces, as the dear child's head recorded its passage with a bump on every stair—Richard afterwards said he counted seven, besides one for the landing—received us with perfect equanimity. She was a pretty, very diminutive, plump woman, of from forty to fifty, with handsome eyes, though they had a curious habit of seeming to look a long way off. As if—I am quoting Richard again—they could see nothing nearer than Africa!

"I am very glad indeed," said Mrs. Jellyby, in an agreeable voice, "to have the pleasure of receiving you. I have a great respect for Mr. Jarndyce; and no one in whom he is interested can be an object of indifference to me."

We expressed our acknowledgments, and sat down behind the door, where there was a lame invalid of a sofa. Mrs. Jellyby had very good hair, but was too much occupied with her African duties to brush it. The shawl in which she had been loosely muffled, dropped on to her chair when she advanced to us; and as she turned to resume her seat, we could not help noticing that her dress didn't nearly meet up the back, and that the open space was railed across with a lattice-work of stay-lace—like a summer-house.

The room, which was strewn with papers and nearly filled by a great writing table covered with similar litter, was, I must say, not only very untidy, but very dirty. We were obliged to take notice of that with our sense of sight, even while, with our sense of hearing, we followed the poor child who had tumbled down-stairs: I think into the back kitchen, where somebody seemed to stifle him.

THE CHILDREN OF DICKENS

But what principally struck us was a jaded, and unhealthy-looking, though by no means plain girl, at the writing table, who sat biting the feather of her pen, and staring at us. I suppose nobody ever was in such a state of ink. And, from her tumbled hair to her pretty feet, which were disfigured with frayed and broken satin slippers trodden down at heel, she really seemed to have no article of dress upon her, from a pin upwards, that was in its proper condition or its right place.

"You find me, my dears," said Mrs. Jellyby, snuffing the two great office candles in tin candlesticks which made the room taste strongly of hot tallow (the fire had gone out, and there was nothing in the grate but ashes, a bundle of wood, and a poker), "you find me, my dears, as usual, very busy; but that you will excuse. The African project at present employs my whole time. It involves me in correspondence with public bodies, and with private individuals anxious for the welfare of their species all over the country. I am happy to say it is advancing. We hope by this time next year to have from a hundred and fifty to two hundred healthy families cultivating coffee and educating the natives of Borrioboola-Gha, on the bank of the Niger."

As Ada said nothing, but looked at me, I said it must be very gratifying.

"It *is* gratifying," said Mrs. Jellyby. "It involves the devotion of all my energies, such as they are; but that is nothing, so that it succeeds; and I am more confident of success every day. Do you know, Miss Summerson, I almost wonder that *you* never turned your thoughts to Africa."

This application of the subject was really so unexpected to me, that I was quite at a loss how to receive it. I hinted that the climate—

"The finest climate in the world!" said Mrs. Jellyby.

"Indeed, ma'am?"

"Certainly. With precaution," said Mrs. Jellyby. "You may go into Holborn, without precaution, and be run over. You may go into Holborn, with precaution, and never be run over. Just so with Africa."

I said, "No doubt"—I meant as to Holborn.

"If you would like," said Mrs. Jellyby, putting a number of papers towards us, "to look over some remarks on that head, and on the general subject (which have been extensively circulated), while I finish a letter I am now dictating—to my eldest daughter, who is my amanuensis—"

THE CHILDREN OF DICKENS

The girl at the table left off biting her pen, and made a return to our recognition, which was half bashful and half sulky.

"I shall then have finished for the present," proceeded Mrs. Jellyby, with a sweet smile; "though my work is never done. Where are you, Caddy?"

"'—Presents her compliments to Mr. Swallow, and begs—'" said Caddy.

"'And begs,'" said Mrs. Jellyby, dictating, "'to inform him, in reference to his letter of inquiry on the African project—' No, Peepy! Not on any account!"

Peepy (so self-named) was the unfortunate child who had fallen down-stairs, who now interrupted the correspondence by presenting himself, with a strip of plaster on his forehead, to exhibit his wounded knees, in which Ada and I did not know which to pity most—the bruises or the dirt. Mrs. Jellyby merely added, "Go along, you naughty Peepy!" and fixed her fine eyes on Africa again.

However, as she at once proceeded with her dictation, and as I interrupted nothing by doing it, I ventured quietly to stop poor Peepy as he was going out, and to take him up to nurse. He looked very much astonished at it, and at Ada's kissing him; but soon fell fast asleep in my arms, sobbing at longer and longer intervals, until he was quiet. I was so occupied with Peepy that I lost the letter in detail, though I derived such a general impression from it of the momentous importance of Africa, and the utter insignificance of all other places and things, that I felt quite ashamed to have thought so little about it.

"Six o'clock!" said Mrs. Jellyby. "And our dinner hour nominally (for we dine at all hours) five! Caddy, show Miss Clare and Miss Summerson their rooms. You will like to make some change, perhaps? You will excuse me, I know, being so much occupied. Oh, that very bad child! Pray put him down, Miss Summerson!"

I begged permission to retain him, truly saying that he was not at all troublesome; and carried him up-stairs and laid him on my bed. Ada and I had two upper rooms, with a door of communication between. They were excessively bare and disorderly, and the curtain to my window was fastened up with a fork.

"You would like some hot water, wouldn't you?" said Miss Jellyby, looking round for a jug with a handle to it, but looking in vain.

"If it is not being troublesome," said we.

"Oh, it's not the trouble," returned Miss Jellyby; "the question is, if there *is* any."

The evening was so very cold, and the rooms had such a marshy smell, that I must confess it was a little miserable; and Ada was half crying. We soon laughed, however, and were busily unpacking, when Miss Jellyby came back to say, that she was sorry there was no hot water; but they couldn't find the kettle, and the boiler was out of order.

We begged her not to mention it, and made all the haste we could to get down to the fire again. But all the little children had come up to the landing outside, to look at the phenomenon of Peepy lying on my bed; and our attention was distracted by the constant apparition of noses and fingers in situations of danger between the hinges of the doors. It was impossible to shut the door of either room; for my lock, with no knob to it, looked as if it wanted to be wound up; and though the handle of Ada's went round and round with the greatest smoothness, it was attended with no effect whatever on the door. Therefore I proposed to the children that they should come in and be very good at my table, and I would tell them the story of Little Red Riding Hood while I dressed; which they did, and were as quiet as mice, including Peepy, who awoke opportunely before the appearance of the wolf.

Soon after seven o'clock, we went down to dinner. The dinner was long, because of such accidents as the dish of potatoes being mislaid in the coal scuttle. Mrs. Jellyby paid no attention to such matters and told us all about the various committees, and the five thousand circulars that were sent out. After dinner, Mr. Jellyby sat in a corner in a state of great dejection. I sat in another and told Peepy, in whispers, the story of Puss in Boots, until Mrs. Jellyby, accidentally remembering the children, sent them to bed. As Peepy cried for me to take him, I carried him upstairs.

"What a strange house!" said Ada, when we got upstairs.

"My love," said I, "it quite confuses me. I can't understand it."

"What?" asked Ada.

"All this, my dear," said I. "It *must* be very good of Mrs. Jellyby to take such pains about a scheme for the benefit of Natives—and yet—Peepy and the housekeeping!"

SISSY JUPE

VI

SISSY JUPE

Dickens called the novel in which Sissy Jupe appears *Hard Times*. It was certainly hard times for children who had to go to the kind of schools that Mr. Thomas Gradgrind believed in. Mr. Gradgrind was a big square man, with a square coat and square shoulders, who thought that he knew all about education. He thought that the children in the schoolroom were like so many little pitchers, and the teacher's business was to fill them with facts.

"Now, what I want is Facts," said Mr. Gradgrind. "Teach these boys and girls nothing but Facts. This is the principle on which I bring up my own children, and this is the principle for these children. Stick to Facts."

Mr. Gradgrind, with two other gentleman, had come to visit the school. Now Sissy Jupe was a bright little girl who would really enjoy using her own mind, but she didn't know how to use Mr. Gradgrind's mind, and she was very much upset when the great man pointed his square finger at her and said:

*   *   *   *   *

"Girl number twenty. I don't know that girl. Who is that girl?"

"Sissy Jupe, sir," explained number twenty, blushing, standing up, and courtesying.

"Sissy is not a name," said Mr. Gradgrind. "Don't call yourself Sissy. Call yourself Cecilia."

"It's father as calls me Sissy, sir," returned the girl in a trembling voice, and with another courtesy.

"Then he has no business to do it," said Mr. Gradgrind. "Tell him he mustn't. Cecilia Jupe. Let me see. What is your father?"

"He belongs to the horse-riding, if you please, sir."

Mr. Gradgrind frowned, and waved off the objectionable calling with his hand.

"We don't want to know anything about that, here. You mustn't tell us about that, here. Your father breaks horses, don't he?"

"If you please, sir, when they can get any to break, they do break horses in the ring, sir."

"You mustn't tell us about the ring, here. Very well, then. Describe your father as a horsebreaker. He doctors sick horses, I dare say?"

"Oh yes, sir."

"Very well, then. He is a veterinary surgeon, a farrier, and horsebreaker. Give me your definition of a horse."

(Sissy Jupe thrown into the greatest alarm by this demand.)

"Girl number twenty unable to define a horse!" said Mr. Gradgrind, for the general behoof of all the little pitchers. "Girl number twenty possessed of no facts, in reference to one of the commonest of animals! Some boy's definition of a horse. Bitzer, yours."

The square finger, moving here and there, lighted suddenly on Bitzer, perhaps because he chanced to sit in the same ray of sunlight which, darting in at one of the bare windows of the intensely whitewashed room, irradiated Sissy. For the boys and girls sat on the face of the inclined plane in two compact bodies, divided up the centre by a narrow interval; and Sissy, being at the corner of a row on the sunny side, came in for the beginning of a sunbeam, of which Bitzer, being at the corner of a row on the other side, a few rows in advance, caught the end. But, whereas the girl was so dark-eyed and dark-haired that she seemed to receive a deeper and more lustrous color from the sun, when it shone upon her, the boy was so light-eyed and light-haired that the self-same rays appeared to draw out of him what little color he ever possessed. His cold eyes would hardly have been eyes, but for the short ends of lashes which, by bringing them into immediate contrast with something paler than them-selves, expressed their form. His short-cropped hair might have been a mere continuation of the sandy freckles on his forehead and face. His skin was so unwholesomely deficient in the natural tinge that he looked as though, if it were cut, he would bleed white.

"Bitzer," said Thomas Gradgrind. "Your defini-tion of a horse."

"Quadruped. Graminivorous. Forty teeth, namely twenty-four grinders, four eye-teeth, and twelve in-cisors. Sheds coat in the spring; in marshy countries, sheds hoofs too. Hoofs hard, but requiring to be shod with iron. Age known by marks in mouth." Thus (and much more), Bitzer.

"Now girl number twenty," said Mr. Gradgrind. "You know what a horse is." . . .

The third gentleman now slipped forth, briskly smiling.

"That's a horse. Now, let me ask you girls and boys, Would you paper a room with representations of horses?"

After a pause, one half of the children cried in chorus, "Yes, sir!" Upon which the other half, seeing in the gentleman's face that Yes was wrong, cried out in chorus, "No, sir!"—as the custom is, in these examinations.

"Of course, No. Why wouldn't you?"

A pause. One corpulent slow boy, with a wheezy manner of breathing, ventured the answer, "Because he wouldn't paper a room at all, but would paint it."

"You *must* paper it," said the gentleman, rather warmly.

"You must paper it," said Thomas Gradgrind, "whether you like it or not. Don't tell us you wouldn't paper it. What do you mean, boy?"

"I'll explain to you, then," said the gentleman, after another and a dismal pause, "why you wouldn't paper a room with representations of horses. Do you ever see horses walking up and down the sides of rooms in reality—in fact? Do you?"

"Yes, sir!" from one half. "No, sir!" from the other.

"Of course no," said the gentleman, with an indignant look at the wrong half. "Why, then, you are not to see anywhere, what you don't see in fact; you are not to have anywhere, what you don't have in fact. What is called Taste, is only another name for Fact."

Thomas Gradgrind nodded his approbation.

"This is a new principle, a discovery, a great discovery," said the gentleman.

"Now, I'll try you again. Suppose you were going to carpet a room. Would you use a carpet having a representation of flowers upon it?"

There being a general conviction by this time that "No, sir!" was always the right answer to this gentleman, the chorus of No was very strong. Only a few feeble stragglers said Yes; among them Sissy Jupe.

"Girl number twenty," said the gentleman, smiling in the calm strength of knowledge.

Sissy blushed, and stood up.

"So you would carpet your room—or your husband's room, if you were a grown woman, and had a husband—with representations of flowers, would you," said the gentleman. "Why would you?"

"If you please sir, I am very fond of flowers," returned the girl.

"And is that why you would put tables and chairs upon them, and have people walking over them with heavy boots?"

"It wouldn't hurt them, sir. They wouldn't crush and wither, if you please, sir. They would be the pictures of what was very pretty and pleasant, and I would fancy—"

"Ay, ay, ay! But you mustn't fancy," cried the gentleman, quite elated by coming so happily to his point. "That's it! You are never to fancy."

"You are not, Cecilia Jupe," Thomas Gradgrind solemnly repeated, "to do anything of that kind."

"Fact, fact, fact!" said the gentleman. And "Fact, fact, fact!" repeated Thomas Gradgrind.

"You are to be in all things regulated and governed," said the gentleman, "by fact. We hope to have, before long, a board of fact, composed of commissioners of fact, who will force the people to be a people of fact, and of nothing but fact. You must discard the word Fancy altogether. You have nothing to do with it. You are not to have, in any object of use or ornament, what would be a contradiction in fact. You don't walk upon flowers in fact; you cannot be allowed to walk upon flowers in carpets. You don't find that foreign birds and butterflies come and perch upon your crockery; you cannot be permitted to paint foreign birds and butterflies upon your crockery. You never meet with quadrupeds going up and down walls; you must not have quadrupeds represented upon walls. You must use," said the gentleman, "for all these purposes, combinations and modifications (in primary colors) of mathematical figures which are susceptible of proof and demonstration. This is the new discovery. This is fact. This is taste."

The girl courtesied, and sat down. She was very young, and she looked as if she were frightened by the matter-of-fact prospect the world afforded.

THE CRATCHITS

VII

THE CRATCHITS

E verybody knows the Cratchits. When Christmas comes people take up *A Christmas Carol* and turn to the account of the Christmas dinner which Bob Cratchit and his family enjoyed in their poor little house in the suburbs of London. Here it is just as Dickens wrote it.

*   *   *   *   *

Then up rose Mrs. Cratchit, Cratchit's wife, dressed out but poorly in a twice-turned gown, but brave in ribbons, which are cheap and make a goodly show for sixpence; and she laid the cloth, assisted by Belinda Cratchit, second of her daughters, also brave in ribbons; while Master Peter Cratchit plunged a fork into the saucepan of potatoes, and getting the corners of his monstrous shirt collar (Bob's private property, conferred upon his son and heir in honor of the day) into his mouth, rejoiced to find himself so gallantly attired, and yearned to show his linen in the fashionable parks. And now two smaller Cratchits, boy and girl, came tearing in, screaming that outside the baker's they had smelled the goose and known it for their own; and basking in luxurious thoughts of sage-and-onion, these young Cratchits danced about the table, and exalted Master Peter Cratchit to the skies, while he (not proud, although his collar nearly choked him) blew the fire, until the slow potatoes bubbling up, knocked loudly at the saucepan lid to be let out and peeled.

"What has ever got your precious father then?" said Mrs. Cratchit. "And your brother, Tiny Tim! And Martha warn't as late last Christmas Day by half-an-hour!"

"Here's Martha, mother!" said a girl, appearing as she spoke.

"Here's Martha, mother!" cried the two young Cratchits. "Hurrah! There's *such* a goose, Martha!"

"Why, bless your heart alive, my dear, how late you are!" said Mrs. Cratchit, kissing her a dozen times, and taking off her shawl and bonnet for her with officious zeal.

TINY TIM AND BOB CRATCHIT ON CHRISTMAS DAY

"We'd a deal of work to finish up last night," replied the girl, "and had to clear away this morning, mother!"

"Well! Never mind so long as you are come," said Mrs. Cratchit. "Sit ye down before the fire, my dear, and have a warm, Lord bless ye!"

"No, no! There's father coming," cried the two young Cratchits, who were everywhere at once. "Hide, Martha, hide!"

So Martha hid herself, and in came little Bob, the father, with at least three feet of comforter exclusive of the fringe, hanging down before him; and his threadbare clothes darned up and brushed, to look seasonable; and Tiny Tim upon his shoulder. Alas for Tiny Tim, he bore a little crutch, and had his limbs supported by an iron frame!

"Why, where's our Martha?" cried Bob Cratchit, looking round.

"Not coming," said Mrs. Cratchit.

"Not coming!" said Bob, with a sudden declension in his high spirits; for he had been Tim's blood horse all the way from church, and had come home rampant. "Not coming upon Christmas Day!"

Martha didn't like to see him disappointed, if it were only in joke; so she came out prematurely from behind the closet door, and ran into his arms, while the two young Cratchits hustled Tiny Tim, and bore him off into the wash-house, that he might hear the pudding singing in the copper.

"And how did little Tim behave?" asked Mrs. Cratchit, when she had rallied Bob on his credulity, and Bob had hugged his daughter to his heart's content.

"As good as gold," said Bob, "and better. Somehow he gets thoughtful, sitting by himself so much, and thinks the strangest things you ever heard. He told me, coming home, that he hoped the people saw him in the church, because he was a cripple, and it might be pleasant to them to remember upon Christmas Day, who made lame beggars walk and blind men see."

Bob's voice was tremulous when he told them this, and trembled more when he said that Tiny Tim was growing strong and hearty.

His active little crutch was heard upon the floor, and back came Tiny Tim before another word was spoken, escorted by his brother and sister to his stool before the fire; and while Bob, turning up his cuffs— as if, poor fellow, they were capable of being made more shabby—compounded some hot mixture in a jug with gin and lemons, and stirred it round and round and put it on the hob to simmer, Master Peter, and the two ubiquitous young Cratchits went to fetch the goose, with which they soon returned in high procession.

Such a bustle ensued that you might have thought a goose the rarest of all birds; a feathered phenomenon, to which a black swan was a matter of course— and in truth it was something very like it in that house. Mrs. Cratchit made the gravy (ready beforehand in a little saucepan) hissing hot; Master Peter mashed the potatoes with incredible vigor; Miss Belinda sweetened up the apple sauce; Martha dusted the hot plates; Bob took Tiny Tim beside him in a tiny corner at the table; the two young Cratchits set chairs for everybody, not forgetting themselves, and mounting guard upon their posts, crammed spoons into their mouths, lest they should shriek for goose before their turn came to be helped. At last the dishes were set on, and grace was said. It was succeeded by a breathless pause, as Mrs. Cratchit, looking slowly all along the carving-knife, prepared to plunge it in the breast; but when she did, and when the long expected gush of stuffing issued forth, one murmur of delight arose all round the board, and even Tiny Tim, excited by the two young Cratchits, beat on the table with the handle of his knife, and feebly cried Hurrah!

THE CRATCHITS

There never was such a goose. Bob said he didn't believe there ever was such a goose cooked. Its tenderness and flavor, size and cheapness, were the themes of universal admiration. Eked out by the apple sauce and mashed potatoes, it was a sufficient dinner for the whole family; indeed, as Mrs. Cratchit said with great delight (surveying one small atom of a bone upon the dish) they hadn't ate it all at last! Yet every one had had enough, and the youngest Cratchits, in particular, were steeped in sage and onion to the eyebrows! But now, the plates being changed by Miss Belinda, Mrs. Cratchit left the room alone—too nervous to bear witnesses—to take the pudding up and bring it in.

Suppose it should not be done enough! Suppose it should break in turning out! Suppose somebody should have got over the wall of the back-yard, and stolen it while they were merry with the goose—a supposition at which the two young Cratchits became livid! All sorts of horrors were supposed.

Hallo! A great deal of steam! The pudding was out of the copper. A smell like a washing-day! That was the cloth. A smell like an eating-house and a pastrycook's next door to each other, with a laundress's next door to that! That was the pudding!

In half a minute Mrs. Cratchit entered—flushed, but smiling proudly—with the pudding like a speckled cannon-ball so hard and firm blazing in half of half-a-quartern of ignited brandy, and bedight with Christmas holly stuck into the top.

Oh, a wonderful pudding! Bob Cratchit said, and calmly too, that he regarded it as the greatest success achieved by Mrs. Cratchit since their marriage. Mrs. Cratchit said that now the weight was on her mind, she would confess she had had her doubts about the quantity of flour. Everybody had something to say about it, but nobody said or thought it was at all a small pudding for a large family. It would have been flat heresy to do so. Any Cratchit would have blushed to hint at such a thing.

At last the dinner was all done, the cloth was cleared, the hearth swept, and the fire made up. The compound in the jug being tasted, and considered perfect, apples and oranges were put upon the table, and a shovelful of chestnuts on the fire. Then all the Cratchit family drew round the hearth, in what Bob Cratchit called a circle, meaning half a one; and at Bob Cratchit's elbow stood the family display of glass. Two tumblers, and a custard-cup without a handle.

These held the hot stuff from the jug, however, as well as golden goblets would have done; and Bob served it out with beaming looks, while the chestnuts on the fire sputtered and cracked noisily. Then Bob proposed:

"A Merry Christmas to us all, my dears. God bless us!"

Which all the family re-echoed.

"God bless us every one!" said Tiny Tim, the last of all.

THE DOLL'S DRESSMAKER

VIII

THE DOLL'S DRESSMAKER

The fact that Dickens when he was only twelve years old was put to work and had to make his own living made him feel old when he was really very young. He had to look after himself as if he had been a man. In *Our Mutual Friend* he gives us a picture of an old young person, Jenny Wren, the Doll's Dressmaker, who talked as if she were forty, when she was only twelve and small for her age. Her father was a drunkard and she had been compelled to act as head of the house.

She was a queer little person with bright, snapping eyes and a sharp tongue. She sat in a little old-fashioned armchair which had a little working-bench before it. She had set up in business as a doll's dressmaker and manufacturer of pin cushions and pen-wipers.

If you were in London you would have to go a long way to find the Doll's Dressmaker. First you crossed Westminster Bridge, and then you came to a certain little street called Church Street, and then to an out-of-the-way square called Smith Square, in the centre of which was a very ugly church. Then you came to a blacksmith-shop and a lumber-yard, and a dealer in old iron. There was a rusty portion of an old boiler that you had to walk around. Beyond that there were several little quiet houses in a row. In one of these houses was the little Doll's Dressmaker. That was the way Bradley Headstone and Charley Hexam found the house where Jenny Wren lived.

They knocked at the door and saw a strange little figure sitting in an armchair.

"I can't get up," said the child, "because my back's bad and my legs are queer. But I'm the person of the house. What do you want, young man?"

"I wanted to see my sister."

"Many young men have sisters. Give me your name, young man."

"Hexam is my name.

"Ah, indeed?" said the person of the house. "I thought it might be. Your sister will be in, in about a quarter of an hour. I am very fond of your sister. She's my particular friend. Take a seat. And this gentleman's name?"

"Mr. Headstone, my schoolmaster."

JENNY WREN, THE LITTLE DOLLS' DRESSMAKER

"Take a seat. And would you please to shut the street door first? I can't very well do it myself, because my back's so bad, and my legs are so queer."

They complied in silence, and the little figure went on with its work of gumming and gluing together with a camel's hair brush certain pieces of cardboard and thin wood, previously cut into various shapes. The scissors and knives upon the bench showed that the child herself had cut them; and the bright scraps of velvet and silk and ribbon also strewn upon the bench showed that when duly stuffed (and stuffing too was there) she was to cover them smartly. The dexterity of her nimble fingers was remarkable, and, as she brought two thin edges accurately together by giving them a little bite, she would glance at the visitors out of the corners of her gray eyes with a look that outsharpened all her other sharpness.

"You can't tell me the name of my trade, I'll be bound," she said, after taking several of these observations.

"You make pincushions," said Charley.

"What else do I make?"

"Pen-wipers," said Bradley Headstone.

"Ha! ha! What else do I make? You're a schoolmaster, but you can't tell me."

"You do something," he returned, pointing to a corner of the little bench, "with straw; but I don't know what."

"Well done you!" cried the person of the house. "I only make pincushions and pen-wipers to use up my waste. But my straw really does belong to my business. Try again. What do I make with my straw?"

"Dinner-mats."

"A schoolmaster, and says dinner-mats! I'll give you a clue to my trade, in a game of forfeits. I love my love with a B because she's Beautiful; I hate my love with a B because she is Brazen; I took her to the sign of the Blue Boar, and I treated her with Bonnets; her name's Bouncer, and she lives in Bedlam.—Now, what do I make with my straw?"

"Ladies' bonnets?"

"Fine ladies'," said the person of the house, nodding assent. "Dolls.' I'm a Doll's Dressmaker."

"I hope it's a good business?"

The person of the house shrugged her shoulders and shook her head. "No. Poorly paid. And I'm often so pressed for time! I had a doll married, last week, and was obliged to work all night. And it's not good for me, on account of my back being so bad and my legs so queer."

They looked at the little creature with a wonder that did not diminish, and the schoolmaster said: "I am sorry your fine ladies are so inconsiderate."

"It's the way with them," said the person of the house, shrugging her shoulders again. "And they take no care of their clothes, and they never keep to the same fashions a month. I work for a doll with three daughters. Bless you, she's enough to ruin her husband!"

The person of the house gave a weird little laugh here, and gave them another look out of the corners of her eyes. She had an elfin chin that was capable of great expression; and whenever she gave this look, she hitched this chin up. As if her eyes and her chin worked together on the same wires.

"Are you always as busy as you are now?"

"Busier. I'm slack just now. I finished a large mourning order the day before yesterday. Doll I work for lost a canary bird." The person of the house gave another little laugh, and then nodded her head several times, as who should moralize, "Oh this world, this world!"

"Are you alone all day?" asked Bradley Headstone. "Don't any of the neighboring children——?"

"Ah, lud!" cried the person of the house, with a little scream, as if the word had pricked her. "Don't talk of children. I can't bear children. *I* know their tricks and their manners." She said this with an angry little shake of her right fist close before her eyes.

Perhaps it scarcely required the teacher-habit to perceive that the doll's dressmaker was inclined to be bitter on the difference between herself and other children. But both master and pupil understood it so.

"Always running about and screeching, always playing and fighting, always skip-skip-skipping on the pavement and chalking it for their games! Oh! *I* know their tricks and their manners!" Shaking the little fist as before. "And that's not all. Ever so often calling names in through a person's keyhole, and imitating a person's back and legs. Oh! *I* know their tricks and their manners. And I'll tell you what I'd do to punish 'em. There's doors under the church in the Square—black doors, leading into black vaults. Well! I'd open one of those doors, and I'd cram 'em all in, and then I'd lock the door and through the keyhole I'd blow in pepper."

"What would be the good of blowing in pepper?" asked Charley Hexam.

"To set 'em sneezing," said the person of the house, "and make their eyes water. And when they were all sneezing and inflamed, I'd mock 'em through the keyhole. Just as they, with their tricks and their manners, mock a person through a person's keyhole!"

An uncommonly emphatic shake of her little fist close before her eyes seemed to ease the mind of the person of the house; for she added with recovered composure, "No, no, no. No children for me. Give me grown-ups."

THE KENWIGSES

IX

THE KENWIGSES

I have always wondered whether I should have liked the Kenwigses if I had met them in New York or Minneapolis. Probably I should not. But I like to read about them, and they somehow seem to be amusing and likeable. That is because they made a part of London once upon a time. They lived in a tumble-down house, in a tumble-down street. All the houses had seen better days and seemed to be nodding at each other as much as to say: "Times are not what they used to be when we were young."

But for all their dreary surroundings, the Kenwigses, big and little, were very cheery people, and had a remarkably good time. The great thing about them was that they admired each other so much, and told each other so. That doesn't seem to be very much. Anybody could do that, but most people don't. I have known very nice people to live together for years without ever telling one another how nice they are. In that way the niceness often disappears. It wasn't so with the Kenwigses. They made the most of each other and got a great deal of satisfaction out of a very little. They were all proud of the family, and didn't care who knew it.

They lived on the first floor of the house, which was never kept in a tidy condition. Mrs. Kenwigs put all her time in keeping the little girls tidy, and I am not sure that any one can blame her for the fact that the entry was always in disorder. Mr. Kenwigs was very proud of his wife, and Mrs. Kenwigs was proud of her uncle, Mr. Lillyvick, whose business it was to collect water-rents in that neighborhood. He would go about with his bills and knock loudly at the doors of all the people who hadn't paid their water-rates, and threaten them in a most terrifying manner. So everyone was afraid of Mr. Lillyvick except Mrs. Kenwigs, who was proud of him. For she was his niece.

We are introduced to the Kenwigs children at a party, which Mrs. Kenwigs made in order to show off her uncle to the admiring neighbors. The reason why the children sat up for the party was because it was held in the sitting-room, which was also the place where they slept. It was a very great occasion, and

MRS. KENWIGS AND THE FOUR LITTLE KENWIGSES

the children were on their good behavior. Uncle Lillyvick was seated in a large armchair by the fire side, and the four little Kenwigses sat side by side on a small bench facing the fire, with their nice little pig-tails tied up with blue ribbons.

"They are so beautiful," said Mrs. Kenwigs, sobbing. It was very easy for Mrs. Kenwigs to sob.

"Oh dear," said all the ladies, "but don't give way, don't!"

"I can't help it," sobbed Mrs. Kenwigs. "Oh, they are too beautiful to live, much too beautiful!"

On hearing this all the four little girls began to cry, too, and hid their heads in their mother's lap. This made a great excitement. At last the little Kenwigses were distributed among the company, so that their mother might not be overcome by the sight of their combined beauty. Then the conversation was taken up again by the older people. Then it threatened to stop, Mrs. Kenwigs turned to Morleena, the oldest of the little girls.

"Morleena Kenwigs, kiss your dear uncle." Morleena obeyed, and then the three other little girls had to do the same thing, and then they had to kiss all the other members of the company. Then Morleena, who had been at the dancing school, had to dance and be admired again by her mother. What with kiss-

ing, and dancing, and being wept over, the little
Kenwigses had a very busy evening, and were the
life of the party.

THE BOY AT TODGERS'S

X

THE BOY AT TODGERS'S

When Mr. Pecksniff and his two daughters came to London, they found their way to Mrs. Todgers's Boarding House. It was early in the morning and they rang two or three times without making any impression on anything but a dog over the way. At last a chain and some bolts were withdrawn, and a small boy with a large red head, and no nose to speak of, and a pair of huge boots under his arm, appeared. The boy rubbed his nose with the back of his shoe brush and said nothing.

"Still abed, my man?" asked Mr. Pecksniff.

"Still abed!" replied the boy, "I wish they wos still abed. They're very noisy abed, all calling for their boots at once. I thought you was the Paper and wondered why you didn't shove yourself through the grating as usual. What do you want?"

The boy was called Bailey, and though he was a little cross when the Pecksniffs came because it was so early in the morning, he was usually the soul of good humor. Indeed, good humor was about the only thing he had, for no one had taken the trouble to teach him good manners.

Bailey would roll up his sleeves to the shoulders and find his way all over the house, and wherever he went he made things lively. He wore an apron of coarse green baize. He would answer the door and then make a bolt for the alley, and in a moment be playing leap-frog, till Mrs. Todgers followed him and pulled him into the house by the hair of his head.

When the two Miss Pecksniffs were sitting primly on the sofa, Bailey would greet them with such compliments as: "There you are agin! Ain't it nice!" This made them feel very much at home.

"I say," he whispered, stopping in one of his journeys to and fro, "young ladies, there's soup to-morrow. She's making it now. Ain't she putting in the water? Oh! not at all neither!"

The next time he passed by he called out:

"I say—there's fowls to-morrow. Not skinny ones. Oh, no!"

Presently he called through the key-hole:

"There's a fish to-morrow—just come. Don't eat none of him!" And, with this warning, he vanished again.

THE BOY AT TODGERS'S

*   *   *   *   *

By-and-by, he returned to lay the cloth for supper, it having been arranged between Mrs. Todgers and the young ladies that they should partake of an exclusive veal-cutlet together in the privacy of that apartment. He entertained them on this occasion by thrusting the lighted candle into his mouth, and exhibiting his face in a state of transparency; after the performance of which feat he went on with his professional duties; brightening every knife as he laid it on the table, by breathing on the blade and afterward polishing the same on the apron already mentioned. When he had completed his preparations, he grinned at the sisters, and expressed his belief that the approaching collation would be of "rather a spicy sort."

"Will it be long before it's ready, Bailey?" asked Mercy.

"No," said Bailey, "it *is* cooked. When I come up, she was dodging among the tender pieces with a fork, and eating of 'em."

But he had scarcely achieved the utterance of these words, when he received a manual compliment on the head, which sent him staggering against the wall; and Mrs. Todgers, dish in hand, stood indignantly before him.

"Oh, you little villain!" said that lady. "Oh, you bad, false boy!"

"No worse than yerself," retorted Bailey, guarding his head, in a principle invented by Mr. Thomas Cribb. "Ah! Come now! Do that agin, will yer!"

"He's the most dreadful child," said Mrs. Todgers, setting down the dish, "I ever had to deal with. The gentlemen spoil him to that extent, and teach him such things, that I'm afraid nothing but hanging will ever do him any good."

"Won't it?" cried Bailey. "Oh! Yes! Wot do you go a lowerin' the table-beer for then, and destroying my constitooshun?"

"Go down-stairs, you vicious boy," said Mrs. Todgers, holding the door open. "Do you hear me? Go along!"

After two or three dexterous feints, he went, and was seen no more that night, save once, when he brought up some tumblers and hot water, and much disturbed the two Miss Pecksniffs by squinting hideously behind the back of the unconscious Mrs. Todgers. Having done this justice to his wounded feelings, he returned underground; whence, in company with a swarm of black beetles and a kitchen candle, he employed his faculties in cleaning boots and brushing clothes until the night was far advanced.

THE BOY AT TODGERS'S

*   *   *   *   *

But it was at the Sunday dinner that Bailey shone in glory. When the hour drew near, he appeared in a complete suit of cast-off clothes several times too large for him, and a clean shirt of extraordinary size. This caused the boarders to call him "Collars." Then Bailey would announce joyfully: "The wittles is up."

When all were seated, Bailey would stand behind the chair winking and nodding with the greatest good humor. His idea of waiting on the table was to stand with his hands in his pockets and his feet wide apart. This was on the whole the best thing to do, for when a dish passed through his hands it was quite likely to drop on the floor.

Mrs. Todgers was always scolding Bailey, who deserved it all, and Bailey was always threatening to leave and be a soldier boy.

"There's something gamey in that, ain't there? I'd sooner be hit with a cannon-ball than a rolling-pin, and she's always a catching up something of that sort and throwing it at me, when the gentlemen's appetites is good. But I ain't going to have every rise in prices wisited on me."

Mrs. Todgers got rid of Bailey after a while, but the boarders never got the same amount of amusement from his successor. The house always seemed a little dull after he left.

THE DOMBEY CHILDREN

XI

THE DOMBEY CHILDREN

In London there is a portion of the huge town that is called the City. People do not live in the City—they do business there. That is where the big banks are and the offices of the great merchants whose ships go round the world. In the City the Lord Mayor of London rules, as he did in the days when the jolly apprentice, Dick Whittington, heard the bells prophesying what he should be.

On one of the streets of the City was a building that had an ancient sign, Dombey and Son. It had been there many years, since the time when the original Dombey had taken his son into partnership. The Dombeys owned a great many ships that sailed to the West Indies and the East Indies, and wherever they could make money on their voyages. Up to this time, each Dombey had been a good business man and had taught his son how to save and how to venture wisely.

So that the Dombeys had become richer and richer. All had gone well with them; but there had come a time when there was a Dombey who hadn't any son. Mr. and Mrs. Dombey had a daughter named Florence, who was a very nice little girl. Her mother loved her dearly, but her father thought she didn't amount to much, because he couldn't put on the sign on his office the words, "Dombey and Daughter." That wouldn't have sounded right in the days of good Queen Victoria. He wanted the name to be always Dombey and Son.

When at last a boy was born, Mr. Dombey was delighted. He dreamed of a time when little Paul would grow up to be a man just like himself, and would take his place in the office and make everybody afraid of him. He should be the Prince while his father was King in the Kingdom of Dombey and Son. All this was very pleasant to think about, and it seemed as if the business in the City would go on forever. But while Mr. Dombey dreamed of what his son would do when he was grown up, he didn't do anything to help him grow. Paul was a poor little rich boy, who lived in a big, uncomfortable house, and was sent to school with other poor little rich boys. I'm sorry for little Paul, but I don't care to read about him very much.

PAUL AND FLORENCE DOMBEY ON THE BEACH AT BRIGHTON

It's a relief to meet the people who didn't have any money, for they seem so much more cheerful than any of the Dombeys. There was Toodles, the husband of little Paul's nurse. Mr. Dombey wanted to find out all about him.

"Mr. What's-your-name, you have a son, I believe."

"Four on 'em, sir. Four hims and a her. All alive."

"Why, it's as much as you can afford to keep them!" said Mr. Dombey.

"I couldn't afford but one thing in the world less, sir."

"What is that?"

"To lose 'em, sir."

"Can you read?" asked Mr. Dombey.

"Why, not partik'ler, sir."

"Write?"

"With chalk, sir?"

"With anything."

"I could make shift to chalk a bit, I think, if I were put to it," said Toodles after some reflection.

"And yet," said Mr. Dombey, "you are two or three-and-thirty, I suppose."

"Thereabouts, I suppose, sir," answered Toodles after more reflection.

"Then why don't you learn?" asked Mr. Dombey.

"So I'm agoing to, sir. One of my little boys is agoing to learn me when he's old enough, and been to school himself."

"Well!" said Mr. Dombey. It was all that he could say. It all seemed so foolish. It would have surprised Mr. Dombey if he had been told that Mr. Toodles's children were more fortunate than his own, and that they were having a great deal better time. But that was what Dickens thought, and I agree with him.

Little Paul was so carefully looked after that he had no adventures. But his sister Florence had better luck. One of her adventures was quite exciting, for she was lost in one of the worst parts of London, and was rescued by a young gentleman who felt the romance of it. At the time Paul was a baby, and Mrs. Toodles had a longing to see her own children. So without asking permission she took Paul and Florence with her along with another nurse named Susan Nipper. They found their way to the poor part of town where her family lived, and all the little Toodleses greeted their mother with shouts, and there was a great celebration. On going home they fell in with a noisy and pushing crowd. Mrs. Toodles of course looked after little Paul, who was very important, but she forgot Florence for a moment. When she looked for her she wasn't there. What followed let Dickens tell.

HOW FLORENCE DOMBEY
WAS LOST IN LONDON

As Susan Nipper and the two children were in the crowd, there came a wild cry of "Mad bull!" With a wild confusion before her, of people running up and down, and shouting, and wheels running over them, and boys fighting, and mad bulls coming up, and the nurse in the midst of all these dangers being torn to pieces, Florence screamed and ran. She ran till she was exhausted, urging Susan to do the same; and then, stopping and wringing her hands as she remembered they had left the other nurse behind, found, with a sensation of terror not to be described, that she was quite alone.

"Susan! Susan!" cried Florence, clapping her hands in the very ecstasy of her alarm. "Oh, where are they! where are they!"

"Where are they?" said an old woman, coming hobbling across as fast as she could from the opposite side of the way. "Why did you run away from 'em?"

"I was frightened," answered Florence. "I didn't know what I did. I thought they were with me. Where are they?"

THE DOMBEY CHILDREN

The old woman took her by the wrist, and said: "I'll show you."

She was a very ugly old woman, with red rims round her eyes, and a mouth that mumbled and chattered of itself when she was not speaking. She was miserably dressed, and carried some skins over her arm. She seemed to have followed Florence some little way at all events, for she had lost her breath; and this made her uglier still, as she stood trying to regain it: working her shrivelled, yellow face and throat into all sorts of contortions.

Florence was afraid of her, and looked, hesitating, up the street, of which she had almost reached the bottom. It was a solitary place—more a back road than a street—and there was no one in it but herself and the old woman.

"You needn't be frightened now," said the old woman, still holding her tight. "Come along with me."

"I—I don't know you. What's your name?" asked Florence.

"Mrs. Brown," said the old woman. "Good Mrs. Brown."

"Are they near here?" asked Florence, beginning to be led away.

"Susan an't far off," said Good Mrs. Brown; "and the others are close to her."

"Is anybody hurt?" cried Florence.

"Not a bit of it," said Good Mrs. Brown.

The child shed tears of delight on hearing this, and accompanied the old woman willingly; though she could not help glancing at her face as they went along—particularly at that industrious mouth—and wondering whether Bad Mrs. Brown, if there were such a person, was at all like her.

They had not gone very far, but had gone by some very uncomfortable places, such as brick-fields and tile-yards, when the old woman turned down a dirty lane, where the mud lay in deep black ruts in the middle of the road. She stopped before a shabby little house, as closely shut up as a house that was full of cracks and crevices could be. Opening the door with a key she took out of her bonnet, she pushed the child before her into a back room, where there was a great heap of rags of different colors lying on the floor; a heap of bones, and a heap of sifted dust or cinders; but there was no furniture at all, and the walls and ceiling were quite black.

The child became so terrified that she was stricken speechless, and looked as though about to swoon.

"Now don't be a young mule," said Good Mrs. Brown, reviving her with a shake. "I'm not agoing to hurt you. Sit upon the rags."

Florence obeyed her, holding out her folded hands, in mute supplication.

"I'm not agoing to keep you, even, above an hour," said Mrs. Brown. "D'ye understand what I say?"

The child answered with great difficulty, "Yes."

"Then," said Good Mrs. Brown, taking her own seat on the bones, "don't vex me. If you don't, I tell you I won't hurt you. But if you do, I'll kill you. I could have you killed at any time—even if you was in your own bed at home. Now let's know who you are, and what you are, and all about it."

The old woman's threats and promises; the dread of giving her offense; and the habit, unusual to a child, but almost natural to Florence now, of being quiet, and repressing what she felt, and feared, and hoped, enabled her to do this bidding, and to tell her little history, or what she knew of it. Mrs. Brown listened attentively, until she had finished.

"So your name's Dombey, eh?" said Mrs. Brown.

"Yes, ma'am."

"I want that pretty frock, Miss Dombey," said Good Mrs. Brown, "and that little bonnet, and a petticoat or two, and anything else you can spare. Come! Take 'em off."

Florence obeyed, as fast as her trembling hands would allow; keeping, all the while, a frightened eye on Mrs. Brown. When she had divested herself of all the articles of apparel mentioned by that lady, Mrs. B. examined them at leisure, and seemed tolerably well satisfied with their quality and value.

"Humph!" she said, running her eyes over the child's slight figure. "I don't see anything else—except the shoes. I must have the shoes, Miss Dombey."

Poor little Florence took them off with equal alacrity, only too glad to have any more means of conciliation about her. The old woman then produced some wretched substitutes from the bottom of the heap of rags, which she turned up for that purpose; together with a girl's cloak, quite worn out and very old; and the crushed remains of a bonnet that had probably been picked up from some ditch or dunghill. In this dainty raiment, she instructed Florence to dress herself; and as such preparation seemed a prelude to her release, the child complied with increased readiness, if possible.

In hurriedly putting on the bonnet, if that may be called a bonnet which was more like a pad to carry loads on, she caught it in her hair which grew luxuriantly, and could not immediately disentangle it. Good Mrs. Brown whipped out a large pair of scissors, and fell into an unaccountable state of excitement.

"Why couldn't you let me be!" said Mrs. Brown "when I was contented. You little fool!"

"I beg your pardon. I don't know what I have done," panted Florence. "I couldn't help it."

"Couldn't help it!" cried Mrs. Brown. "How do you expect I can help it? Why, Lord!" said the old woman, ruffling her curls with a furious pleasure, "anybody but me would have had 'em off, first of all."

Florence was so relieved to find that it was only her hair and not her head which Mrs. Brown coveted, that she offered no resistance or entreaty, and merely raised her mild eyes toward the face of that good soul.

"If I hadn't once had a gal of my own—beyond seas now—that was proud of her hair," said Mrs. Brown, "I'd have had every lock of it. She's far away, she's far away! Oho! Oho!"

Mrs. Brown's was not a melodious cry, but, accompanied with a wild tossing up of her lean arms, it was full of passionate grief, and thrilled to the heart of Florence, whom it frightened more than ever. It had its part, perhaps, in saving her curls; for Mrs. Brown, after hovering about her with the scissors for some moments, like a new kind of butterfly, bade her hide them under the bonnet and let no trace of them escape to tempt her. Having accomplished this victory over herself, Mrs. Brown resumed her seat on the bones, and smoked a very short black pipe, mowing and mumbling all the time, as if she were eating the stem.

When the pipe was smoked out, she gave the child a rabbit-skin to carry, that she might appear the more like her ordinary companion, and told her that she was now going to lead her to a public street, whence she could inquire her way to her friends. But she cautioned her, with threats of summary and deadly vengeance in case of disobedience, not to talk to strangers, nor to repair to her own home (which may have been too near for Mrs. Brown's convenience), but to her father's office in the City; also to wait at the street corner where she would be left, until the clock struck three. These directions Mrs. Brown enforced with assurances that there would be potent eyes and ears in her employment cognizant of all she did; and these directions Florence promised faithfully and earnestly to observe.

At length, Mrs. Brown, issuing forth, conducted her changed and ragged little friend through a labyrinth of narrow streets and lanes and alleys, which emerged, after a long time, upon a stable-yard, with a gateway at the end, whence the roar of a great thor-

oughfare made itself audible. Pointing out this gateway, and informing Florence that when the clocks
struck three she was to go to the left, Mrs. Brown,
after making a parting grasp at her hair which seemed
involuntary and quite beyond her own control, told
her she knew what to do, and bade her go and do it:
remembering that she was watched.

With a lighter heart, but still sore afraid, Florence
felt herself released, and tripped off to the corner.
When she reached it, she looked back and saw the
head of Good Mrs. Brown peeping out of the low
wooden passage, where she had issued her parting
injunctions; likewise the fist of Good Mrs. Brown
shaking toward her. But though she often looked back
afterward—every minute, at least, in her nervous rec-
ollection of the old woman—she could not see her
again.

Florence remained there, looking at the bustle in
the street, and more and more bewildered by it; and
in the meanwhile the clocks appeared to have made
up their minds never to strike three any more. At last
the steeples rang out three o'clock; there was one close
by, so she couldn't be mistaken; and—after often
looking over her shoulder, and often going a little
way, and as often coming back again, lest the all-
powerful spies of Mrs. Brown should take offense—

she hurried off, as fast as she could in her slipshod shoes, holding the rabbit-skin tight in her hand.

All she knew of her father's offices was that they belonged to Dombey and Son, and that that was a great power in the City. So she could only ask the way to Dombey and Son's in the City; and as she generally made inquiry of children—being afraid to ask grown people—she got very little satisfaction indeed. But by dint of asking her way to the City after a while, and dropping the rest of her inquiry for the present, she really did advance, by slow degrees, toward the heart of that great region which is governed by the terrible Lord Mayor.

Tired of walking, repulsed and pushed about, stunncd by the noise and confusion, anxious for her brother and the nurses, terrified by what she had undergone, and the prospect of encountering her angry father in such an altered state; perplexed and frightened alike by what had passed, and what was passing, and what was yet before her, Florence went upon her weary way with tearful eyes, and once or twice could not help stopping to ease her bursting heart by crying bitterly. But few people noticed her at those times, in the garb she wore; or if they did, believed that she was tutored to excite compassion, and passed on. Florence, too, called to her aid all the firmness and self-reliance of a character that her sad experience had prematurely formed and tried; and keeping the end she had in view steadily before her, steadily pursued it.

It was full two hours later in the afternoon than when she had started on this strange adventure, when, escaping from the clash and clangor of a narrow street full of carts and wagons, she peeped into a kind of wharf or landing place upon the riverside, where there were a great many packages, casks, and boxes strewn about; a large pair of wooden scales; and a little wooden house on wheels, outside of which, looking at the neighboring masts and boats, a stout man stood whistling, with his pen behind his ear, and his hands in his pockets, as if his day's work were nearly done.

"Now then!" said this man, happening to turn round. "We haven't got anything for you, little girl. Be off!"

"If you please, is this the City?" asked the trembling daughter of the Dombeys.

"Ah! it's the City. You know that well enough, I daresay. Be off! We haven't got anything for you."

"I don't want anything, thank you," was the timid answer. "Except to know the way to Dombey and Son's."

The man who had been strolling carelessly toward her, seemed surprised by this reply, and looking attentively in her face, rejoined:

"Why, what can you want with Dombey and Son's?"

"To know the way there, if you please."

The man looked at her yet more curiously, and rubbed the back of his head so hard in his wonderment that he knocked his own hat off.

"Joe!" he called to another man—a laborer—as he picked it up and put it on again.

"Joe it is!" said Joe.

"Where's that young spark of Dombey's who's been watching the shipment of them goods?"

"Just gone, by the t'other gate," said Joe.

"Call him back a minute."

Joe ran up an archway, bawling as he went, and very soon returned with a blithe-looking boy.

"You're Dombey's jockey, an't you ?" said the first man.

"I'm in Dombey's House, Mr. Clark," returned the boy.

"Look ye here, then," said Mr. Clark.

Obedient to the indication of Mr. Clark's hand, the boy approached toward Florence, wondering, as well he might, what he had to do with her. But she, who had heard what passed, and who, besides the relief of so suddenly considering herself safe at her journey's end, felt reassured beyond all measure by his lively youthful face and manner, ran eagerly up to him, leaving one of the slipshod shoes upon the ground and caught his hand in both of hers.

"I am lost, if you please!" said Florence.

"Lost!" cried the boy.

"Yes, I was lost this morning, a long way from here—and I have had my clothes taken away, since—and I am not dressed in my own now—and my name is Florence Dombey, my little brother's only sister—and, oh dear, dear, take care of me, if you please!" sobbed Florence, giving full vent to the childish feelings she had so long suppressed, and bursting into tears. At the same time her miserable bonnet falling off, her hair came tumbling down about her face: moving to speechless admiration and commiseration, young Walter, nephew of Solomon Gills, ships' instrument-maker in general.

Mr. Clark stood rapt in amazement: observing under his breath, *I* never saw such a start on *this* wharf before. Walter picked up the shoe, and put it on the little foot as the Prince in the story might have fitted Cinderella's slipper on. He hung the rabbit-skin over his left arm; gave the right to Florence; and felt, not to say like Richard Whittington—that is a tame comparison—but like Saint George of England, with the dragon lying dead before him.

"Don't cry, Miss Dombey," said Walter, in a transport of enthusiasm. "What a wonderful thing for me that I am here. You are as safe now as if you were guarded by a whole boat's crew of picked men from a man-of-war. Oh, don't cry."

"I won't cry any more," said Florence. "I am only crying for joy."

"Crying for joy!" thought Walter, "and I'm the cause of it ! Come along, Miss Dombey. There's the other shoe off now! Take mine, Miss Dombey."

"No, no, no," said Florence, checking him in the act of impetuously pulling off his own. "These do better. These do very well."

"Why, to be sure," said Walter, glancing at her foot, "mine are a mile too large. What am I thinking about! You never could walk in *mine*! Come along, Miss Dombey. Let me see the villain who will dare molest you now."

So Walter, looking immensely fierce, led off Florence, looking very happy; and they went arm in arm along the streets, perfectly indifferent to any astonishment that their appearance might or did excite by the way.

THE DOMBEY CHILDREN

*　　*　　*　　*　　*

Then , though it was growing dark and foggy, Florence was perfectly happy, and Walter felt that he was a knight escorting a princess to her father's castle.

PAUL DOMBEY AT BRIGHTON

L ittle Paul Dombey was only six and very small for his age, when his father sent him to a boarding school at Brighton. The head master's name was Blimber, and he prided himself on giving information to his pupils at all times. Here is a scene at the dinner table.

*　　*　　*　　*　　*

Doctor Blimber was already in his place in the dining room, at the top of the table, with Miss Blimber and Mrs. Blimber on either side of him. Mr. Feeder in a black coat was at the bottom. Paul's chair was next to Miss Blimber; but it being found, when he sat in it, that his eyebrows were not much above the level of the table-cloth, some books were brought in from the Doctor's study, on which he was elevated, and on which he always sat from that time—carrying them in and out himself on after occasions, like a little elephant and castle.

Grace having been said by the Doctor, dinner began. There was some nice soup; also roast meat, boiled meat, vegetables, pie, and cheese. Every young gentleman had a massive silver fork, and a napkin; and all the arrangements were stately and handsome. In particular, there was a butler in a blue coat and bright buttons, who gave quite a winey flavor to the table beer; he poured it out so superbly.

Nobody spoke, unless spoken to, except Doctor Blimber, Mrs. Blimber, and Miss Blimber, who conversed occasionally. Whenever a young gentleman was not actually engaged with his knife and fork or spoon, his eye, with an irresistible at traction, sought the eye of Doctor Blimber, Mrs. Blimber, or Miss Blimber, and modestly rested there. Toots appeared to be the only exception to this rule. He sat next Mr. Feeder on Paul's side of the table, and frequently looked behind and before the intervening boys to catch a glimpse of Paul.

Only once during dinner was there any conversation that included the young gentlemen. It happened at the epoch of the cheese, when the Doctor, having taken a glass of port wine and hemmed twice or thrice, said:

THE DOMBEY CHILDREN

"It is remarkable, Mr. Feeder, that the Romans—"

At the mention of this terrible people, their implacable enemies, every young gentleman fastened his gaze upon the Doctor, with an assumption of the deepest interest. One of the number who happened to be drinking, and who caught the Doctor's eye glaring at him through the side of his tumbler, left off so hastily that he was convulsed for some moments, and in the sequel ruined Doctor Blimber's point.

"It is remarkable, Mr. Feeder," said the Doctor, beginning again slowly, "that the Romans, in those gorgeous and profuse entertainments of which we read in the days of the Emperors, when luxury had attained a height unknown before or since, and when whole provinces were ravaged to supply the splendid means of one Imperial Banquet."

Here the offender, who had been swelling and straining, and waiting in vain for a full stop, broke out violently.

"Johnson," said Mr. Feeder, in a low, reproachful voice, "take some water."

The Doctor, looking very stern, made a pause until the water was brought, and then resumed:

"And when, Mr. Feeder——"

But Mr. Feeder, who saw that Johnson must break out again, and who knew that the Doctor would never come to a period before the young gentlemen until he had finished all he meant to say, couldn't keep his eye off Johnson; and thus was caught in the act of not looking at the Doctor, who consequently stopped.

"I beg your pardon, sir," said Mr. Feeder, reddening. "I beg your pardon, Doctor Blimber."

"And when," said the Doctor, raising his voice, "when, sir, as we read, and have no reason to doubt— incredible as it may appear to the vulgar of our time— the brother of Vitellius prepared for him a feast, in which were served, of fish, two thousand dishes——"

"Take some water, Johnson—dishes, sir," said Mr. Feeder.

"Of various sorts of fowl, five thousand dishes."

"Or try a crust of bread," said Mr. Feeder.

"And one dish," pursued Doctor Blimber, raising his voice still higher as he looked all round the table, "called, from its enormous dimensions, the Shield of Minerva, and made, among other costly ingredients, of the brains of pheasants——"

"Ow, ow, ow!" (from Johnson).

"Woodcocks,——"

"Ow, ow, ow!"

"The sounds of the fish called scari,——"

"You'll burst some vessel in your head," said Mr. Feeder. "You had better let it come."

"And the spawn of the lamprey, brought from the Carpathian Sea," pursued the Doctor, in his severest voice; "when we read of costly entertainments such as these, and still remember, that we have a Titus,"

"What would be your mother's feelings if you died of apoplexy!" said Mr. Feeder.

"A Domitian,——"

"And you're blue, you know," said Mr. Feeder.

"A Nero, a Tiberius, a Caligula, a Heliogabalus, and many more," pursued the Doctor; "it is, Mr. Feeder—if you are doing me the honor to attend—remarkable; VERY remarkable, sir——"

But Johnson, unable to suppress it any longer, burst at that moment into such an overwhelming fit of coughing, that, although both his immediate neighbors thumped him on the back, and Mr. Feeder himself held a glass of water to his lips, and the butler walked him up and down several times between his own chair and the sideboard, like a sentry, it was full five minutes before he was moderately composed. Then there was a profound silence.

"Gentlemen," said Doctor Blimber, "rise for grace! Cornelia, lift Dombey down"—nothing of whom but his scalp was accordingly seen above the table-cloth. "Johnson will repeat to me to-morrow morning before breakfast, without book, and from the Greek Testament, the first Epistle of Saint Paul to the Ephesians. We will resume our studies, Mr. Feeder, in half-an-hour."

*　　*　　*　　*　　*

No wonder that poor little Paul looked forward longingly to the happy Saturdays, for then Florence always came at noon, and they had long walks on the great beach, and watched the waves come in. Then Paul forgot about Doctor Blimber and Nero, and Tiberius and the rest, and only knew how much he loved his sister.

ON THE WAY TO
GRETNA GREEN

XII

ON THE WAY TO GRETNA GREEN

Harry was eight and Norah was seven. They lived on Shooters Hill, six or seven miles from London. Harry's father, Mr. Walmer, had a big place called the Elms. The children read fairy-stories and delighted in princes and dragons and wicked enchanters, and kings who had fair daughters and offered them to any knights who were brave enough to come and take them. And they liked to read about lovers who ran away to Gretna Green and were married and lived happily ever after. Just where Gretna Green was they didn't know, but it must be a very romantic place to run away to. Cobbs, the gardener, heard them talking about it all as they sat under a tree. They intended to keep bees and a cow, and live on milk and honey.

Cobbs left Mr. Walmer, and went to work at the Holly Tree Inn up in Yorkshire. One day the coach drew up and two little passengers got out. Harry and Norah were on their way to Gretna Green.

"We'll stop here," said Harry to the landlord. "Chops and cherry pudding for two." Then they went to the sitting room.

Cobbs found them there. Master Harry, on an enormous sofa, was drying the eyes of Miss Norah with his pocket handkerchief. Their little legs were entirely off the floor.

"I see you a-getting out, sir," said Cobbs. "I thought it was you. I thought I couldn't be mistaken in your height and figure. What's the object of your journey, sir? Matrimonial?"

"We are going to be married, Cobbs, at Gretna Green. We have run away on purpose. Norah has been in low spirits, Cobb, but she'll be happy now that we have found you to be our friend."

"Thank you, sir, and thank you, miss, for your good opinion. Did you bring any luggage with you?"

The lady had got a parasol, a smelling-bottle, some buttered toast, eight peppermint drops, and a small hair-brush. The gentleman had got half a dozen yards of string, a knife, three or four sheets of writing-paper, an orange, and a china mug with his name on it.

"What may be the exact nature of your plans, sir?" said Cobb.

THE RUNAWAY COUPLE

"To go on," said the boy, "in the morning and be married to-morrow."

"Just so, sir," said Cobb. "Would it meet your views if I was to accompany you?"

When Cobbs said this, they both jumped for joy again, and cried out: "Oh, yes, Cobbs, yes!"

"Well, sir," said Cobbs, "if you will excuse my having to give an opinion, what I should recommend would be this. I'm acquainted with a pony, sir, which, put in a phaeton which I could borrow, would take you and Mrs. Harry Walmer Junior (myself driving, if you approved), to the end of your journey in a very short space of time."

They clapped their hands and jumped for joy.

"Is there anything you want, just at present, sir?"

"We should like some cakes after dinner," answered Master Harry, "and two apples and jam. With dinner we should have toast and water. But Norah has been accustomed to half a glass of currant wine for dessert, and so have I."

"It shall be ordered at the bar, sir," said Cobbs.

"Cobbs, are there any good walks in this neighborhood?"

"Begging your pardon, sir," said Cobbs, "there is Love Lane. And a pleasant walk it is, and proud shall

I be to show it to yourself and Mrs. Harry Walmer Junior."

"Norah, dear," said Master Harry, "put on your bonnet, my sweetest darling, and we'll go there with Cobbs."

It was very pleasant walking down Love Lane gathering water-lilies, but as the afternoon came on they both became a little homesick. Master Harry kept up nobly, but Mrs. Harry Walmer Junior began to cry, "I want to go home." When Harry's father and Norah's mother appeared upon the scene, every one was happy. Harry and Norah had been on the way to Gretna Green, though they never got there.

THE INFANT
PHENOMENON

XIII

THE INFANT PHENOMENON

In our day the movies and TV have made it possible for the people who live in the city and the people who live in the country to see and hear the same things. Our amusements are very much alike. But it was not so in Dickens's day. The great actors were in the theatres of the large cities; but companies of strolling players were on the roads. They carried their stage scenery with them and did their own advertising. They did not have to compete with those who could act better.

Dickens enjoyed these cheerful wanderers who went about giving entertainments to people who were easily pleased. When Nicholas Nickleby and his friend Smike were trudging along on the road from London to Portsmouth they fell in with Mr. Vincent Crummles and his dramatic company. Nicholas had almost come to the end of the little money with which he started, and he was very glad when Mr. Crummles invited him to share his supper at the inn. When Nicholas had told Mr. Crummles his story he was invited to join the company, at a salary which while not large was sufficient to keep him from starving. In this way he became acquainted with the Infant Phenomenon. She was the daughter of Mr. and Mrs. Crummles and was the pride of the family. Nicholas was introduced to her when they came to the theatre in the next town. It was a very dingy little theatre on a back street. Mrs. Crummles led the way to the stage.

There bounded on to the stage from some mysterious inlet, a little girl in a dirty white frock with tucks up to the knees, short trousers, sandled shoes, white spencer, pink gauze bonnet, green veil, and curl-papers; who turned a pirouette, cut twice in the air, turned another pirouette, then, looking off at the opposite wing, shrieked, bounded forward to within six inches of the footlights, and fell into a beautiful attitude of terror, as a shabby gentleman in an old pair of buff slippers came in at one powerful slide, and chattering his teeth, fiercely brandished a walking-stick.

"They are going through the Indian Savage and the Maiden," said Mrs. Crummles.

"Oh!" said the manager, "the little ballet interlude. Very good, go on. A little this way, if you please, Mr. Johnson. That'll do. Now!"

THE INFANT PHENOMENON

The manager clapped his hands as a signal to proceed, and the savage, becoming ferocious, made a slide toward the maiden; but the maiden avoided him in six twirls, and came down at the end of the last one upon the very points of her toes. This seemed to make some impression upon the savage; for, after a little more ferocity and chasing of the maiden into corners, he began to relent, and stroked his face several times with his right thumb and forefinger, thereby intimating that he was struck with admiration of the maiden's beauty. Acting upon the impulse of this passion, he (the savage) began to hit himself severe thumps in the chest, and to exhibit other indications of being desperately in love, which being rather a prosy proceeding, was very likely the cause of the maiden's falling asleep; whether it was or no, asleep she did fall, sound as a church, on a sloping bank, and the savage perceiving it, leaned his left ear on his left hand, and nodded sideways, to intimate to all whom it might concern that she *was* asleep, and no shamming. Being left to himself, the savage had a dance, all alone. Just as he left off, the maiden woke up, rubbed her eyes, got off the bank, and had a dance all alone too—such a dance that the savage looked on in ecstasy all the while, and when it was done, plucked from a neighboring tree some botanical curiosity, resembling a small pickled cabbage, and offered it to the maiden, who at first wouldn't have it, but on the savage shedding tears relented. Then the savage jumped for joy; then the maiden jumped for rapture at the sweet smell of the pickled cabbage. Then the savage and the maiden danced violently together, and, finally, the savage dropped down on one knee, and the maiden stood on one leg upon his other knee; thus concluding the ballet, and leaving the spectators in a state of pleasing uncertainty, whether she would ultimately marry the savage, or return to her friends.

"Very well indeed," said Mr. Crummles; "bravo!"

"Bravo!" cried Nicholas, resolved to make the best of everything. "Beautiful!"

"This, sir," said Mr. Vincent Crummles, bringing the maiden forward, "this is the Infant Phenomenon— Miss Ninetta Crummles."

"Your daughter?" inquired Nicholas.

"My daughter—my daughter," replied Mr. Vincent Crummles; "the idol of every place we go into, sir. We have complimentary letters about this girl, sir, from the nobility and gentry of almost every town in England."

"I am not surprised at that," said Nicholas; "she must be quite a natural genius."

THE INFANT PHENOMENON

"Quite a—!" Mr. Crummles stopped; language was not powerful enough to describe the Infant Phenomenon. "I'll tell you what, sir," he said; "the talent of this child is not to be imagined. She must be seen, sir—seen—to be ever so faintly appreciated. There; go to your mother, my dear."

"May I ask how old she is?" inquired Nicholas.

"You may, sir," replied Mr. Crummles, looking steadily in his questioner's face, as some men do when they have doubts about being implicitly believed in what they are going to say. "She is ten years of age, sir."

"Not more?"

"Not a day."

"Dear me!" said Nicholas, "it's extraordinary."

It was; for the Infant Phenomenon, though of short stature, had a comparatively aged countenance, and had moreover been precisely the same age—not perhaps to the full extent of the memory of the oldest inhabitant, but certainly for five good years. But she had been kept up late every night, and put upon an unlimited allowance of gin and water from infancy, to prevent her growing tall, and perhaps this system of training had produced in the Infant Phenomenon these additional phenomena.

Nicholas was invited to dinner with the Crummles family at their lodgings. Mrs. Crummles, who always talked as if she were on the stage, received him in a most dignified way.

"You are welcome," said Mrs. Crummles, turning round to Nicholas when they reached the bow-windowed front room on the first floor.

Nicholas bowed his acknowledgments, and was unfeignedly glad to see the cloth laid.

"We have but a shoulder of mutton with onion sauce," said Mrs. Crummles, in the same charnel-house voice; "but such as our dinner is, we beg you to partake of it."

"You are very good," replied Nicholas, "I shall do it ample justice."

"Vincent," said Mrs. Crummles, "what is the hour?"

"Five minutes past dinner-time," said Mr. Crummles.

Mrs. Crummles rang the bell. "Let the mutton and onion sauce appear."

The slave who attended upon Mr. Bulph's lodgers disappeared, and after a short interval reappeared with the festive banquet. Nicholas and the Infant Phenomenon opposed each other at the pembroke-table, and Smike and the Master Crummleses dined on the sofa-bedstead.

"Are they very theatrical people here?" asked Nicholas.

"No," replied Mr. Crummles, shaking his head, "far from it—far from it."

"I pity them," observed Mrs. Crummles.

"So do I," said Nicholas; "if they have no relish for theatrical entertainments, properly conducted."

"Then they have none, sir," rejoined Mr. Crummles. "To the Infant's benefit, last year, on which occasion she repeated three of her most popular characters, and also appeared in the Fairy Porcupine, as originally performed by her, there was a house of no more than four-pound-twelve."

"Is it possible?" cried Nicholas.

"And two pound of that was trust, pa," said the Phenomenon.

"And two pound of that was trust," repeated Mr. Crummles.

The public did not always appreciate the genius of the Infant Phenomenon, but that made no difference to the admiring father. When Nicholas suggested that perhaps a boy phenomenon might be added to the company, Mr. Crummles answered solemnly: "There is only one Phenomenon, sir, and that is a girl."

HOW TO COPE
WITH STORMS

——————Dietrich von Haeften——————

SHERIDAN HOUSE

This edition published 1997 by
Sheridan House Inc.
145 Palisade Street
Dobbs Ferry, NY 10522

Library of Congress Cataloging-in-Publication Data

Haeften, Dietrich von.
    [Sturm was tun? English]
    How to cope with storms / Dietrich von Haeften.
      p.   cm.
    Includes index.
    ISBN 1–57409–032–1 (pbk.)
    1. Windstorms– –Safety measures. 2. Sailing– –Safety measures.
3. Heavy weather seamanship. 4. Marine meteorology. I. Title.
QC943.H2513 1997
623.88– –dc21   97–980
                                                            CIP

Printed in Great Britain

ISBN   1–57409–032–1

Contents

Introduction

Being here and wishing you were out there is always preferable to being out there and wishing you were here.

This piece of wisdom, left to us by some unknown nautical philosopher is worth reflecting on as you read this book in the comfort of your living room.

To quote Adlard Coles from his classic account of experiences of storms at sea, *Heavy Weather Sailing*:

> Gales are rarely pleasant experiences, except for the sense of exhilaration in their early stages, and of elation when they have passed. The intermediate part is often one of anxiety and tiredness, but, whether one likes it or not heavy weather at some time or another is the lot of most of us, whether cruising or ocean racing.

No experienced sailor wishes to be in a storm. It is potentially damaging to his boat and a great physical and mental strain for skipper and crew. And it is by no means unreasonable to assume that something could go wrong. When someone at the bar tells glamorous stories of sailing in wild seas – much of it can be attributed to the beer and a vivid imagination! In reality, we are talking about hard work, major discomfort and danger. On a crazily pitching and heaving boat, normal tasks become tough struggles. Lungeing for a hold somewhere; fighting against the wildly flapping sailcloth; fumbling with a knot which suddenly will not tie; cursing cold fingers and that horrible icy wetness creeping down your neck.

Into one's thoughts creep anxiety and even fear: Does the helmsperson see the huge wave piling up behind us? Watch out! Wow, those leeward shrouds are whipping about, I hope the crosstrees can take the strain! Have they ever been as loose as this before? Just pray that the mast is OK. Then there's the desperate desire to check the position when you've only done it a few moments ago – have we still got plenty of sea to leeward? I can't go below to check now ...

Routine helps. With plenty of experience under your belt, you'll be less likely to get worried about a storm and stay much calmer.

Still, it is unlikely that you'll ever get blasé about heavy weather – big seas can always command respect.

Most of us are amateurs. We are mainly at sea during the summer season when gales are rare. But, because of this, we rarely get practical experience of heavy weather. Nothing can replace real experience, but knowing some theory about coping with storms will help.

There are no hard and fast rules for dealing with heavy weather when sailing but the aim of this book is to give practical suggestions and stimulate thought. I want to put forward scenarios and discuss them. Then, at home in your armchair, you can reflect on this advice so that when you next go to sea you are equipped with greater knowledge to deal with challenging situations.

1   The power source

Wind, and therefore gales, are the result of a process that begins with the heat of the sun. The process is governed by the laws of physics and, more particularly, meteorology. Let us take a brief look at this science.

Warm air rises

A hot-air balloon, like that of the Montgolfier brothers, floats upwards because the air inside it is heated by fire. The warm air is lighter than the cold air outside the balloon and it begins to rise. The principle is the same as that for a ship – it will float as long as it weighs less than the amount of water it displaces. The balloon, including the hot air inside, weighs less than the volume of the surrounding air that it displaces. And so it rises.

In terms of physics, air gets lighter when it warms up because it expands. Its molecules get farther apart when warm. The density becomes less and, with it, the weight of a given volume. That is why warm air rises above cool air.

In the air surrounding the earth this principle of the hot-air balloon applies wherever air temperatures differ; where some parts are warmer than others. What causes these variations in air temperature?

How the air absorbs heat

Only to a very limited extent do the rays of the sun heat up the air directly. They mainly heat up the surface of the earth, and this in turn heats the air above. The surface of the earth heats up the air like a radiator heats a room.

Land and sea, forest and heathland, sand and marshes, all absorb the sun rays to a different extent. Surface and colour are important factors (black heats up best), but the material is also important. Under the same amount of sun, stones and sand warm up five times as much, fields twice as much as water. So, depending on the surface structure, the earth develops quite different temperatures and, accordingly, radiates differing amounts of heat into the air.

Another reason for variations in heat absorption is cloud. Cloud cover varies with time and place, though average amounts depend on climate.

Finally, heat absorption also depends on the angle at which the sun's rays strike the surface of the earth. The earth is round and towards the poles this angle becomes progressively lower. Accordingly, reflection of the rays becomes greater and the amount of heat absorbed is smaller.

The origin of wind

When air rises, more air has to come in from all sides to take its place. The ensuing movement of air parallel to the surface of the earth is what we know as wind.

How a gale forms

For the wind to reach gale force a lot more energy is needed. Variations in the warming of the earth by the sun and subsequent absorption of the heat by the air are not enough. But additional energy is available in abundance, when the air is very moist, in the form of *latent heat*. Vast amounts of energy stored in this form can travel with the air across huge distances before being released, by the right combination of circumstances, in the shape of a gale.

Latent heat

Perhaps you have wondered why boiling water takes so long to boil away. Even after reaching boiling point, a lot of energy is still needed to turn all the water to steam. The scientific explanation is as follows: to heat up one gram of water from zero to boiling point 418·68 J of energy are required; to turn one gram of water into vapour 2,500 J are needed. In other words, six times as much heat is needed to turn water into vapour as to boil it.

Basically the same thing happens with evaporation, even though the water never gets hot and, as it occurs at the water surface only, the process takes longer. The amount of heat absorbed is the same, whether the water vapour is created by evaporation or boiling. (It is this heat absorption that makes you feel cold when you first climb, steaming, out of a hot bath.)

Condensation, the process whereby water vapour turns back into water, is the opposite of evaporation. Accordingly, in condensation the latent heat absorbed by evaporation is released back into the air.

While water is in the form of vapour the heat is latent. It is present in the air, but you cannot see it or feel it. Every body of air that contains vapour also contains this latent heat.

The amount of latent heat in the air depends on the amount of water vapour in it. The amount of water vapour it can contain in turn depends on the temperature. At 15° Celsius, it can be up to 13 grams of water per cubic metre of air. The latent heat of one gram of water is enough to heat up one cubic metre of air by 2°. So, a saturated mass of air at 15° could, through condensation of all the water it contained, heat up by as much as 26° Celsius!

Causes of condensation

Why does condensation happen? We have already said that the ability of the air to absorb water is dependent upon temperature. That is why washing dries more quickly in warm air than in cold. Warm air can absorb more water than cold air. Cold air is saturated earlier.

When saturated air is cooled down, the excess water has to be shed. At first, this water will appear in the form of extremely small particles as fog or cloud. If the concentration is high enough, these particles will group together to form drops, which then descend as rain.

Table 1.1 Air saturation level at different temperatures

Air temperature (°C)	−5	0	5	10	15	20	25	30
Saturation level (g/m^3)	3	5	7	9	13	18	23	30

Air cools as it rises

This can be explained by two facts. First, air warms up when compressed. We all know this phenomenon from using a bicycle pump, which does not get warm through friction, but due to compression of the air inside it. Conversely, the air escaping through the valve feels colder than the tyre itself. This is due to the expansion and

3

consequent cooling of the air when it is released from the tyre.

Second, atmospheric pressure decreases with increasing height. If you imagine the weight of air pressing down from above, it is easy to understand why.

If temperature decreases with decreasing pressure, and if pressure decreases with increasing height, then, accordingly, temperature must also decrease with increasing height. Putting aside local differences due to the weather, the general rule is that for every 1000 m of altitude the air temperature decreases by 6.5°C, based on the assumption of 15°C at sea-level and –56.5°C at a height of 11 000 m (above which this rule doesn't apply anymore).

So if air rises through the atmosphere it will cool down, according to this rule. If it descends it will correspondingly warm up.

The release of latent heat

Obviously, where skies are blue, condensation is not taking place. This is because here the air is drier the higher you go, so it never reaches saturation point at any level.

If for some external reason there is now an upward movement of the air, for example because the air meets rising ground or a mass of colder air, or simply due to warming up, like the hot-air balloon, condensation will take place as the higher, colder layers of air are reached.

Now the latent heat is released. For each gram of condensed water, this is enough energy to warm up two cubic metres of air by 1°C. The air thus warmed will rise further, like the hot-air balloon. It will gradually cool down on its way upwards, but will nevertheless maintain a generally higher temperature than the surrounding air. So, the air rises further, until it has reached saturation point again (even though it has lost some of its original humidity), restarting the process of condensation. Now more latent heat is released, and the whole process is repeated over and over again, until no vapour is left in the air.

The flue pipe effect

Depending on the amount of water vapour in the air, the amount of latent heat can be quite substantial. This energy is transformed into vertical acceleration via the warming up of the air. As condensation continues, the same chain of events is repeated at every level. This adds up to an effect that could be described as a giant flue pipe, sucking air upwards at tremendous speed. At ground level air is drawn towards the flue pipe from all directions. The greater the effect, the stronger the resulting winds at ground level, the more violent the storm. The flue pipe is the powerhouse of the gale.

It is popularly believed that wind is created by air rising due to warming by the sun. This view needs to be modified. While such an effect actually exists, it must be stressed that the main energy of a storm is let loose by condensation. The gale derives its power from the humidity of the air.

2 High and low pressure

Vertical air circulation

Areas of high and low pressure are part of the vertical circulation of air in our atmosphere. We have already seen how the rising parts of this circulation cause wind. There the air was less dense because it was warm. Lower density also means lower pressure. Accordingly, this area of rising air is called an area of low pressure, or simply a *low*.

Air cannot go on rising for ever. What goes up must come down. When there is no more latent heat to be released by condensation, the air will cool at high altitude and the vertical flow will start to become a horizontal flow. As the air continues to cool, its density and weight increase. Consequently, this air will in due course begin to descend once more towards the surface of the earth where it will, as it were, form a heap of relatively dense air of correspondingly higher pressure. This is an area of high pressure or, in short, a *high*.

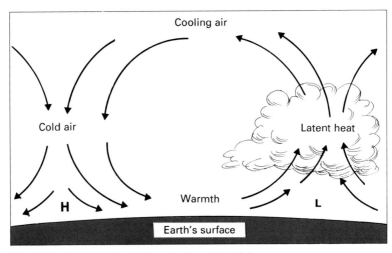

Fig 2.1 Vertical air circulation. L = low, H = high.

Like a heap of potatoes which will tumble down sideways if piled up too high, the air in this heap will start to flow away sideways. In principle, it will flow towards the nearest area of low pressure, where the space underneath the rising air needs to be filled up. Thus, the cycle is complete.

The planetary wind system

The distribution of highs and lows follows a theoretical pattern which is worth studying, even if in practice it is nearly impossible to see it in the real world because of all the irregularities. The pattern is global (hence the term *planetary* wind system) and takes into account the rotation of the earth and its orbit round the sun, but ignores the fact that its surface is not uniform.

As can be seen in Fig 2.2, in equatorial latitudes the intensity of the sun is highest. The hot air rises and so the tropical low pressure areas are created. At high altitude the air flows north and south, loses its warmth and descends in the so-called *horse latitudes* as an extended area of high pressure. Like the potatoes in the heap, the air flows away sideways, partly to the south to complete the circle and partly to the north to develop a new circulation in the northern hemisphere.

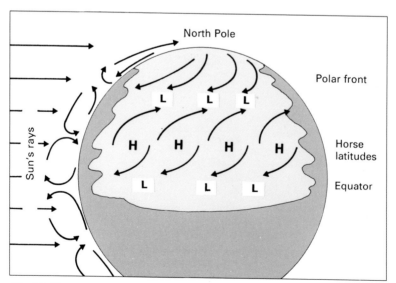

Fig 2.2 Planetary wind system.

Due to an effect known as the *Coriolis force*, the airflow at ground level to the north of this high pressure is, in fact, deflected north-eastwards by the earth's rotation, while the airflow to the south is deflected to the south-west.

Let us follow the first airflow as it moves north-eastwards towards higher latitudes and meets an opposing airflow roughly in the latitude of central Europe. This opposing airflow is part of the air circulation of the north pole, which is generated by the relative warmth of the area around the pole compared to the pole itself. The south-going airflow from this circulation is itself deflected south-westwards before it encounters the first airflow approaching from the opposite direction.

The collision zone of these two air masses is called the *polar front* or the *polar convergence*. More than the name, the actual collision is of interest to us because, when air masses of different temperature meet, as they do here, the cold air forces the warm air upwards. We already know what happens next – condensation, release of latent heat, ascending air currents and so on. Lows are born, lots of them, along the entire polar front if topographic influences did not sometimes disturb the pattern.

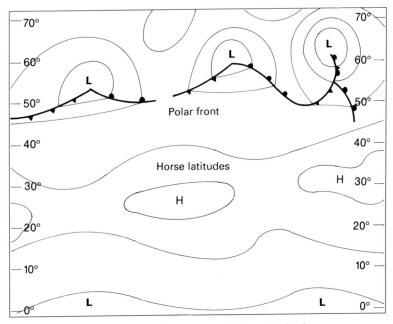

Fig 2.3 Typical distribution of pressure at different latitudes.

In practice, we can often relate highs and lows to the planetary wind system, which should please the theoretically minded. The big influential high pressure systems in summer, the Azores high and the Bermuda high, are typical results of air descending over the horse latitudes. The lows of the north Atlantic, notably the Iceland-low, are parts of the chain of lows along the polar convergence zone.

According to the time of year, the wind belts of this planetary system shift either north or south. Only during spring and autumn is the sun directly over the equator. In summer it shifts north by the angle of the earth's inclination (23.5°) and in winter it moves south by the same amount. However, the wind belts lag behind by about three months and only move to and fro by about 10° of latitude.

These belts of the planetary wind system should not be considered in isolation. The entirely different thermal conditions of land and sea mean that the vertical circulation is very vigorous in some regions and dictates the weather patterns of entire continents or oceans, while in other regions it is insignificant due to the lack of energy. It would be going too far to investigate the causes of these divergences, although this is another very interesting area of meteorology.

Winds around a low

The first thing we notice is that the wind does not blow straight towards the centre of a low, but is deflected (to the right in the northern hemisphere) by the Coriolis effect. Thus the air spirals around the low, in an anti-clockwise direction in the northern hemisphere. Conversely, in the southern hemisphere the spiral is clockwise, but we will stick to the northern hemisphere for the time being.

As the air circulates around the low, the pressure difference, on one hand, and centrifugal force, on the other, work against one another. Where there is a steep fall of pressure, the air is drawn more towards the centre of the low; where the fall is gradual, more air is drawn away from it. In the first case, the wind speed increases; in the second, it decreases. (In keeping with the basic laws of physics, the rotational force remains constant.) We can now see that in a low pressure system the wind tends to follow the iso-bars, even where they are irregular. This is why you can read the wind direction from the isobars, after allowing for a deflection of 10° to 25° towards the centre of the low due to surface friction. We can also see why, on the side of a low where the pressure falls most

9

steeply, where the airflow is drawn inwards and where, by defini-
tion, the isobars are closest to one another, the wind speeds are
always highest.

Sharp corners in the isobars indicate a change of wind-direction,
which is made possible by the airflow in the warm sector being
forced to rise above colder at the front. As the low approaches, the
wind speed often increases in jumps mainly due to the strong vertical movements of the condensation process. It is worth noting that
at the cold front the entire process of condensation is concentrated
in a very small zone, which is why all weather phenomena are more
violent here than in the larger area of the warm front.

Winds around a high

Imagine for a moment the isobars of a weather map as the contours
of a relief map. In most weather patterns you would see a hilly,
rolling landscape of a particular kind. The hills would have gently
rounded tops. In between, you would find deep valleys like craters.
In contrast to the broad hilltops, the craters would have only small
diameters.

Now, projecting the model of the vertical air circulation onto this
landscape, we see that the airflow spreads out over a large area
when descending over a high pressure area, but in the low it has to
squeeze upwards through a small aperture. Wind speeds vary
accordingly. The wind is slack in the high, where the gentle pressure gradient creates no energy. The right-hand deflection due to
the Coriolis effect only appears at the outer fringes of the high,
because of the low wind speeds. It is only on its way towards a low
that the wind speeds up again (around the craters on our relief
map), to reach a maximum in the spiralling flow around the low.

Wind information on weather maps

The landscape of highs and lows is shown on the weather map. The
heights, or isobars, show wind speed and direction at every point.
But the weather chart is only a momentary snapshot. In reality, the
pressure systems are on the move. In our latitudes their main
direction of movement is from west to east, from which they can
diverge from time to time, mainly to follow the polar front. They
can also realign themselves, causing one side either to lag behind
or draw ahead. The entire relief is constantly bulging and undulat-
ing in itself.

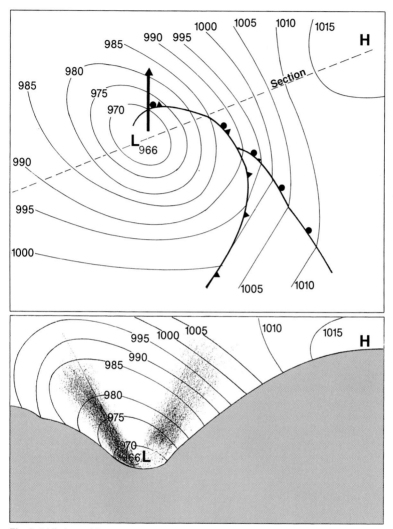

Fig 2.4 High and low pressure on a weather chart (above) and what they would look like as an actual ridge and trough on a relief map (below) if the isobars were height contours.

The present weather is an interpolation between the previous weather map and the forecast. To extract one's own forecast from a weather map is only possible with the utmost caution as an extrapolation from already known movements and trends. This method is too

11

unreliable for any prediction for more than 12 hours ahead. Amateurs should leave these forecasts to the professional meteorologists.

With the aid of a barometer you can try to identify which part of a weather system is overhead. This can be done quite similarly to fixing your position at sea using a row of soundings. The 'soundings' with the barometer are taken by noting its reading at regular intervals. Normally this will be done at two-hour intervals and the readings entered in the yacht's log. Easier to use and clearer is the barograph, which records the pressure as a continuous curve. I recommend every yachtsman to invest in one, as even without a weather map the barograph gives a clear indication of coming changes in the weather. However, to be able to recognise these indications it is essential to have had quite a lot of practice at watching the weather in relation to the barograph.

Once you have found your position in the weather system, it is possible to establish the weather pattern over the entire area. You will then be able to predict what the wind will do, what wind to expect on your present course and what you would find in neighbouring areas, should you elect to head there instead.

3 Wind strength

As we turn our attention specifically to gales, it is time to be more precise about this frequently misused term. Meteorologists talk of a 'gale' when mean winds of at least force 8 are encountered, which is 34 knots or more. Force 6 and 7, corresponding to wind speeds of 22 to 33 knots, are termed 'strong breeze' and 'near gale' respectively. Not everybody has an anemometer on board to measure the wind speed exactly and find out when the wind has officially reached gale force. But a subjective assessment of weather conditions is, of course, perfectly adequate and, from the point of view of safety, what really matters. Most people tend to overestimate the strength of wind and waves, and there is no harm at all in that.

Personally, I have come to call anything which feels uncomfortable a 'strong breeze', and then anything which starts to become frightening a 'gale'. Obviously, there are certain indicators to help with one's estimate of wind speed, but these differ depending on the area you are in and even vary from boat to boat. There are some notorious boats whose rigs start to hum in a force 5, and others where you can never hear any noise from the rigging above the slam-

Table 3.1 Beaufort scale

Force	Max Speed (kn)	(mph)	Description	Sail guide
1	1–3	1–3	Light air	Calm
2	4–6	4–7	Light breeze	Near calm
3	7–10	8–12	Gentle breeze	No 1 jib
4	11–16	13–17	Moderate breeze	No 1 jib
5	17–21	18–24	Fresh breeze	No 2 jib
6	22–27	25–30	Strong breeze	1st reef, No 2 jib
7	28–33	31–38	Near gale	2nd reef, No 3 jib
8	34–40	39–46	Gale	3rd reef, storm jib
9	41–47	47–54	Strong gale	3rd reef, storm jib
10	48–55	55–63	Storm	Storm jib
11	56–63	64–72	Violent storm	Storm jib
12	over 64	over 73	Hurricane	Storm jib

ming of the hull into the seas. The sea is similar. In shallow water you can have nasty breaking seas in a force 5, whilst in the really deep sea, you can have a relatively comfortable ride in a force 8.

Measuring wind speed

Don't place too much trust in the anemometer. What you read on the display is the apparent wind, the accuracy depending on the calibration of the instrument, further influenced by the movement of the mast. The latter can be reduced by damping the instrument. The true wind can be found out by constructing a vector diagram on a piece of paper (not the chart please!).

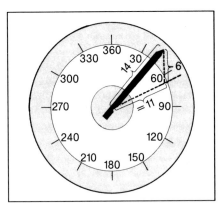

Fig 3.1 Estimating true wind speed and direction from an apparent wind indicator.

If you are good at estimating distances, you can use a simple trick to construct an imaginary vector diagram directly on the display of your wind direction indicator (Fig 3.1). The instrument's needle is the vector of the apparent wind, which in this example is 14 knots. The boat's speed is 6 knots. From the tip of the needle, imagine a speed vector pointing downwards of 6/14 the length of the needle, which is not quite half as long. Then, imagine a line from the centre of the dial to the end of the speed vector. This will be the vector of the true wind. The direction of the true wind will correspond to this line (in this example about 70°) and the true wind speed can be estimated in relation to the needle's length (about 11 knots). With some practice, this works surprisingly well!

Estimating wind speed from isobars

We have already seen that wind speed increases as the isobars get closer together. Meteorology actually has a formula by which this relation can be fairly accurately expressed mathematically – wind speed is inversely proportional to the distance between the isobars and the sine of the latitude. The former determines the amount of energy available, while the latter determines the Coriolis effect, which will be non-existent at the equator and at a maximum near the pole.

$$\text{Wind speed (kn)} = \frac{\text{interval between isobars (mb)}}{\text{distance between isobars (nm)}} \times \frac{556}{\text{sine latitude}°}$$

For example: on latitude 30° if the isobars are 160 nautical miles apart, on a weather map with an interval of 4 millibars between isobars, the wind speed is 27.8 knots.

$$\frac{4}{160} \times \frac{556}{\text{sine }30°} = \frac{4}{160} \times \frac{556}{0.5} = 27.8$$

When looking at a weather map, I always watch out for two critical distances between isobars. These are the ones which, on my latitude, indicate winds of force 6 or force 8. You can calculate these critical figures each time you need them, but you can also work them out once and for all for the latitude of your main cruising area. On British weather maps isobars are normally drawn at intervals of 4 millibars, while on German weather maps they are shown every 5 millibars and on Italian ones at only every 8 millibars.

Table 3.2 Approximate distance between isobars denoting strong breeze and gale at different latitudes (for British weather maps)

Latitude °	Distance (nm) Strong breeze	Gale
10	580	380
20	300	190
30	200	130
40	160	105
50	130	85
60	115	75
70	110	70

For the English Channel the critical distances are about 130 and 85 nautical miles respectively. If the isobars are about as close together as that, it indicates strong breeze at 130 nautical miles and gale at 85 nautical miles. Eighty-five miles is roughly the distance from Start Point to the Needles or from Portsmouth to Le Havre. Approximations like these help us to interpret weather maps instantly. Obviously, the parallels of latitude would give a more accurate measurement of distance, but they are seldom shown on a weather map.

4 Evolution of a gale

Rapid fall of pressure

In the latitude of northern Europe, if the barometer falls at more than one millibar per hour, all warning lights should be at red. This rate of fall is typical of an approaching gale at the normal travelling speed of depressions. You will be in the path of the approaching depression and stand a good chance of being in the centre of the storm.

The approaching gale on the weather chart

This rather resembles a target, with numerous concentric rings, becoming more tightly spaced towards the centre. To be a bit more scientific, it is a crater-like area of low pressure, perhaps down to 980 or 960 mb in our latitudes. It may be fed by an intense high of 1025 to 1035 mb in its warm sector, not more than 800 to 1200 miles distant, and is often further fuelled by an Arctic high to the north-west. The pressure difference from the associated highs to the low is around 5 to 7 mb per 100 miles.

A gale in northern European latitudes frequently develops from a wave on the polar front over the North Atlantic (Fig 4.1, 1st day). With pressure deepening it approaches the British Isles, while the fronts become more clearly defined and gradually swing into the warm sector (2nd day). Depending on the intensity of the high and the energy contained in the air masses involved, the low will either deepen or become shallower. If it continues to deepen the second front (the cold front) will tend to overtake the first (the warm front). It will force the mass of warm air to rise off the earth's surface above the cold air. This is called *occlusion* (3rd day).

In the course of its progress the depression rotates. The fronts swing out in front, while the centre of the low lags behind, trailing a trough of low pressure in its wake. The slowing down of its progress means that the low centre can affect areas even when the frontal system is already several hundred miles ahead. The dent in the isobars at the rear of the low (4th day) indicates the trough.

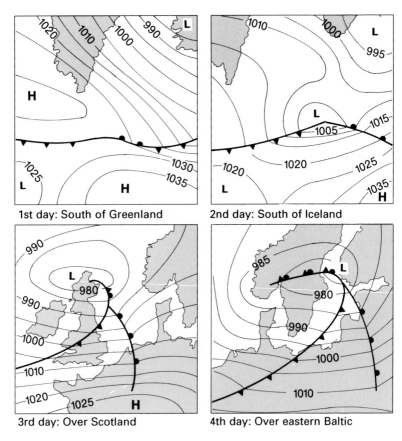

1st day: South of Greenland

2nd day: South of Iceland

3rd day: Over Scotland

4th day: Over eastern Baltic

Fig 4.1 Development of a gale depression in the North Atlantic.

Normally, the depression begins to fill after three or four days, having covered a distance of one to two thousand miles. This is due to the general equalization of air pressure, but also arises from the increased friction over the continental land surfaces as the low passes over middle and northern Europe.

The path of the depression

The only good thing about a deep depression is its comparative dependability. This kind of depression will always, more or less, follow the same pattern. If enough data from its area of origin, the North Atlantic, is available, its development can be forecast fairly accurately. The contribution of weather satellites is of enormous value in this respect. Formerly, the weather data available from the North Atlantic was, by comparison, rather patchy.

The speed of a deep depression can be very high. Two thousand nautical miles in 48 hours is perfectly possible. This equals more than 40 knots! The area of the gale can have a diameter of 500 nautical miles. The immediate consequence is that a yacht will rarely have the opportunity to get right out of the way of a gale. In 12 to 18 hours, the gale will have passed, while in the same time you would have covered only 60 to 90 miles. So all we can do is make some attempt to stay at least a little away out of the direct path of the storm.

Moreover, hurricane-evasion tactics cannot really be applied in the comparatively confined waters of northern Europe. Even sailing only 60 to 90 miles will usually bring you to land and the remaining question then is whether you can find shelter. But this is a whole subject on its own and will be discussed in Chapter 16, where we will look at planning a course ahead for a storm.

Passage of the fronts

To the south of the low you will experience a gradual veering of the wind which will increase as the pressure falls. The fronts, particularly the cold front, are heralded by heavy rain, a change in temperature and a sudden veer of the wind. At the front the wind will increase with frequent gusts, then decrease again. In the middle of a gale the typical cloud formations of a warm front can not really be distinguished from the towering clouds of a cold front or an occluded front. Fragments of low cloud and a lot of spray will turn everything an indeterminate grey. And sometimes the warm front does not even exist, because it may have occluded already with the cold front.

After the cold front you will normally experience the weather typical of the rear of a depression, with decreasing winds and lessening rain. For the storm-tossed crew this is the first respite. Clear indications of this situation are the fall in temperature and the new wind direction from the north-west.

A trough

If, after the normal signs of the passage of a cold front, pressure falls again and the wind backs, a trough is following the front and the situation will deteriorate once more. The trough amounts to a deep cut extending from the centre of the low into the ridge of pressure behind it. In this case, there will be an unusually strong fall in pressure with correspondingly high winds. These can last from two to five hours even, until the trough has gone through. Only when the wind veers again and pressure starts to rise will conditions become more settled. But only the wind may die down. The sea will often remain rough and, depending on the circumstances, may even worsen. This is due to the sudden change of wind direction as the trough passes, into the north-western and sometimes even veering past north, so that a new wave pattern develops on top of the existing swell. We will discuss these cross seas in Chapter 8, where we turn our attention to waves and swell.

Troughs often do not receive enough attention on weather charts. Due to the lack of clear symbols, such as exist for fronts, troughs do not readily catch the eye. And the signs of an approaching trough are also not obvious at sea, as the threatening clouds and heavy showers do not differ much from the aftermath of the preceding cold front. The Fastnet Race disaster of 1979 was due to a typical trough, and afterwards there was much discussion about whether the warning signs of the trough had been taken seriously enough.

North of the depression

To the north of a passing depression the whole picture is less dramatic. This is the sector of polar air which has by nature less energy. Moreover, normally we do not encounter any fronts here. The wind will back continuously. If it starts to blow from the south, we are in the path of the storm. But if the strong wind develops from the south-east, or perhaps east-south-east, we stand a good chance of keeping our distance from the storm.

As before, the wind increases with decreasing pressure and vice versa. Once the wind is back in the north it will be time to unbatten the hatches.

5   Effects of land

The distance between a high and low could be the span of an entire continent. The speed of the airflow between them is fundamentally determined by the pressure difference. Nevertheless, the shape of the earth's surface can substantially change both the direction and the speed of the flow. We will not discuss here the thermal effects of land and sea breezes, which are well known anyway, and instead concentrate on those influences that are relevant to gales.

Funnelling

The funnelling effect of a narrow strait between two areas of high ground is obvious and well known. The constriction generates higher winds (Fig 5.1).

The Strait of Bonifacio, between Corsica and Sardinia, is a typical example. In medium to strong winds you will normally encounter wind two forces higher in the straits than in the open sea.

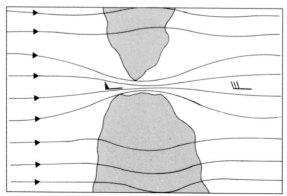

Fig 5.1 Funnel effect in a narrow strait.

Headlands

The effect around a headland is really the same as the strait effect, only in this case nature seems to forget that the restriction is only

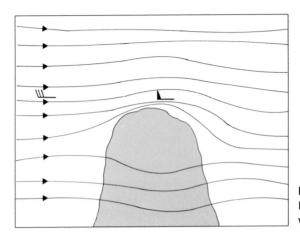

Fig 5.2 Effect of a headland on wind speed.

on one side. In any case, the result is the same (Fig 5.2).

Cap Corse, the northern tip of Corsica, is a notable example of this phenomenon and always produces an extra force or two of wind.

To leeward of a headland you should also be prepared for strong gusts. Friction as the air passes the land generates rotating air currents which are felt quite far out to sea, disturbing an otherwise stable airflow. On one side the rotation adds to the general wind speed, while on the other it reduces it. The difference between the two wind speeds can easily reach 10 to 15 knots, which is roughly two forces. These alternating squalls and calmer periods are an additional hazard for the harassed yachtsman.

Katabatic winds

These winds, sometimes referred to as 'white squalls', deserve a special mention simply because some quite outrageous stories are told about them. They will, it is often said, capsize boats and pin them to the water, because they blow straight downwards.

Like all winds, katabatic winds blow parallel to the earth's surface. It is their origin alone which has led to their reputation. They are formed by air masses that have cooled down over the tops of mountains and become denser and heavier than the surrounding air. The air then rolls down the mountain side gathering speed as it does so. By the time it reaches the open sea it will have acquired considerable force. Depending on the volume of cold air it will be experienced either as a heavy squall or as a local gale (Fig 5.3).

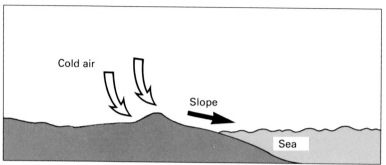

Fig 5.3 Katabatic winds.

Perhaps the best-known katabatic wind is the Mistral. It origi-
nates in the cold air high up in the French Alps. Due to the circulation around an area of low pressure over Genoa, this cold air is
set in motion towards the Rhone valley. On its way, it accelerates
due to its greater weight. As it crosses the coast over the Rhone
delta it is still under the influence of the Genoa low so that the high
wind speeds can be sustained even out to sea. Thus, the Mistral can
often reach as far as south-west Sardinia or even further.

Lesser squalls occur everywhere around the Mediterranean in
the lee of mountainous coasts. They only affect small areas, maybe
only a quarter to one nautical mile in width, but here it will blow
very hard indeed! Harder in any case than the wind out to sea, from
which one was perhaps hoping to shelter under the lee of the land.
More than one unwary yachtsman has been dismasted in a sudden
white squall when cruising along an otherwise quiet weather shore.

If for some reason one is forced to sail close to leeward of a mountainous shore it pays to keep a very sharp lookout ahead. White
squalls are easily recognised by the disturbed water. From a distance, they look like either a black or a white carpet, according to
how the light shines off the sea.

Thermal squalls

There is another type of strong wind which can produce a sudden
local storm. It can appear without prior warning in an area of uniform pressure and disappear as quickly as it comes. It is caused by
the rising of a pocket of hot air that has stayed at the earth's surface for a long time, due to an unexplained immobility of the air
mass. There is no cloud, no front, no swell – nothing to warn of the
strong wind to come. Maybe a very sensitive barograph would show

a small dent in its graph, but this is obviously useless as a warning.

The yachtsman in warmer latitudes never belays his sheets too permanently. When scanning the horizon, he will always pay special attention to any suspicious shadow. Or, to be precise, in the area just before the horizon. The horizon itself becomes indistinct when this fair weather gale approaches.

6 Thunderstorms

Thunderstorms are the most likely occasions for the cruising yachtsman, who normally confines his sailing to fine summer weather, to experience really strong winds, albeit of short duration.

Summer thunderstorms in our latitudes can develop gusts of up to force 10, so it is worth sparing them a thought or two. In meteorological terms, they are a localized and extreme case of a rising airflow fuelled by the release of latent heat through condensation. Two elements are required - air with an unusually high moisture content and a trigger in the form of a rising air current. Huge billowing clouds are formed, towering higher and higher into the sky. As condensation takes place, the upward motion becomes violent, sucking in air from all around and causing a line of squalls around the base of the cloud.

Rain normally starts only when the storm is well developed and marked by the dramatic cloud formation with its characteristic anvil top (which, incidentally can attain heights of as much as 6 to 10 miles). The rain when it comes is sudden and torrential, so much so that it actually cools the air in the middle of the cloud, causing that to descend with it. When it reaches sea level the rush of air turns outwards where it collides with the air being sucked in from outside, before rejoining the upward flow once again.

Lightning is the result of turbulence within the thunder cloud leading to separation of positive and negative charges, followed by a sudden and violent discharge of this electrical energy. Lightning itself has no influence on the wind in a thunderstorm, but can have quite an effect on the mood on board. The firework display can be quite alarming at sea, but that is a different subject.

The question of protecting your boat from a lightning strike would also go far beyond the scope of this book. We will limit ourselves to two observations. First, the chances of being struck by lightning at sea are really extremely small. It is amazing how often lightning strikes the sea around a yacht, but always misses the yacht itself. Second, even if lightning does strike the mast, apart from a loud bang nothing much will happen as long as it is properly earthed and no one is holding on to the shrouds. The crew are

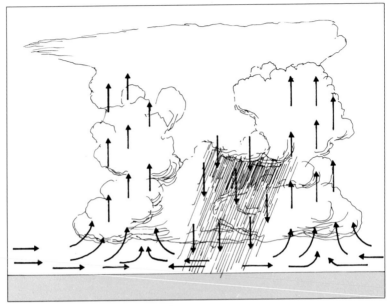

Fig 6.1 Section through a thunderstorm.

normally not endangered by lightning, but electric or electronic equipment is likely to be damaged.

Warning signs

Thunderstorms never come out of the blue. The weather conditions are distinctive. Sometimes, you can even *smell* a thunderstorm. They generally develop somewhere beyond the horizon and then approach from there. Very seldom will you watch a thunderstorm build up and then move away. Only the inexperienced think that, as a thunderstorm is downwind, it will recede. They are fooled by the surface wind direction, according to which a thunderstorm is always to leeward since the enormous amount of air that is sucked into it easily overrides the general wind direction, in which the thunderstorm itself is moving.

Actually, a thunderstorm follows the direction of the winds at medium height which, with a bit of practice, can be read from the movements of the clouds at that height. If this is not possible, you have to refer to the overall weather picture for the region.

Winds in a thunderstorm

As long as the storm is some distance off, you will enjoy a pleasant sailing breeze and perhaps tend to ignore its approach, which may then take you by surprise. When it starts to grow dark under the massive clouds; the vertical wall of cloud is directly above you and before rain is in sight, you are then in the region of the squalls which surround the storm in a large circle. The wind may freshen so rapidly that it can reach 30 to 40 knots (force 7 to 9) within seconds. At first, the direction of the wind will change little, maybe 30° to 40°. But as you get closer to the centre, the wind will suddenly change completely. You are then within the area of the central downdraft, which is confirmed by the heavy rain.

Until the thunderstorm has finally moved on, it will remain very squally with frequent and sudden changes in wind direction. Intervening calms for a few seconds often precede these changes.

Heavy seas do not normally occur. The thunderstorm is too localized for that. The waves do not have enough time to build up. Moreover, the changes in direction are so frequent that the normal wind-driven seas cannot really develop. Lastly, the heavy showers literally flatten the sea. In all probability, wave heights stay below three feet.

Thunderstorm tactics

You will probably be able to recognize the line of squalls well in advance. Depending on light conditions, the sea under the squalls looks either dark or light, but in either case clearly different from normal.

In busy sailing waters, the squalls are even easier to see. Just keep a look-out ahead, to where you think the danger will come from, and when the boats there start to heel over it is time to do something.

As the wind will quickly reach its full force it does not make sense to reef down in stages as usual. Sail area has to be reduced quickly and radically. If you find reefing too troublesome, don't hesitate to lower all sail and just motor through the storm. If you use this tactic, the engine needs to be powerful enough, because you could find yourself having to motor upwind and in a thunderstorm this can be quite arduous.

Motoring through the storm has the added advantage that you can then concentrate on your navigation, which could become critical. It is a lot easier to keep your bearings when you don't have to worry about tacking and leeway.

7　Tropical cyclones

Meteorology of a cyclone

The region around the equator is occupied by a belt of low pressure and rising air (see Fig 2.2). The winds that blow here, the trade-winds and monsoons, are warm and have a high moisture content. In other words, they are full of potential energy. Unlike at the polar front, no frontal systems develop here, as the opposing air masses only differ slightly in temperature. Also, the rotational force that is essential for the forming of a cyclonic low is not available. The air in northern (and southern) latitudes obtains this rotation from the meeting of opposing air masses along the polar front. Lows as we know them in our latitudes cannot develop on the equator. The equatorial belt of low pressure remains simply a belt.

Although the release of latent heat is quite vigorous, as energy is available in large quantities, wind speeds are actually rather low. Again, this is due to the missing rotational effect along the equator.

This changes when, in the northern summer, the low pressure area shifts to the north. Then it enters a region where the Coriolis effect comes into play and provides the surface airflow with the vital rotation. With the warmth of the sea also being carried north by the equatorial current, we have the ingredients for a tropical cyclone.

Physics states that speed of rotation increases as the radius decreases. Over the sea, where there is not much surface friction to slow the rotation, this principle applies with full effect. The ideal state, where centrifugal and centripetal forces are equal, comes close to realization. It is comparable to the so-called 'bath tub effect', where the water seems to circle endlessly around the waste pipe without going down it. Something similar happens with the unfettered circulation of hurricane force winds around the hub of a cyclone.

The hollow at the centre of the cyclone is the *eye*. Its diameter is between three and thirty miles and it is free of wind. But the sea is boiling, having just come through the full force of the hurricane and, furthermore, being the meeting point of swell from

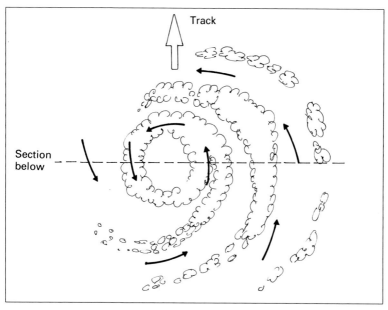

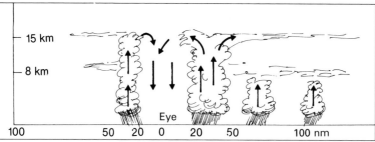

Fig 7.1 A tropical cyclone. The lower diagram shows a section through the cyclone along the broken line.

all directions. The confusion of cross seas is unimaginable.

Initially, the cyclone is only about ten miles across, but as it ages it can become as large as 50 miles in diameter. Away from the cyclone the wind decreases quickly if the system is a young one, but less so if the cyclone is well developed. Depending on the age and type of cyclone, the distance from the eye to the outer zone of winds around force 8 varies between 50 and 500 miles.

In the northern hemisphere, the surface wind blows in an anti-clockwise inwards spiral towards the inner part of the cyclone (which may be elliptical instead of round). This is where the condensation which fuels the whole system is most concentrated. Accordingly, torrential rain occurs in this region, while further out the rain is more like that of a warm front.

High above, air that has been sucked up by the hurricane is ejected from the system and forms spindrift clouds extending outwards in a spiral. These make the hurricane visible from a long way off.

A minority of this expelled air falls back within the eye of the cyclone and forms a miniature high pressure area. This explains the light winds and clear sky in the eye.

When and where do cyclones occur?

Whenever the equatorial low pressure area (or, to be precise, the *intertropical convergence*) attains latitudes between 15° and 25° due to seasonal factors and at the same time a warm ocean current delivers water temperatures above 26.5°C, tropical cyclones have a good chance to develop. These circumstances occur with regularity in certain regions so that an average figure for the number of cyclones to be expected annually can be calculated with some accuracy.

In the Caribbean and the neighbouring western Atlantic the hurricane season begins at the end of May, peaks in September and

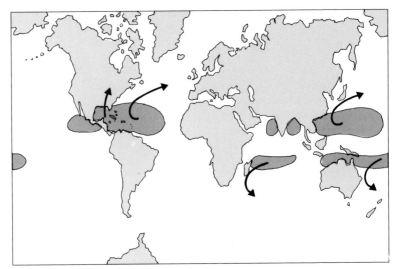

Fig 7.2 Areas of origin and typical tracks of cyclones.

terminates in November. In the north-eastern Pacific the season is quite similar, while in the monsoon areas of south-east Asia, a cyclone-free period does not exist. In any case, it is advisable to check the pilot books for the areas in which you are cruising. Most of these have detailed statistics for local areas, which should be duly consulted when planning a voyage.

Movement of cyclones

Elementary physics teaches us that an object will continue to rotate until slowed down by friction. In practice, this means that as long as cyclones stay out over the open sea they can last for a long time. Over land, because of the increased friction, they quickly lose their energy and, before long, their identity.

Their tracks across the oceans follow established patterns. In general, they follow the course of an inclined parabola with an east-west axis. In the northern hemisphere they travel westwards initially and then swing north and north-east. The apex of the parabola normally lies in the horse latitudes. The storm will cut through this belt between the two areas of high pressure. It may circle a particularly warm high pressure system if one is available. Should the cyclone survive as far as the polar front, it will most probably merge with the frontal system of a local low and form a joint depression.

In its area of origin, the travelling speed of the cyclone is low, in fact under ten knots. As it turns away from the equator it becomes faster. When passing through the high pressure belt, it slows to a crawl, after which the system accelerates again to as much as 30 knots on its way to the polar front (about the same speed as northern depressions).

Of course, there are cyclones which do not conform to the standard. For no obvious reason, they suddenly veer away from the expected course and frustrate attempts to avoid them. Hurricane *Carrie* in 1957 was one example, which went down in history for sinking the sail training ship *Pamir* in the course of a totally abnormal career.

The dangerous quadrant

Viewed from the centre of the cyclone (in the northern hemisphere), the forward right-hand quadrant is the most dangerous. The wind direction in the right-hand half of the storm coincides with the

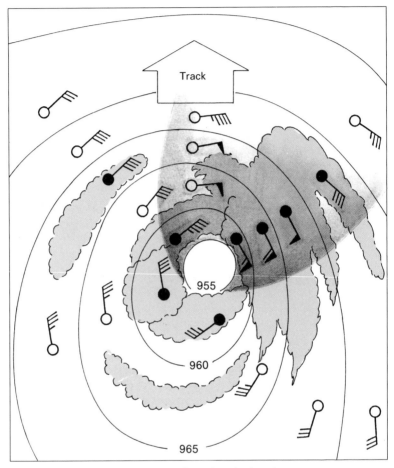

Fig 7.3 Dangerous quadrant (northern hemisphere).

direction of travel of the cyclone, so wind speeds are higher there. Moreover, the isobars tend to be closer together and condensation, the storm's main energy supply, tends to be especially vigorous in that quadrant.

The *dangerous quadrant* covers an area about 30 to 40 miles in diameter. This, above all, is the area to avoid. If you know the structure of a cyclone it is possible to locate yourself in relation to it by observing pressure, wind speed and direction, and thus try to avoid the danger.

Cyclone avoidance tactics

While most other storms can be weathered at sea providing you are in a well-found yacht with a competent crew, it is preferable to steer well clear of the path of a tropical cyclone.

In the United States there is an excellent hurricane warning system that broadcasts positions and predicted tracks of hurricanes on various frequencies. These warnings are invaluable. I recommend plotting the known positions of the hurricane in sequence on a large plotting chart, so you study its path to date. Similarly, I would pencil in all the predictions and later compare these with the actual path. In this way, an idea would emerge of the accuracy of the predictions. Using knowledge of the basic structure and movement of cyclones, you could then evaluate the predictions and plan your route accordingly.

Proper hurricane-avoidance tactics go beyond the competence and experience of the average cruising yachtsman, but here is some basic advice:

Plan ahead at appropriate time intervals, for example, every 12 hours. Pencil in the predicted position of both the eye of the storm and the yacht at these times. Make a note against the ship's position of the expected wind force and direction at each point, depending on the storm's position at that moment. Think what courses are

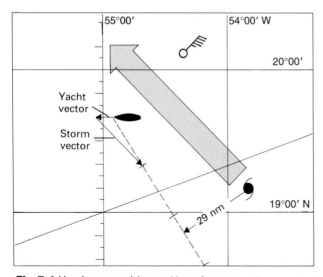

Fig 7.4 Hurricane avoidance. Use of a vector diagram to determine the safest course.

then open to you. Choose a course that will keep other options open, in case the storm deviates from its predicted path.

If it is not possible to keep completely out of the storm's way, the chosen course must be the one that puts the maximum distance between you and the expected track of the storm. A simple vector diagram on a plotting chart is useful for this. From your present position draw the vector for your course and speed made good over the ground. From the end of that vector, draw the *reverse* vector for the course and speed of the cyclone. A third line, starting at your present position and passing through the end of the second vector, will show you how soon and how far away the storm will pass, provided your information on the position and course of the cyclone is reliable.

In Fig 7.4 the yacht is sailing due west at 8 knots. The hurricane is tracking north-west at 30 knots. The vectors for these courses and speeds have been drawn on the chart and the end of the second vector shows where the yacht will be, relative to the storm, in one hour's time (for this purpose, the storm is regarded as having remained in its original position). The broken line, marked off at hourly intervals, shows that the hurricane will pass within 29 miles of the yacht in about 2 hours 20 minutes. It is also possible to see that a more south-westerly course would take the yacht farther away from the storm, though it would pass it slightly sooner.

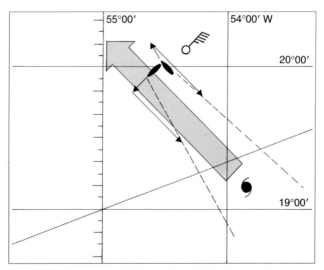

Fig 7.5 Safest courses in the path of a hurricane. The two yachts avoid the eye by the same distance.

The analysis of escape courses is extremely critical when the cyclone is coming straight towards you. In this situation you have a choice between two courses - either to run before the wind across the path of the storm or to reach away from it on starboard tack (assuming you are in the northern hemisphere). The first alternative will take you nearer to the left-hand quadrant; the second, nearer to the right-hand. The dividing line which determines which of these choices is best does not lie straight down the track of the storm, but, depending on the speed of the yacht and the storm, a little off to the right.

Fig 7.5 shows two critical cases, assuming that in both the speed of the yacht is the same. The vector diagram indicates that, for the yacht more or less directly in the path of the storm, the downwind course is best. For the yacht slightly to the right of the storm's track, the reaching course is correct. In this example, the dividing line, along which either course would be equally good (or bad), lies about 5° to the right of the hurricane's track.

Of course, it is also possible to imagine situations where exact navigation is not possible and where neither the yacht's nor the storm's position is certain. In this, not so unusual, case one can use this rule of thumb: *reach away from the storm on starboard tack in the northern hemisphere or on port tack in the southern hemisphere. Exception: if you believe that you are directly in the path of the storm, start by sailing downwind as fast as possible.*

Using the rule of thumb you might not be steering the ideal course, as it is more of an emergency measure than a complete substitute for the vector diagrams described above.

8 Waves

A few observations and definitions to start with. The *wave height* is the vertical distance from the trough of the wave to its crest. The *wave length* is the distance from crest to crest. On board a sailing yacht estimating the wave height is extremely difficult. Normally, the height of eye in a sailing yacht's cockpit will be around 2 m. If you see the crests of the waves just in line with the horizon, their height will be 2 m. If the crests of the waves are in line with the horizon from a height of 3 m, then the wave height is also 3 m; and so on. Personally, I would not necessarily climb the mast to estimate the heights of larger waves, although it would be possible.

The *wave velocity* is the speed of the waves, not of the water. The water itself, disregarding current and wind drift, does not move apart from oscillating at the frequency of the waves. The wave is a systematic deformation of the water's surface, moving horizontally. When a wave has risen in one spot, a new one will rise next to it, while the first subsides again. Next to the second, a third will rise, and so on. The material of the wave itself does not travel. At each stage the wave is made from new water.

Small waves, big waves

When describing the state of the sea, we really mean the form of the waves. Wave height, wave length, wave period (the time interval between crests) and wave velocity are the parameters used to describe the waves.

Waves get higher with time, with increasing wind and with increasing length of fetch. While the height of the waves reacts more to wind speed, the development of wave period, length and velocity really require a long fetch of open water. This is why you find long rolling waves in the open ocean, while inshore waves are generally shorter and steeper.

Increasing lengths of time and fetch have quite a substantial effect on wave development at first, becoming progressively less. In a force 8 the sea is fully developed after it has been blowing for 37 hours across a distance of 520 miles. In a force 9 this state is reached at 52 hours and 960 miles. In a force 10 it takes 73 hours and 1,570 miles. In the following table for wind speeds of 30, 40 and 50 knots, the wave parameters for three differing fetches are shown. This is average data for deep water which gives us an insight into wave mechanics. It goes without saying that nature can develop some quite different seas to these average ones.

Table 8.1 Wave characteristics at different wind strengths and lengths of fetch.

Wind			Wave			
speed (kn)	force	fetch (nm)	height (m)	length (m)	period (sec)	velocity (kn)
30	7	20	2.4	61	6.3	19
30	7	50	3.5	90	7.6	23
30	7	200	4.5	120	9.0	26
40	8	20	4.0	88	7.6	23
40	8	50	6.0	141	9.3	29
40	8	200	8.0	169	10.1	33
50	10	20	6.0	126	9.0	27
50	10	50	10.0	190	11.0	34
50	10	200	14.0	263	13.0	39

Waves in shallow water

Wave characteristics change in shallow waters between 50 and 20 m in depth. As the movement of the surface water extends some distance below the surface, contact with the sea bed lessens the velocity. Despite this, the wave does not lose its energy, and a wave coming in from deeper water will retain its period and height as it moves into the shallows. Only the wave length, and hence the velocity, are reduced.

Table 8.2 Change in characteristics as a wave enters shallower water.

Water depth (m)	Wave			
	height (m)	length (m)	period (sec)	velocity (kn)
50+	5	120	8	29
25	5	90	8	22
10	5 (breaks)	70	8	17
5	5 (breaks)	51	8	12

The steepness of the wave, expressed by the ratio of height to length, increases with decreasing water depth. In our example, from 1:24 in deep water to 1:14 in 10 m depth and 1:10 in 5 m.

This phenomenon of the wave becoming steeper in shallower water is general. It is the reason for the heavy seas on bars and sandbanks. The Dogger Bank is a notorious example.

The steepness of the seas is a major source of the discomfort on a yacht. Steep seas throw the yacht about more and it becomes increasingly difficult to control. At a height-length ratio of 1:14, waves begin to break.

Breaking seas

While regular wave movement, particularly a long swell, can be a pleasant, almost soothing motion, breaking seas spell trouble.

When waves move into shallow water, or when different waves systems meet, the height–length ratio rises. From 1:14 upwards, the wave becomes too steep to stay together. At first, only the crest breaks, as it is here that the wind has most effect. In a fully-fledged breaking sea the entire wave crashes forwards into the trough. The wave's energy is dissipated in foam and swirling water. Waves break regardless of their height, only the steepness is significant. In the waters around northern Europe, waves break from force 6 upwards, in deeper water from force 7 to 8. In the open ocean it is possible to experience waves of heights of 12 to 14 metres in a force 9 or 10. Due to their great length they do not break. Only when overlapping wave patterns push individual waves to even greater heights do these break. And then stupendously! These exceptional waves are sometimes called, rather loosely, 'freak waves'.

Breakers of small to medium height can be shrugged off, but breakers of any size are doubly dangerous for yachts. First, there is the impact of the mass of water hitting the boat. This has been measured at 5 to 10 tons per sq m. This is a force that liferafts or dinghies stowed on deck often cannot withstand. Second, the yacht can be rolled down the steep face of the wave and crash beam-on into the trough. Estimates have been made about the frequency of breaking seas. For normal seas in deep water, they range from 4 per cent in a force 7 to 12 per cent in a force 11. For seas crossing a short fetch of open water, the percentage is higher than for seas which have travelled a long way.

In the western Baltic, for example, a storm will seldom generate seas higher than 4 to 5 m. Larger seas are limited by the shallowness of the water. On the other hand, the wave lengths are shortened considerably which results in short, steep seas. They can be as steep as the large seas of the open ocean which is why the seas in these enclosed waters can be so treacherous.

Surface flow

The surface water follows a circular path, viewed from the point of view of a cork bobbing on the waves (Fig. 8.1). The oncoming wave draws the water towards itself and upwards, and drops it again after passing through. So there is a horizontal component as well as a vertical one, resulting in a circular movement. The velocity of the water particles during this process can be calculated from the diameter of the circle (the height of the wave) and the wave period.

Table 8.3 Orbital speed of surface water particles in waves of different height and period.

Wave height (m)	2	4	6	8	10	12	14
Wave period (sec)	6.0	7.8	9.2	10.2	11.1	12.0	12.9
Orbital speed (kn)	1.8	3.1	4.0	4.8	5.5	6.1	6.6

The *orbital* speed is in effect the velocity of the surface current on the crest of the wave and in the trough. On the crest the water flows in the direction of the wave, but in the trough the current is reversed. With a wave height of 6 m, the water will flow at about 4 knots. Unlike a normal current, which will not be noticed on board much, this alternating surface current has a marked effect. It is most noticeable on courses with or into the waves.

The yacht's inertia means that its speed over the ground does not vary as much as the reversals of surface current. Instead, the changes are experienced as an alternate increase and decrease in the speed at which water passes the hull, in time to the waves. The shorter the wave-period, the less the yacht will react to the changes of surface flow, and so the speed through the water will change all the more. Variations of plus or minus 3 knots are not unusual. Quite a lot, if you think what this means for the handling of the yacht.

Waves and currents

If the tide is with the wind the wave length will increase. If it is against the wind, the wave length will decrease.

Reduced in length, the wave makes up for it in the vertical plane. The wave's energy is channelled into increased height. With a 2 to 3 knot current running against the wind, this can mean an increase in height of 150 to 200 per cent. So we have a double effect: the wave is shorter, and it is higher. The result is a steep breaking

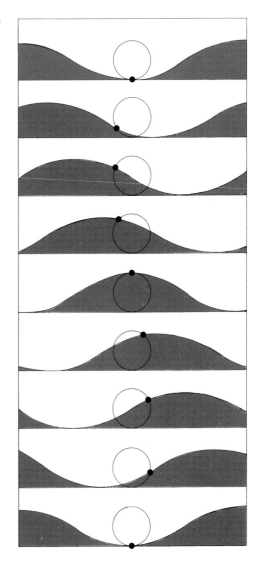

Fig 8.1 Orbital motion of a water particle at the surface. Wave movement is from left to right.

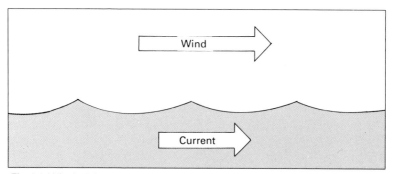

Fig 8.2 Wind with current.

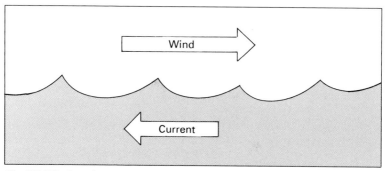

Fig 8.3 Wind against current.

sea where tide meets wind in an estuary or off a headland. On the other hand, when the tide turns, the effect is to smooth out the seas.

Interference and cross-seas

Whenever two or more wave systems are superimposed on one another, variations in wave size will develop. When they coincide, two waves will form a wave twice as high; two troughs will form a trough twice as deep; and a wave and a trough will cancel each other out. The resulting wave system will have areas of higher waves and areas of lower waves. In the language of physics this effect is known as *interference*.

These varying wave heights make cross-seas uncomfortable. Depending on the circumstances, some truly enormous waves can be formed.

Superimposed wave systems occur after drastic changes in wind

41

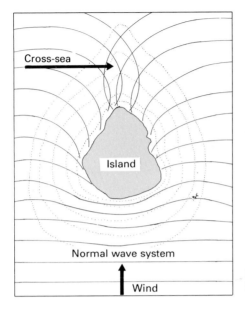

Cross-sea

Island

Normal wave system

Wind

Fig 8.4 Cross-seas in the lee of an island.

direction, as happens with the passing of a front or a depression. They also form when a new wave system develops on top of an old swell and when a regular wave system is distorted by the lie of the coastline. This is why surprisingly big seas can be encountered in the lee of small islands, where the refracted waves converge once more. Another example is Cap Corse. Whenever the Mistral blows, a significant cross-sea will develop in the lee of the cape. (This effect is enhanced by the small island of Giraglia.)

Interference effects probably explain many of the 'freak waves' which have been recorded throughout seafaring history, including in recent times. Although truly 'freak' seas do undoubtedly occur, many of them would perhaps be more accurately described as extreme of the normal wave-making processes.

Breakers

In water depths of 2 to 5 m (or 4 per cent of the wave length), waves of a special form, breakers, develop. The proximity of the sea bed disturbs the orbital motion and both wave length and height are reduced. As the water shallows further, the wave stumbles and breaks. The velocity of the crest of a breaker is significantly higher

As waves reach shallow depths, they become shorter and steeper.

than the normal orbital speed of a wave. (This can be explained by the fact that the orbit is deformed to an ellipse owing to the lack of depth. Velocity in an ellipse is greatest along its long sides.)

Breakers of the type just described only occur where water depth is 4 per cent or less of wave length. However, breakers of a kind are also encountered wherever seas break due to diminishing depth, which can happen in water 10, 20 or 30 m deep. Strictly speaking, this is a slightly different use of the term.

Waves in reality

In order to understand wave mechanics we have looked at waves in an analytical way. This perhaps gives the impression of an orderly system. This, however, is far from the case as the sea state, in reality, is often very different. The sea is often chaotic. The interaction of countless factors produces waves of an infinite variety of different forms, so that the scientifically-minded yachtsman will probably have difficulty matching them to theory.

Waves do not march down on you in neat rows, but approach in an irregular confusion. It may be nearly impossible to identify the main wave crest in order to determine the wave length. And perhaps the next wave does not materialize at all, only to be followed by a mountainous sea. There are also seas with no reverse slope. The crest goes by, but there is no trough behind it. Extraordinary, but true.

It is the way the sea appears through human eyes that matters. Subjective impressions determine the reactions of skipper and helmsman. Undoubtedly, these impressions differ from strict reality. Excitement, concentration, effort, fear and fatigue distort the senses. Subconsciously we can be nervous and exhilarated at the same time. The one certain thing is that neither feeling is conducive to objectivity. Very few people will accurately judge a 5 or 10 second interval between two wave crests. With so much going on it seems more like half a minute. No matter. The half minute *is* reality from the sailor's point of view.

9 The yacht in a gale

What happens when a yacht is caught out in a gale? And what *would* happen if we didn't adopt tactics or special measures to prevent it? What are the dangers? How do the major problems of heavy weather arise?

Let us take this subject in a systematic way, step by step, making a distinction between the effects of wind and sea, although in practice they will nearly always act together.

Stress factors in strong winds

All loads imposed on the rig by the wind increase by the square of the wind speed, in proportion to the sail area. In other words, to retain the same load the sail area would have to be reduced by 75 per cent in twice the wind speed, and by nearly 89 per cent in three times the wind speed.

If this was all, the problem of strengthening winds could be solved by reefing alone. But there are other forces apart from the wind. First, the drive that even an unreefed rig provides in 15 knots would not be sufficient to propel the yacht against the force of a storm and heavy seas. Therefore, in 45 knots of wind one would not reef down to 11 per cent of the original sail area. The storm jib of a yacht that normally carries 60 square metres of sail will be larger than 6.6 square m, which would be exactly 11 per cent. The extra load is dealt with by the use of heavier sailcloth, which also solves the problems below.

The main problem is the flogging of the sail in the wind. Especially in heavy weather, the helmsman's concentration will be centred on the oncoming seas, and it is inevitable that the sails will flap once in a while. But spilling wind in a storm imposes tremendous strain on the cloth and seams.

Violent rolling whips the mast to and fro. For the sails, this means additional stress, alternating tensile loads and flogging; making quite a severe test every time a wave passes.

All mechanical loads that apply in normal manoeuvres are multiplied in a storm. Gybes under storm jib happen quickly and, sometimes, inevitably. Only someone who has heard the crack like a rifle shot can appreciate the immense strain that is put on sail and sheets.

A constant rain of spray into the foresail is normal. Not normal is a solid mass of green water flying into it. This is the ultimate test for any sail and if it can bear this load it will withstand any amount of wind pressure as well.

The effect of too much sail

The stability of a yacht is critical for the amount of wind pressure that the rig has to stand. A yacht with a moderate stability will heel over when wind pressure increases. The effective sail area exposed to the wind is reduced and the load on the rig remains within reasonable limits. Theoretically, the effective pressure of the wind on the sails is reduced by the cosine of the heeling angle and thus tends towards zero at 90°. Theoretically.

In practice, a yacht will go out of control before the wind has heeled her right over. With increasing heel, the centre of effort of the rig goes from amidships to outboard and to leeward, while the centre of forward resistance is still amidships. The combined forces

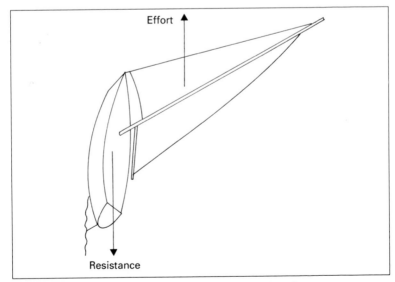

Fig 9.1 Cause of weather helm in a heavily-heeled yacht.

now produce a turning moment which creates so much weather helm that the rudder can not compensate anymore. In addition, the rudder comes further and further out of the water, so that eventually the yacht will luff up into the wind. Or even be taken aback, as if trying to tip her crew into the sea.

It is impossible to tear working sails in good condition by wind pressure alone. If it happens, nevertheless, it will either be down to some sail-handling mistake so that the sail has been chafed or caught up somewhere, or to the fact that the sail was old and worn out.

The decrease in tensile strength through wear is considerable. But instead of throwing a sail away one will probably continue to use it, without realising that it may have only 30 per cent of its original strength. This is normal practice, but the sail will not stand up to excessive loads.

Pitching

This problem lies not in the wind, but in the seas. Even small seas that do not break, say of a height of 3 to 5 m are a test of boat and crew. The motion of the waves is not passed on to the yacht as a whole, but first to the bows, then to the stern, or the other way around. The boat will never be entirely parallel to the surface of the waves. Stem and stern are lifted alternately. If the stem is up, the stern will be down, and vice versa. There are also lateral movements, but these are not experienced quite as badly.

Pitching and pounding are not only stressful for the yacht and crew, they also slow the boat down considerably. When the bows slam down into the sea, masses of water have to be pushed aside.

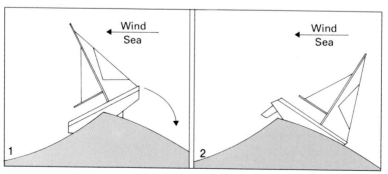

Fig 9.2 Pitching.

The energy used for this is subtracted from the forward momentum of the yacht.

Depending on her course and speed, a yacht can more or less easily accommodate the pitching motion of the waves. The closer to the wind and faster the boat is sailed, the more often it tends to overshoot the waves. The bows will then slam down into the next trough with considerable force. Under these conditions nobody can sleep in the forward berths and you have the unsettling feeling that sooner or later something will break.

Rolling

In addition to the other problems of heavy weather, most modern yachts have cross-sections with a high proportion of *form stability* (stability created by the shape of the hull). In contrast to stability created by ballast, which will hold the boat upright in relation to the vertical, form stability will hold the boat at right-angles to the

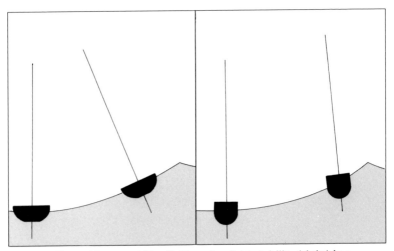

Fig 9.3 Effect of form stability (left) and weight stability (right) in a beam-sea.

water surface. If this happens to be sloping, not horizontal, the boat will be sloping too! Modern dinghy-type hulls tend to follow the inclination of every wave in the sea.

Boats which respond to the roughness of the sea in this way are uncomfortable to sail in. Moreover, working on deck is not made any easier. The crew may have to go without hot food and any repairs could be extremely difficult to carry out. The chances of sea-sickness are also increased.

Excessive rolling is also not without its problems aloft. The danger is that something might work loose. It has been known for the leeward shrouds to detach themselves from the crosstrees. There is a story of a three-masted full-rigged sailing ship which lost her rigging while becalmed in a high swell off Cape Horn.

The motion of a boat in a sea should not be taken lightly. Sea-sickness affects nearly everyone sooner or later. For the point of view of safety, seasickness obviously means less available crew. If, due to seasickness, the helmsman is the only person who remains more or less fit, he or she will not be able to cope. Helming for hours on end, and doing the odd job on the foredeck in between, is too much for one person, at least for the average cruising yachtsman.

Yawing

A yacht that does not maintain a straight course in a sea is said to be *yawing*. It has to be counteracted by the rudder. Excessive yawing can be too much for the helmsman to correct and result in loss of control. Therefore, it is of paramount importance for effective sailing to keep yawing to a minimum.

Yawing is caused by a combination of two effects of the waves. First, gravity tends to push the yacht's stern, as it lifts on a following wave, down towards the trough, resulting in a tendency to broach. (The same thing happens to the bows in a head-sea.) The helmsman must counter this as every wave approaches.

Second, when the seas are on the quarter, bow and stern are pushed in opposite directions by the wave's surface water flow, first to one side, then to the other. On the front of the wave, this turning moment increases the tendency to broach, while on the back of the wave the tendency is reversed.

These turning forces catch a yacht running down the face of a wave at a particularly vulnerable moment. The helm may already be hard over. As the crest approaches, the direction of the surface current means that the flow of water past the rudder slows down, reducing its effectiveness. It is essential that the rudder retains enough effectiveness to keep the yacht on course. Otherwise, a broach will result.

In a big sea, broaching can be decidedly dangerous. The yacht will round up very sharply, eventually tripping over her keel and ending up on her beam ends under the weight of wind and water.

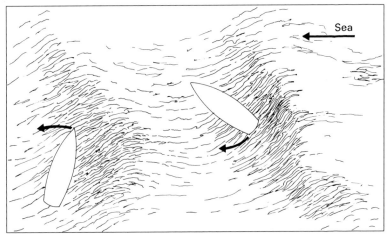

Fig 9.4 Yawing effects of waves on bow (left) and stern.

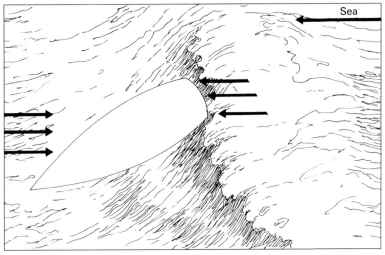

Fig 9.5 Broaching forces.

Scooping water on board

Nosediving into approaching waves is primarily a problem for
motor boats that are driven too fast. It seldom happens to sailing
boats, although when beating into a steep sea it can occur that the
bows bury themselves in an oncoming wave and a lot of water is

Fig 9.6 Submerging the bow.

scooped on board. This tendency increases with the boat's speed and of the approaching seas. It makes it harder for the yacht's pitching to accommodate the wave motion.

Luckily, with nosediving not much boat speed is lost. The reason for this lies in the surface water flow which, in the trough, is running in the same direction as the boat and stops the bow from digging too far into the wave. (The flow also reduces the rudder's effectiveness somewhat, but this is less important on this point of sailing.)

Running downwind, water is not normally scooped over the bow. The reason is simply that in a following sea it could only happen if the yacht was actually moving faster than the waves. The closer the boat's speed gets to the wave speed, the slower the waves approach the boat. And the easier it is for the yacht to adapt to the wave motion.

Something akin to nosediving does happen downwind, only at the stern. If the following seas for some reason change rhythm and

Fig 9.7 Submerging the stern.

the stern cannot rise to the next crest, the water will flood over the stern into the cockpit. Provided they are not breaking seas, these incursions are entirely harmless as they do not have any kinetic energy. Normally there will be no damage. As long as the cockpit drains are working, the water will be long gone before the next sea comes aboard.

The yacht in a breaking sea

The situation becomes much more serious if the seas build up and start to break. It is worth remembering that for this to happen, not only the height of the waves, but the ratio of height to length is important. In the North Sea or Baltic, breakers can develop in wave heights of only 3 to 5 m. Luckily, these seas are less dangerous as they are less massive.

Two things happen when one is caught in a heavy breaking sea. First, tons of water pour on to the deck, sweeping away things in its path like an avalanche. Often the cockpit will fill with water; the horse-shoe lifebuoys will be left dangling over the stern (if they were lashed to the stern pulpit) and the Dorade ventilators will be washed away. In some cases, even a dinghy that was lashed to the

It is essential to keep the yacht from turning beam-on in a huge following sea such as this.

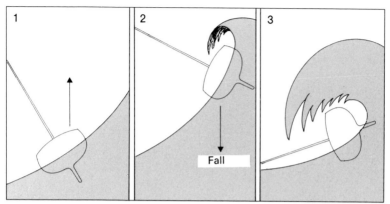

Fig 9.8 Falling off a breaking wave.

deck may be swept off. If someone happened to be on the foredeck, he will have been knocked off his feet and have had some anxious moments trying to cling to the boat. Everyone will normally be soaking wet under their oilskins.

Second, not only does water fall on to the boat; often the boat itself falls. It tumbles down the front of the wave, which only a moment before was lifting it up, and is engulfed by the breaking sea when it reaches the trough.

Falling off a wave is at its most dangerous if the yacht is beam-on to the sea. The side of the hull will hit the bottom of the trough with destructive force. The damage will obviously be on the leeward side: stove-in windows or portholes, bent stanchions and damage to the joint between deck and hull. Anyone whose harness is not hooked on securely will be in serious danger of being washed overboard, while below decks there is a severe danger of broken bones. Heavy objects, such as batteries, tanks, tool boxes, pots and pans can come loose and shoot across the cabin. Wherever these projectiles land the damage can be substantial. It has also been known for an engine to come loose, although I know that in that case fatigue of the engine mountings was to blame. But who always has brand-new engine mountings in his boat?

Yachts which capsize when falling off a breaking wave may also be rolled right over. Once the mast is parallel to the water and a breaking wave hits the upturned side of the hull, a roll-over is quite possible. It is equally possible to imagine the disastrous results of one.

Falling off a wave is less dangerous if the wave strikes at the stern. The yacht will then fall bow-down towards the trough. The impact will not be as severe. If she holds her course before the waves, the bow will appear again and the yacht will carry on sailing. If not, we have the start of a broach, as already described above. But this time we have the added effect of the breaking wave, which vastly increases the tendency to capsize.

Another unpleasant situation is when a yacht loses way when trying to climb up the face of a breaking sea and subsequently falls off the wave stern-first. Few helmsmen will be able to keep control of the helm when this happens. The rudder will be hard over (if it is still there at all) and the yacht will again go beam-on to the seas. Again with all the consequences described above.

10   Design features for heavy weather

A yacht designed solely for use in heavy weather would probably look like a submarine. The heavy cylindrical hull of a submarine is safe in almost any sea, while its steel plates can withstand almost any punishment (including depth charges!). The rig is extremely compact and strong. The short mast, in the form of a periscope, can even be retracted. Ideal!

However, we have to compromise. Our yacht has to have good sailing abilities, offer some comfort, be easily handled, look nice and not be too expensive – all at the same time. Safety is one of the prime considerations in this compromise, but the other things cannot be neglected.

The fact that safety sometimes has to be compromised is seldom acknowledged. But if safety was the only consideration, sailing would not be much fun.

From the starting point of the typical family cruiser, we will look at all aspects of safety on board and the compromises involved. We will take the boat piece by piece and examine it for heavy weather suitability. Which are the features of the boat that determine her suitability for heavy weather? How does the overall picture change if we change certain elements? How do they all interact?

Size of yacht

If one is looking for points in favour of larger yachts, heavy weather ability is fairly high on the list. Obviously, an ocean liner of 300 m in length is less troubled by seas than a 10 m fishing boat. The larger mass makes a positive contribution to the boat's motion in a seaway. So it does with yachts. Larger yachts drive through the seas more easily, they are less liable to veer off course and can maintain higher speeds when running before a gale. They also offer their crew more protection in the cockpit and below decks. They can be better equipped and are easier to steer.

The list of arguments in favour of a larger yacht is a long one. That is why ocean crossings in very small boats are considered as outstanding, enterprising feats. I believe that without reason one does not want to expose oneself to this kind of experience.

Standing rigging

Only in racing yachts is it necessary to calculate the exact strain on the rigging in order to be able to reduce weight and windage aloft. For cruising yachts the rule is always that one size larger can do no harm. And we can also afford to forego sophisticated and vastly expensive features such as rod-rigging. A sense of geometry and basic engineering principles will easily enable one to see where strong forces are at work. The smaller the angle at which a stay joins the mast, the higher the load. This problem arises on most modern yachts, where the base of the shrouds is well inboard to allow the genoa to be sheeted in closer. To avoid too small an angle between mast and shrouds one or more sets of spreaders are used. With the introduction of spreaders the angle of the shrouds to the mast increases and the load becomes acceptable once more. But the number of shrouds has now increased. For example, a double spreader rig has upper, lower and intermediate shrouds. And it is the sum of the loads on all the shrouds that is critical in terms of the load on the hull where the shroud plates are attached, and of the compression load on the mast and mast step. The loads at these critical points increase in relation to mast length and the horizontal distance from the shroud plates to the base of the mast, regardless of the number of spreaders.

This should be kept in mind when comparing dimensions of shrouds and their attachments. And it is especially important to examine how the load on the mast is transmitted to the hull. It should be distributed as widely as possible towards the sides of the hull, using stiffeners and bulkheads.

The cross-section of the hull in the area of the mast and shrouds is liable to serious deformation. The windward shrouds pull the hull upwards; the heel of the mast pushes down in the middle. The entire section is distorted into a parallelogram. This is why, in some yachts, doors and lockers get stuck when the boat is heeled. Only strong bulkheads and stiffeners in this area can counteract these loads.

Stays are less problematic, since their angle to the mast is larger. However, sometimes the weak points lie in the attachment to the hull. The rugged look of a stemhead fitting can be pure illusion, if it is not secured to the hull properly. I have several times seen stemhead fittings that have been pulled off the hull. One critical point is that the holes for the bolts, by which the fitting is fastened to the hull, are continuously exposed to spray and water. Once water is allowed to penetrate into these holes, in a timber hull, deterioration can happen very quickly.

Double forestays are a good thing, but they should also have separate fittings at the bow and at the masthead. Stays often break at these fittings.

Whether you have a grooved forestay or a conventional hanked-on foresail should make no difference to the strength of the stay. When changing headsails in heavy weather, I personally feel that it is easier to hank on a foresail rather than feed the luff into the groove. But maybe I am just not used enough to these modern inventions.

Mast and halyards

The material of the mast is not really an issue any more. Modern aluminium masts are so advanced that the good old spruce mast is almost a thing of the past. However, again you should bear in mind, when deciding dimensions, that you are not racing. Generous sections with ample reserves of strength inspire confidence.

When masts are bent fore-and-aft by the lower shrouds to flatten the mainsail, problems arise with compression loads. When the mast is bent in this way, the compression forces tend to become bending loads, and proper use of the runners is necessary to preserve the mast. Also, mast sections will be on the small side in order for the mast to be able to bend in the first place, as the designer will assume that the runners will be correctly adjusted. In heavy weather masts of this type present an extra risk.

Spreaders are trouble-free in normal use. This can change in heavy weather. Due to the violent motion of the boat, the slack leeward shrouds flap backwards and forwards. This movement is passed on to the spreader and from there, aided by the leverage of the spreader itself, to its attachment point on the mast. The strength of this attachment for the spreaders is critical for the heavy weather suitability of a yacht.

Halyards running inside the mast are often condemned for safety reasons, although they do have other points in their favour. At all events, spare halyards should be rove, preferably more than just one, though it will be extremely unlucky if more than two halyards break in one gale. Afterwards, you can reeve the new halyards at your leisure.

Halyards led aft to the cockpit help with reefing or changing sail.

But they should run through as few sheaves and blocks as possible, since otherwise the friction will be too great. A free-running halyard is important for lowering a sail swiftly. If you have to pull it down fold by fold, you'll end up in a dangerous predicament on the foredeck.

Sails

It can be left up to the sailmaker to decide the cut of the sails, as well as other details and the type and weight of cloth. The amateur cannot really be the judge of this. Still, it is important to be able to spot poor quality sails and reject them. Often money is saved in the wrong place. This especially applies to the seldom used storm sails, although these will incur the highest labour costs if they are made properly. Eyelets, for example, have to be laboriously sewn in and reinforced by hand. This quality has its price, but it is worth paying as a torn storm jib can defeat your entire strategy for coping with a storm. And the alternative strategy may be far more inconvenient, if it exists at all.

In any case, I would strongly recommend a sail wardrobe with an adequate choice of sails for stronger winds. To change straight down from the working jib to the storm jib is a big step, for instance. It would probably be better to have a No 2 jib, high cut from the heavier cloth of a storm jib. Such a foresail is ideal for strong winds in summer, which seldom exceed force 8. If a No 2 jib is not available most skippers will probably hold on to the working jib for too long and delay the decision to change down to the storm jib – an unnecessary extra strain on boat and crew.

The mainsail has to be made from a cloth that can cope with the loads of at least a force 8, for which the highest row of reefing points is intended. Weak points are again around reinforcements, eyelets and grommets. The reefed-down mainsail is, on most yachts, still within reach of breaking seas. This is why *trysails* are used. These are very high cut sails hoisted in place of the main attached at the luff to the mast and then sheeted loose-footed, like a foresail, through the spinnaker blocks. The cloth of such a sail used to resemble a heavy tarpaulin and was very difficult to handle. On longer voyages I would now have a trysail made from modern cloth on board.

'Jiffy' reefing, with hooks for the luff and a leech pendant is, in my view, the safest and most effective way of reefing. Normally it only takes a few seconds to put in a reef in this way, and the sail will also set properly afterwards.

Under no circumstances would I use roller reefing. The mechanism for turning the boom is prone to problems; the sail sets badly after reefing; the luff rolls up into an awkward bundle around the boom; the foot of the sail cannot be hauled taut; and the kicking strap is hard to rig. Roller reefing must have been invented for some other purpose, as it is useless for sailing.

In-mast reefing systems are a different matter. If they function properly, they do just the right job. They avoid the difficulties of working at the foot of the mast; the reefed sail sets reasonably well; and the foot can still be trimmed, although not the luff. The main advantage of these systems is the ability to reef without leaving the cockpit which is easy if done in the right way.

In-mast reefing can become dangerous in strong winds if the system is not operated properly. If, for instance, the yacht is not pointing straight into the wind and the mainsheet is not free enough when unrolling the main, the sail will catch the wind and come surging out of the mast before anybody on board knows what's happening. This can happen so quickly that the mechanism inside the mast is damaged. The full main will knock the yacht down or flog itself to pieces. With the machinery inside the mast damaged, the question will be what to do next.

A similar view applies for roller-furling headsails. They are widespread these days, as again they save the harassed cruising yachts-

This big cat is running on minimal sail in a very lively sea. *Photo: Barry Pickthall/PPL.*

man work on the foredeck. More important, they reduce the risk that is always present when somebody has to go forward in a gale. But these roller-furling headsails also have to be ha̶n̶d̶l̶e̶d̶ ̶w̶i̶t̶h̶ care. More than once I have seen headsails ripped to shreds because the furling line had either broken or been accidentally released in a strong wind. In this situation, it can be very difficult to get the remaining shreds of sail down on deck and feed in a new sail.

Another serious drawback of roller-furling headsails is the fact that when reefed they, too, set badly and the thick bulge around the forestay disturbs the flow of the wind. If you need to point as high as possible, this could be a fatal handicap.

If you do not want to lose the roller-furling foresail and its advantages, a solution can be found in the form of a detachable inner forestay which should be fastened to the deck aft of the forestay about 20 per cent nearer to the mast and which can then carry a hanked-on No 2 jib or storm jib. When not in use this stay can be detached from the deck so that it will not be in the way of the genoa when tacking.

A second advantage of this inner foresail is its closeness to the main, which enhances the airflow between jib and main and improves windward performance substantially. Steering is in no way impaired by this sail plan, as the jib is more effective and produces more drive. The inner foresail can be got ready well in advance, while you are still sailing under genoa. The stay can be fixed to the deck and the sail hanked on, ready to hoist, tied down with thin, breakable sail ties. When the wind strengthens you can furl the genoa and hoist the heavy weather jib, both from the cockpit.

Hull construction

The relative merits of different hull materials are debated with an almost religious fervour among sailors. Personal taste, maintenance, re-sale value, and many more considerations determine the choice of material, all of them irrelevant to our question of heavy weather suitability. All of the materials used for boatbuilding today have proven themselves under extreme conditions. It is more important to differentiate when it comes to the design and construction method. One should avoid types with extremely light displacement. They have been developed for another purpose. I would be sceptical of the claims made for them in many sales brochures. An ultra-light yacht requires sophisticated techniques of construction. On the other hand, a heavily built boat needs to be constructed strongly throughout. The entire construction is only as strong as its weakest point. Potential weak spots are the bonding of hull to deck, the fastening of the keel, the attachment of stemhead fittings, shroud plates and steering gear.

Bow shape

Some yachts pitch like a rocking horse, while others glide through the waves as effortlessly as a dolphin. Why is this? Whenever the bow meets a sea it buries itself in the water. Drag increases and speed is lost. A series of short, steep waves can bring a yacht to a complete standstill.

This is why the bows of a yacht have to be sharp. The bows should cut through the seas rather than shoulder them aside. To avoid burying themselves too deeply in the sea they have to be light. The main weight of any yacht should be concentrated amidships. The anchor chain, normally stowed right forward and often weighing up to four hundredweight, does not improve the heavy-weather performance of a yacht (alas, alternatives are difficult to organize). Many designers tried successfully to minimize the burying of the bows by having flat sections in the bows to create hydro-dynamic lift. But the burying is stopped at the cost of slamming, which is painful for the boat and for the crew. The ideal configuration for the bow is a shallow V-shape with a fine entry and little weight in the ends of the boat.

Cross-sections

The righting moment of any yacht is a mixture of weight and form stability. Long slim yachts with S-shaped sections have a high proportion of weight stability, while wide hulls with shallow sections have a higher proportion of form stability. In the latter case, the weight of the keel can be reduced. As form stability improves sail-carrying at low angles of heel and thus increases the efficiency of the sail plan, nobody wants to miss out on form stability these days. But, as already said, the yacht with a high degree of form stability tries to remain perpendicular to the surface of the water, and its angle of heel is largely determined by the steepness of the waves. This rolling with the waves is not only uncomfortable, but it makes the mast swing to and fro which constantly disturbs the flow of the wind across the sails. It is only the sails that prevent excessive rolling of this type of boat, as anyone will discover when motoring or, better still, when becalmed in a swell.

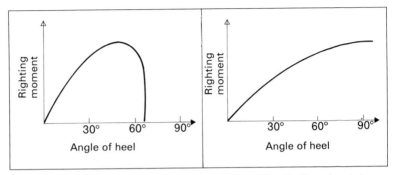

Fig 10.1 Stability curves for yacht with form stability (left) and weight stability (right).

The yachts with a high proportion of weight stability orientate themselves relative to the gravitational pull of the earth, which is the true vertical. Waves approaching beam-on would normally not disturb these boats so much.

The yacht that relies on form stability is dangerous if rolling is extreme. As in sailing dinghies, stability increases when heeled up to a certain point, beyond which it decreases and then actually becomes negative. Weight stability, however, increases with the sine of the heeling angle up to a 90° heel.

For a hull that possesses both types of stability, the stability curves are simply combined. Depending on the proportion of both elements, the higher stability can be nearer the beginning or the

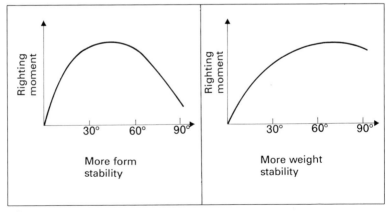

Fig 10.2 Stability curves for combinations of form stability and weight stability.

end of the curve. For safety, a good margin of stability at angles of heel approaching 90° is essential to avoid the worst in a broach.

Modern racing yachts, whose lines are increasingly being copied in normal production boats, have a high risk of capsizing. A little residual stability at 90° is not enough to right the boat when it falls off a wave.

And that is not all. If the worst happens and the yacht capsizes and turns right over, the form stability has a very unpleasant result. In Fig 10.3 you can see an alarming similarity between a capsized yacht of that type and a dinghy sailing normally. The capsized yacht is just as stable as the dinghy. Before righting herself, she would have to be heeled over by another big wave far enough for the centre of gravity to move back past the centre of buoyancy. Only then will she turn over again, this time back the right way up. This is why you hear accounts like: '... It was an age before she righted herself again.'

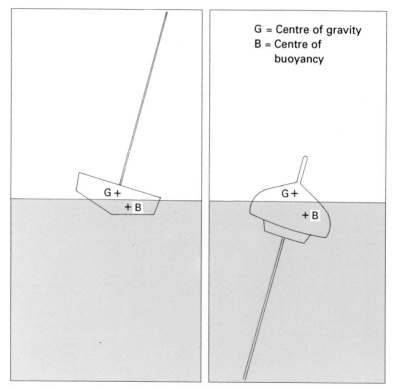

Fig 10.3 Comparison of sailing dinghy (left) and upturned yacht.

The subject of stability can be summed up as follows: form stability and heavy weather ability are opposite poles. Every yacht combines both types of stability in her lines. The proportion of each type is a major index of the heavy weather ability of a yacht.

Hull profile

Here we are concerned with controlling the yawing tendencies experienced in a heavy sea. While the rudder is responsible for the active control of these movements, the passive reduction of these tendencies can be achieved by the shape of the yacht's underwater profile. This is important because it ensures that in heavy weather the helmsman does not have too much difficulty holding the boat more or less on course. On the other hand, the underwater profile should not be such as to seriously reduce the effectiveness of the rudder.

Course stability is achieved by a long keel which resists sideways movement at both bow and stern. On the other hand, a long-keeled boat does not accord with the concept of modern fast family yachts. The long-keeled yacht has too much drag and inadequate windward performance. The latter would be optimized in a boat with a deep narrow fin with the rudder far apart from the keel, which is a design which also answers readily to the helm. Again, we have to find a compromise between these two extremes, although there must surely be wide scope for personal preferences. One compromise could be a moderately long fin keel combined with a powerful rudder.

Another compromise has to be found in the bow and stern overhangs. While long overhangs help to reduce pitching, they unfortunately increase yawing. They offer easy targets for cross-seas and a long lever for pushing the ends of the boat off course.

Steering system

The remaining yawing movements have to be counteracted by the helm. For this purpose, a well-balanced steering system is necessary which provides good steering control without excessive load on the helm over a wide range of speeds. Nowadays we have perfectly balanced rudders with optimized profiles that meet these demands. With conventional rudders there is always the problem of too much load at high speeds, which can become a severe handicap when running before high seas and strong winds.

Where strength is concerned, we have to rely on the skill of yacht designers, since substantial forces are at work on the rudder which have to be borne by the hull. Often a skeg is regarded as the solution for this, regardless of its drawback in producing an unbalanced, or only partially balanced, rudder. Whether a skeg is more likely to prevent the rudder breaking off than a strong stock I do not know, but I would always prefer a broken rudder stock to a skeg torn out of the hull with the water pouring in.

The important thing is that the rudder should be deep enough. The further aft it is, the deeper it has to be. Two reasons for this: first, the danger of the rudder coming out of the water when the yacht is heeled over or pitching heavily; second, the surface flow on a wave is considerably less, even at one or two metres depth, which enables the rudder to be much more effective down there.

I would take a very close look at the mechanical components of the steering system. In a cable steering system, the quadrant should have a large radius, so that stretch in cables only causes a minor amount of play at the blade. A loose steering system in heavy weather can deteriorate quickly due to the strains on the rudder and maybe even cause a cable to jump off a sheave. Also important are the rudder stops which need to be very strong, but flexible.

With hydraulic steering gear, I would prefer a long arm. The loads on the pivot and mountings of the cylinder are less and the danger of breakage is reduced.

The dinghy

There are yachts whose dinghies are successfully stowed on deck all their life. But unless they are very large yachts, I would still have my reservations about this, especially out on the ocean. However, the dinghy should at least be stowed keel upwards or have a strong tent-like cover so that no water can get inside. Lashings should be diagonal, as vertical lashings are sometimes exposed to a heavy strain. A dinghy that breaks loose on deck will damage everything around it.

Dinghies in davits are also dangerous if the yacht is not very large. Somebody once told me that if you can afford to have your dinghy in davits, you can also afford to cut it loose in heavy weather, which is one solution.

There is no way of towing your dinghy in bad weather, even if it is a heavy and stable boat. If it capsizes (and there will be ample opportunity for this) the painter will instantly break and the dinghy will be lost. Maybe this is not as bad as it sounds. Another danger is to be overtaken by the dinghy. When going down the face of a wave a dinghy surfs with ease, while the yacht will remain in displacement mode. So the dinghy shoots towards the yacht at great speed, and a collision is the result. You will be thankful if it is only an inflatable.

As a tender, my preference is for an inflatable which is deflated and stowed away in a locker. As an encouragement to follow this procedure I allow myself an electric pump, because then there is no excuse for not deflating it and stowing it away after use.

Similarly, the outboard motor belongs in a locker in which it can be secured or lashed safely. It is generally important to have a means of lashing the contents of all large lockers, so that things will not get broken in heavy weather.

On deck

Dorade vents (these days mostly made from soft plastic) get catapulted off their bases on deck not only by flogging sheets, but also by breaking seas. Against the seas, even a framework of solid bars over the vent is no protection. It has to be screwed off and replaced by a firmly fitting cap. These caps are a standard accessory for use on these vents, but in practice they are seldom to hand when needed.

Portholes, windows and hatchcovers are normally of sound construction these days. One exception are forehatches which become larger and larger so that sails and spinnakers can be handed below decks more easily. This is convenient for normal use, but these hatches pose some risks. More than once there have been reports of hatches coming open in heavy weather because the locking mechanisms were too weak. In extreme situations, things can crash against the hatchcover from the inside, and if the catches are too small, they will eventually give. Another possibility is that, due to the heavy loads to which the hull is subjected, the deck around the hatch can bend and break the catches. But, regardless of the cause, there is a simple remedy for these hatchcovers: fit stronger catches with really solid bolts.

The same applies to lockers which can come open at less than 90° of heel if they are not secured. Not only is it really dangerous for the crew groping for a handhold in the cockpit if the lockers suddenly fly open and then shut again when someone has his or her hand on the coaming of the locker. A few tons of water can also find their way into the locker, as the boat will be heeling far over at the time.

The lifelines on most production yachts these days are perfectly high and strong enough. It is, however, wise to fit netting between the upper lifeline and the toe rail to prevent sails, spinnaker booms and crew members who might have lost their footing being washed overboard under the lifelines.

Jackstays on deck seem to be standard equipment on any seaworthy yacht, but they must be fitted in such a way that nobody can trip when treading on them. Personally, I am not a great admirer of jackstays along the entire deck. Once hooked on, you generally cannot reach the mast or the boom to work on them. You have more freedom of movement if one or two lines are attached to the mast and then led loosely back to the cockpit. If any crew member needs to go forward, the loose end of this line can be attached to their harness. If this person should go overboard, he or she will be trailing in the water roughly alongside the cockpit and can be pulled on board to leeward if they are on that side. If they are on the windward side, the boat is hove-to first before they are rescued.

On some yachts the liferaft is stowed and secured on deck just forward or aft of the mast. Here it is easily accessible for use, but by the time it is needed it may have already gone overboard, because in that position the raft is exposed to every sea that sweeps the deck. It is better to stow the liferaft somewhere in the cockpit, if possible in a specially designed locker.

Some cruising yachts have a gallows to support the boom across the front of the cockpit. In addition to supporting the boom when the mainsail is lowered, the gallows also gives a secure handhold for anyone entering or leaving the cabin. Last but not least, it can serve as an aft fixing point for the sprayhood which, if fitted well, gives excellent shelter against wind and waves for the crew in the cockpit.

Turning to the cockpit itself, this should not be too large, in order to minimize the amount of water it will hold if a sea breaks into it. The cockpit drains have to be vast. An open stern is the best drain of all and looks quite sporty, but I would still not recommend it. Too many winch handles, torches and binoculars have already been lost through one. But cockpit drains should have the diameter of a man's arm. The feeling of sitting waist-deep in a cockpit full of water that takes ages to empty out is quite unique – especially if the next breaking sea comes aboard before the first has drained away. This is enough to make anyone start to think about more effective cockpit drains.

Companionways that are low enough to let water from the cockpit down below are seldom found these days. A few years ago we had to think about that, too.

In the cockpit people are always looking for handholds. To discourage them from holding on to the steering wheel, a solid bar should be fitted forward of it. On both sides of the cockpit there should be handholds, as well as small lockers for all those small items that are constantly needed. The helmsman should have more than one attachment point for his harness, so he can either secure himself close to the wheel or to a longer line for more freedom of movement.

Large-diameter wheels are more of a hindrance than a help on a cruising boat. It is not easy to squeeze past the huge wheels that are fashionable today. And if someone is thrown against one a heavy strain is put on the hub. Hopefully, it will be strong enough. If not, it would not be the first time a wheel has broken.

Doghouses and other such high structures are rare today. From the point of view of heavy weather, they are a potential weakness. Just imagine what happens to these mahogany constructions when the yacht falls off a 5 m wave. Steel covers secured over the windows help, but only as long as the entire doghouse is not torn off. So it is perhaps a good idea to have a watertight bulkhead between the doghouse and the rest of the interior with a secure hatch. In an emergency you can then at least sail on without the doghouse.

Below decks

From nightmares of torn-off doghouses to more common considerations. Below decks the seaworthy yacht is practical throughout, without any fancy accessories. Everything has to be stowed in such a way that it remains in place even when the yacht is heeled right over, and not stationary, but moving violently in a sea. Most of the common types of fastener burst open. Floor boards fly across the boat, followed by the provisions stowed in the bilge. Seldom have I seen floorboards securely fastened down.

All joinery must be solid enough to withstand a hefty knock from someone falling against it. And to ensure that this is not too painful, all sharp corners should be rounded off and there should be no sharp-edged or fragile instruments or lights hanging from the ceiling.

All heavy items, such as batteries, tanks, tool boxes, spare propellers and spare anchors should be lashed down securely to stop them from becoming missiles in the event of knock-downs. There are also boats with ballast stowed loose in the bilge. This is extremely dangerous.

The berths on modern cruising boats are designed for gentle

holiday sailing. But it must also be possible to get some sleep in heavy weather. For this, berths are needed more like those found on traditional yachts: about 65 cm (26 in) wide, aligned fore-and-aft and with solid boards to stop the occupant rolling out. Lee cloths are not quite as effective for the same purpose, but suffice. Not all berths on board need be as functional as these. When it blows hard the crew will use 'hot berths' anyway, taking turns in only those berths that are suitable for the conditions. These berths are located amidships or aft, where the motion is not quite as bad. They also need to be isolated from comings and goings in wet oilskins that could take place in the galley or navigation area, and against sounds from deck. Excited cries from deck wake up everyone, even if there is quite a din going on in the background.

The traditional quarter berths right beside the companionway are no good. They are notoriously wet because every time someone goes up or down the companionway a load of water splashes on to the berth. For this reason someone once put a shower curtain up around their quarter berth. This may be a bit unconventional, but it helps!

Talking about getting wet, right at the foot of the companionway there should be a designated wet area, the 'wet lock'. From here, the chart table, galley, heads, electrical system and instruments should be accessible. There should be a locker for foul weather gear here, too. The idea is to stop people from crawling around the boat in dripping wet oilskins.

The engine

Not so long ago, yachtsmen did not take this subject seriously. Now it is generally accepted that an engine contributes to the boat's safety, even, and especially, in heavy weather.

The power of the engine should be adequate for the size of boat. The only drawback is the cost which rises sharply with the available horsepower. The increased fuel consumption can be ignored as long as you do not use it on full power. The real advantage lies in the safety value of the reserve engine power. This is not needed for speed, but for more control when manoeuvring or when motoring against wind and sea. In both cases we are talking about low speeds. To be able to utilize the extra power in these circumstances the propeller has to have a good bite in the water. A propeller with a larger diameter is more efficient and, if it is a folding one, can also be used on sailing boats. Most yachts have propellers too small for their large engines.

It is said that diesel engines cannot run when the boat is heeling. This is not entirely true. All modern marine diesels operate safely up to a certain angle of heel which can be found in the handbook. But this is in static conditions. In a seaway the oil will be washed continually into the sump and, moreover, the angle of heel is not constant. The pump will frequently draw some air which, unlike a break in the flow of diesel, is of no consequence as oil will always follow.

The more serious problem lies with the supply of fuel. Even modern diesel pumps cannot cope with air in the system. But air can enter the system when fuel starts to slop around in the tank. It can happen that around the end of the fuel pipe the diesel is displaced and instead air is sucked into the system. The engine will then stop. The system will then have to be bled which is no easy task, especially in any kind of sea. Of course, the engine will always suck in air when you most urgently need it to work. Such is life.

So it is advisable to make the fuel supply wave-proof. This can be done in two ways: either you have a gravity feed from a tank above the engine which can be refilled from the main tank; or you can have a sump tank underneath the main tank which is automatically always full of diesel. It is then impossible for air to enter the fuel system, no matter how violent the motion of the boat.

You can save yourself a lot of trouble if both engine and the entire electrical system are mounted well clear of bilge water. But do not forget that, in heavy seas, bilge water will climb up the sides of the boat. I have experienced bilge water splashing onto the V-belt and then being sprayed all over the engine by it. When the engine was needed next later, the starter would not work. Electrical equipment, dynamos, starters and, especially, mains connections do not appreciate salt water showers!

Bilge pumps

An automatic bilge pump is often considered a perfect solution. I think it is only second best, as you have no indication of the amount of leakage. A warning system which gives an audible alarm when too much water is in the bilge is actually much better. The two systems can be combined by a two-way switch.

You should not neglect the bilge pump. Leaks do not necessarily happen in heavy weather, but chances are higher that some hose will work loose, not to mention the danger of colliding with cargo lost from the decks of a freighter. All-important is the capacity of the pumps. At least three separate systems should be installed:

1 A submersible electric pump with large capacity, located in the bottom of the bilges and with an outlet well above waterline because of the danger of back flow.

2 As a back-up, a large-capacity manual membrane pump in the cockpit that also draws from the bottom of the bilge.

3 An electric pump with diverter valves that can pump out isolated areas of the bilge.

Can we combine all these features?

With the bilge-pumping system, this checklist comes to a somewhat arbitrary conclusion. It could go on, going further into details, but for our purposes this shall suffice. It enables us to measure the heavy weather ability of a yacht in comparison with others, to identify weak points, and suggest remedies.

It would be pointless to try and combine all the features desirable in heavy weather in a single specification. It is a matter of personal preference how much significance is attached to individual features. How much, for example, poor directional stability is traded off against good pitching characteristics. Knowledge of the technical and physical background is important in order to understand what happens to a yacht in a gale. It is important to know why a yacht reacts in a certain manner and to know the reason for a particular characteristic of the boat. Understanding the problem is the key to solving it.

11   To go or not to go?

After the event it's always easy to be wise: 'We really should have stayed in harbour. There was enough warning of what was coming.' Imagine the situation: you are tied up in a safe harbour, but want to get under way again. A bad forecast makes you hesitate. Minds are torn between 'safety first' and 'wasting the holiday'.

Caught in such a situation, a debate will inevitably follow. Sailors are by nature too much obsessed by sailing to give in too easily. The good old principle of 'when in doubt don't' is put aside while you concentrate on dispelling your doubts, or at least try to.

Weather forecasts

How is the weather really going to develop? Even the best forecast is worthless if we don't know the basics. To make sure that you definitely receive the relevant forecast for your area you make a list of weather stations and broadcasting times from the almanac. And to ensure that you don't miss the next forecast, you set the alarm clock. Blank weather maps covering the forecast areas are obtained. If you can't buy them – you can always draw them yourself and photocopy them.

The decision to set sail should never be based on one forecast alone. The current weather pattern should be studied. Previous forecasts should be integrated into the decision-making process. Thus, even before starting a voyage and during time in harbour, someone should be keeping a record of the forecasts.

In harbour, you don't even need a weather fax on board to get hold of weather maps. You can often get them from the harbour master or sometimes from the local newspaper.

There is no harm in also tapping unconventional sources for weather information, such as fishermen or other local pundits. They often use indicators for their personal forecasts that are unknown to scientists. The rate of accuracy is surprisingly high, if not always one hundred per cent.

Incidentally, a possible approach to unravelling forecasts in a foreign language is to record the forecast on a cheap tape-recorder.

You can then invite all self-declared linguists on board to listen to it sentence by sentence to decipher the meaning.

Perhaps also worth mentioning is my personal feeling about the official forecasts. In most meteorological services the morning forecast is compiled by the night shift and the evening forecast by the day shift. Over a period of several days you'll get to know the individual forecasters in a meteorological sense. You may then be able to distinguish between optimists and pessimists, traditionalists and innovators. However, it is a matter for personal judgement whether to allow a correction factor based on these assumptions. And if you do, always bear in mind the risk of a change in shifts!

Finally, you try and assemble an overall picture from all the different weather information collected. In this, the reliability of individual items of information has to be borne in mind and their origin. I would tend to trust an official forecast more than the weatherman in a tabloid newspaper. But I do regard the often repeated and well-meant recommendation always to believe the worst available forecast, as quite naïve.

The decision to leave

The final assessment of the weather is now compared to the proposed route. From where will it blow? How does this relate to the course? Sailing into a force 6 is hard work, while running before a force 7 can be thrilling.

How long is the fetch for the seas to build up? How deep is the water and what are the seas expected to be like? How able is the ship, and the crew? How long will the weather and the trip go on for? Can we sail in watches? How much sea room do we have to leeward in case we have to bear off, heave-to or even run before the gale? (Twelve hours hove-to cost 50 miles leeway, as a rule of thumb. See Chapter 16.) What are the alternatives along the route, in terms of shelter under the lee of the land or another harbour? Can you turn back if it gets too rough and where is the point of no return?

Once these questions have been considered it's time to discuss the plan with the crew. Everyone on board has to share the decision of whether to leave or not. The skipper has to analyze the reactions of the crew. Is the enthusiastic mood real or is it brought about by a minority? Often enthusiasm is put on as no one wants to be the one to spoil things. This can be put to the test by the skipper arguing against leaving and carefully observing the reactions.

It is also important to reduce the argument to essentials and leave all peripheral issues aside. 'What do we really want to do?' is a question designed to get to the heart of things. If this is not enough, it sometimes helps to consider what happened on previous occasions when conditions were similar.

It would be asking too much to expect complete self-revelation from everyone on board. It is good enough if the responsible person, the skipper, gains a passing insight into the souls of his crew and tries to assess the prevailing mood as accurately as possible.

Lastly, it may be sensible to try and reach a consensus by suggesting alternative routes or even other means of transport to reach the intended goal of the voyage. If these alternatives are available, it is always much wiser to consider them.

If doubts remain you can always depart and sail to the point where it really starts to get rough. Possibly in this way feigned enthusiasm can be unmasked. I remember one such occasion. In that particular case, however, morale on board soared and we sailed on, which turned out to be the right decision.

12 Gales in harbour

By deciding to stay in harbour, you'll probably have chosen the lesser worry, but a worry it can still be. Even in harbour, heavy weather can cause substantial damage.

Short steep wavelets in harbour make yachts rock. The boats are heeled by the wind and masts touch each other. Rigging gets entangled. Mooring lines can break. Anchors drag. Neighbouring yachts get too close to your own and, at some stage, an unmanned boat drifts like a mine through the anchorage. An unnerved new arrival in harbour loses control during manoeuvres and on the other boats fenders and boat-hooks come out. The old saying, 'you've made your bed and now you must lie in it', is as true in a marina as anywhere. Many factors have to be considered when mooring the boat in preparation for a gale.

Lying alongside

Unless the wind is blowing offshore, lying alongside is mainly a problem of fendering. The fenders tend to work about between jetty and topsides, and sometimes even burst. They have to be checked constantly and often held in position by extra lines. There have to be enough fenders to distribute the weight of the boat between them and they have to be attached horizontally so that they follow the yacht's fore-and-aft movements. Bow and stern lines have to be long to allow for pitching, the boat being held in position by the springs.

The mast should be positioned well away from neighbouring masts so that when rolling they do not crash into each other.

Bear in mind that, even in non-tidal waters, the depth in harbour can be changed drastically during strong winds. A rise in sea level can present problems if the boat rises above quay level and the fenders cannot be submerged. Again, creative thinking helps. Maybe even lines passed under the bottom of the boat to keep the fenders down and in place.

It can be extremely difficult or even impossible to leave a berth in an emergency if an onshore gale is pinning you into it. A wise skipper will therefore lay out an anchor to windward using the dinghy.

Rafting up

The main problem when yachts are rafted several deep are the loads on the whole unit when the wind is fore-and-aft. The raft will then normally deform, like a banana, which places huge loads on head or stern lines. If smaller boats are lying nearer to the jetty, the loads become even bigger where the mooring cleats are smaller.

This problem is helped by taking lines ashore from the outer yachts. But for them to be efficient there has to be enough space fore-and-aft, otherwise the angles will be detrimental and the lines will just pull the boats towards the pier and not hold them against the wind. One can imagine the loads put on the innermost boats in this case. If the adjacent raft is too close it is better to try and pass a line ashore through that raft, instead of making fast to it. In the latter case, fenders and lines of the other raft would be put under extra strain. The outermost yachts should lay anchors out to windward or, if the opportunity is available, make fast to a strong point to windward.

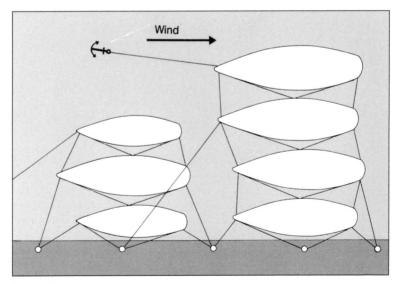

Fig 12.1 Yachts moored abreast for strong winds.

Securing a stern-to 'Mediterranean' mooring

This well-known way of mooring up is sometimes referred to as the 'Roman Catholic' way of berthing as it is almost exclusively used in Mediterranean harbours without jetties or pontoons. As long as the holding ground is good enough and the ground tackle adequate, this way of mooring in harbour in a gale is actually better than lying alongside.

It is essential that the anchor is well placed and has a secure hold. You can check this by putting strain on to the anchor, but wait a while to give the anchor time to bed in. If in doubt, the best plan is to up-anchor immediately and try again, this time using more chain. If you want more security or peace of mind, a second anchor on a long warp and a length of chain can be laid out well upwind. A weight on the line would be useful to hold the warp down and thus keep it out of the way of any traffic in the harbour.

It is always an advantage to have long stern lines, so that the stern is about 3 to 5 m away from the pier. The anchor chain then

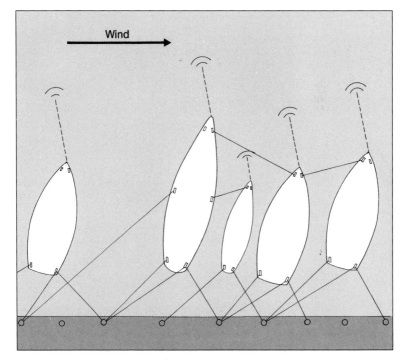

Fig 12.2 Securing yachts moored stern-to.

does not have to be pulled quite as tight and the boat has some freedom of movement with the waves. It will then not jerk the lines as
sharply, which is easier on rope, chain and cleats.

If the wind blows across the bows, the bows of the boats must be
made fast to one another and, wherever possible, secured to windward. These transverse lines can run across the entire harbour, as
long as other traffic is not obstructed. The lines can also be led diagonally across other boats, as with the raft. The important thing is
to keep a long distance between the attachment point and the stern
to avoid excessive strain on the anchor.

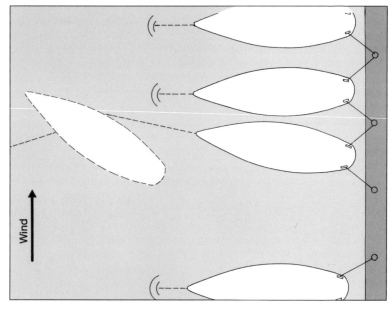

Fig 12.3 Crossing the anchor chain of the next boat.

When moored stern-to, the escape route is always open. Getting
under way normally presents no problems, regardless of wind
direction. The only real danger is being pushed down to leeward
across the anchor chain of the next boat. Then you are helpless,
drifting across the bows of the other yachts without being able to
use the engine. To avoid this embarrassing situation, you have to
give your boat a good kick ahead with the engine as soon as you are
free of fenders and mooring lines. Running over your own anchor
chain is less important. The vital thing is to get the stern out of the
danger zone of other chains and warps, so that the boat can turn

into the wind clear of the other yachts. (See also Chapter 18, Manoeuvres in harbour.)

Avoiding chafe

No matter where or how you are berthed, ropes and fenders have to be watched constantly during a gale. Not all problems of chafe can be solved with pieces of plastic hose or old carpet.

Fig 12.4 Round turn and two half-hitches.

The universal favourite knot of most yachtsmen, the bowline, if used for mooring to rings, eyes or smallish cleats, concentrates chafe over a very short section of rope. So in this case one, or more, round turns and two half hitches is better.

Lines passed through a ring ashore and brought back on board are only useful for getting under way quickly, when they can be slipped from on board. They do not give any additional security. The doubling of the rope is deceptive. At the point of chafe it is only single.

If you want to run out double mooring lines for extra security, the second warp should be parallel to the first, but not taut. In this case only the first line will chafe. If it breaks, the second is as good as new and will then take the strain.

As a protection against chafe on the quay edge, I can recommend a series of hitches tied with another rope around the warp. This will withstand chafe for quite a while and not slip (Fig 12.5).

But a still better way to avoid chafe is to find suitable points to make fast to in the first place. Here, creativity is called for. You can include old tyres, wooden piles and even the lamp post in your calculations on this subject. Finally, don't forget the possibility of using a length of anchor chain at the shore end of a warp.

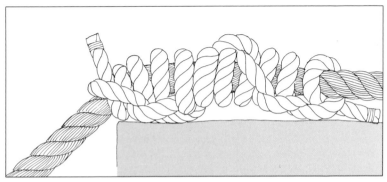

Fig 12.5 Method of protecting a warp from chafe with a series of hitches.

Fenders

Normally, the manufacturer of fenders expects his products to be simply hung over the side in the position where the yacht might contact something hard. Over the years sailors have found many ways to increase the effectiveness of fenders. Again, this is mainly a question of creativity. Three examples are shown here.

The squeaking and working of fenders between two yachts is greatly reduced by connecting fenders in a chain. The fenders in this case are free to roll up and down and are primarily held in position horizontally.

If a yacht lying alongside a quay is moving a lot, the fenders must be concentrated amidships to create the maximum possible distance between boat and pier. The single fenders fore and aft only

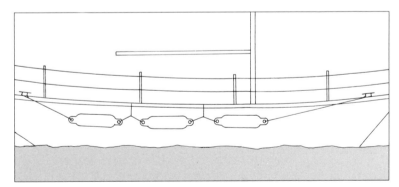

Fig 12.6 Fenders connected in a chain.

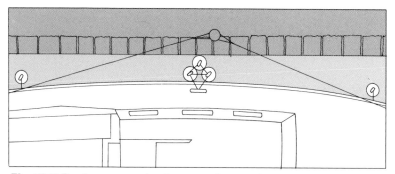

Fig 12.7 Fenders grouped to increase distance from the quay.

serve to fend off occasional bumps. Amidships, a pair of fenders are tied together with a third fender hung outside them. In this way, the rope holding together the inner fenders cannot chafe against the quay.

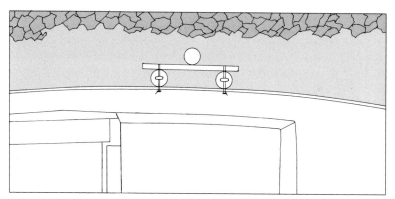

Fig 12.8 Arrangement of two fenders lashed to a plank for lying alongside a pile.

If the yacht is lying against a pile any fender will eventually work its way out from between the two. The solution is to have two fenders spanned by a plank which then rests against the pile.

Dinghy at the ready

It is advisable to have the dinghy in the water, so that should the need arise you can lay out more warps or anchors. Even if your own yacht is tied up snug and secure, you can sometimes use the dinghy to help others. In the last analysis, it increases the security of your own boat if your neighbour is properly secured. As so often in life, altruism and self-interest are in the end combined.

The dinghy should have an outboard of around 4 hp or you should be good at rowing. Otherwise, you may not be able to make way to windward and end up in some remote downwind corner of the harbour.

I once watched a small boy in an Optimist dinghy sailing to and fro in a harbour in a strong wind, helping to lay out lines and warps. I must say that I was impressed.

It takes a bit of practice to lay out an anchor in the dinghy. Everything has to be stowed in the order of letting go and off you go to windward. The warp should pay out of the dinghy as you go along and the chain and anchor should ideally be thrown in when the warp is more or less tight. Make sure, of course, that you do not have a foot or a paddle caught in the rope.

This operation is less straightforward if you have to lay out chain instead of rope. This is only possible in shallow water up to 3 or 4 m deep. Otherwise, the weight of the chain is such that it will just fall out in one big heap on the bottom. Moreover, the dinghy will probably not be able to make any headway against the pull of the chain.

There is a way of laying out lines to windward without a dinghy. You take a walk around the harbour, tie a fender on to the end of your rope and let it drift to downwind towards the boat. If the rope is too heavy more fenders will have to be attached to it, which will incidentally help you to see it in the water.

Using the engine

If the anchor drags, a whole raft of yachts drifts sideways before the wind or if, lying before bow anchor, the bow is blown on to the neighbour, you can sometimes become quite helpless. These are situations in which it can be impossible to swiftly bring out another line or anchor.

In a tight corner you should include the engine in your calculations. It does not matter that it may have to run for hours on end. People run their engines for hours just to cool down their refrigerator.

Of course, mooring lines may have to be adjusted to keep the boat in the right place once the engine is running. Normally, you will motor against a spring in order to turn bow or stern into the wind. It will sometimes help if you make a little drawing to understand the effects. The possibilities are surprisingly extensive.

Sometimes, when moored up in a row stern-on, for example, it may be necessary for neighbouring yachts also to run their engines. In this way, whole rafts of yachts have been saved in the past. And if anyone sniffs at this solution, don't worry. Diesel fumes are not noticeable in a gale!

Getting out of trouble

It may become too dangerous in harbour if the anchor drags, if the motion becomes too violent or if you are in danger of being crushed by the boat next door. It may then be sensible to leave and move to another mooring. Of course, manoeuvres in a gale require careful handling and can have unfortunate consequences. But you should never categorically rule out this option, and carefully consider the risks and benefits. Sometimes you are more secure at anchor in the outer harbour. The boat will be tossed by the waves, but there are no dangers from quay walls or neighbouring yachts.

It may, under really threatening conditions, be better to leave and weather the storm at sea, rather than be caught in the chaos in harbour. This can sometimes happen in Mediterranean harbours, when the first yachts up-anchor due to dragging and accidentally dislodge other yachts' anchors at the same time. Then these boats, too, have to up-anchor, during which operation other anchors may be disturbed, and so on. A whole chain reaction can be set in motion, and from such chaos I, too, would prefer to escape out to sea.

Watches in harbour

The conclusion is that problems in gales do not arise exclusively out at sea. Even in harbour there is scope for mistakes or doing things in the right way. The crew of a yacht sheltering in harbour must be ready to take appropriate action and it is advisable to maintain a system of watches in harbour, as lines can break, anchors drag or fenders get out of position.

The owners of boats on permanent moorings often do not have the opportunity to see to their yacht quickly in the event of a gale. Therefore, yachts without crew on board have to be far better secured, as is possible in most modern marinas. In some small harbours in the Mediterranean, where it is not possible, one is accordingly not allowed to leave a yacht unattended for any length of time.

13 Preparations for heavy weather at sea

A change of scenario. Your yacht is somewhere at sea. The horizon has a threatening look. The forecast is south-west 7 increasing, and the glass is falling.

Recognizing the danger

It is vital to recognize and accept at an early stage that heavy weather is coming. In northern latitudes the weather normally builds up slowly so that generally one is not taken by surprise by gales, unless you choose to ignore the signs. Wishful thinking where bad weather is concerned can be dangerous. Of course, you cannot start to nail boards over your windows at the first sign of any squall, but you should carefully consider the facts and weigh the odds.

You are more likely to be caught out further south, for example, in the Mediterranean. A gale force squall can overtake you in minutes without any prior warning, out of blue skies and with a rock steady barometer. Luckily, these sudden gales seldom exceed force 8, possibly 9. Still, if one does not react quickly a sail can be blown out. One crew were dozing in the sunny cockpit when a squall pounced. The next minute a sail was in shreds. This was on a ketch under the north coast of Elba.

It pays to know about the climatic conditions of the area you are in. In some guides one finds extraordinary descriptions and statistics which make interesting reading.

Apart from the forecasts, there are certain signs of approaching weather which can only be interpreted with some experience. Often it begins with a sort of intuition. Something seems different, but you cannot really tell what it is. Sometimes it might be a watery sun, possibly with an ominous halo around it, or ragged high clouds moving in ahead of something, or an unusual wind direction. A clear indicator is an unnatural swell that does not coincide with the prevailing wind. This is followed sooner or later, by dark looming clouds, or else the swell will have been a false alarm.

The RDF set can give quite a good indication. Especially on medium wave you can clearly hear the electrical discharges of an approaching gale. In the tropics you can even take a bearing on the null in the crackling and thus determine the direction of the cyclone over surprisingly large distances.

Storms are not all alike. Preparations for a storm in northern latitudes might not need to be as thorough as for those in the tropics. Moreover, the general seaworthiness of a yacht and her gear should relate to the area where she is cruising. It would be overdoing things to prepare a yacht cruising in the Baltic for knock-downs. It is rather unlikely that a yacht will fall off a breaking sea in the Kiel Fjord, but somewhere off the Bermuda it could indeed happen.

Briefing the crew

If your crew are old hands, nothing much has to be discussed before a gale as everyone will know what to expect and what to do. The only need is to get organized. Tasks have to be allocated to individual members of the crew.

With a less experienced crew it is advisable to allow time for a preparatory briefing. This is of great psychological value, apart from the more straightforward organizational purpose. The crew will be far more confident during heavy weather if no unspoken fears are gnawing away inside. The briefing has to be as open, clear and as personal as possible. Everyone must be reassured by the knowledge that, whatever happens, an answer is available. Everyone must know exactly his or her function and have confidence that he or she are up to it and that the others on board can rely on them to play their part.

New and inexperienced crew should not be ignored. Their particular tasks must be tailored to their experience. They must know that others will make allowances, but that their contribution is important.

Apart from discussing the expected course of events, hypothetical questions should be put and answered. This could, on one hand, paint a frightening picture. But, on the other hand, such things are better discussed than left to individual imaginations.

Those who so far have not had seasickness may now be going to get it. Everyone knows that being seasick is no disgrace. But deep down inside? If the skipper or some other experienced hand has ever been seasick, this is the time to admit it.

The purpose of the discussion should not be misunderstood. A skipper who cannot stop talking gets on the nerves of the crew who may want actions, not words. Monologues without feedback are dangerous.

Watchkeeping

So we come to the practical steps. Due to the extra strain, it is advisable to change the watchkeeping routine to create short watches, but also long enough rest periods. On normal cruising yachts the watch on deck should consist of two persons: one on the helm and one taking care of navigation and everything else that has to be done. The two take turns at each job and the entire watch lasts two hours. Depending on the number of crew on board, at least four hours off watch is then hopefully possible. With a crew of only four persons or less, the whole exercise can become quite arduous.

When reshuffling the watches for heavy weather, the experience of individuals should be taken account of. It is essential to have one experienced hand in each watch, so that those of lesser experience can learn from him or her. Moreover, the skipper can relax as he knows that each watch has at least one person with enough experience to handle the situation.

To exclude a navigator or a cook from the watch routine is, in my opinion, a luxury which I would trade for longer periods off watch.

Apart from watchkeeping, a situation requiring all hands on deck has to be anticipated in which again everyone on board has to have his or her specific task. But it is often not necessary for the entire crew to scramble on deck if the watch need more hands, so I would suggest an intermediate stage of 'two hands on deck'. Two extra people, in addition to the two already on deck, are normally enough for operations such as reefing or changing sail. If the two extra hands are called for it should be clear who is meant. I would generally allocate this standby role to the watch that has just been relieved, as they know best what is where on deck. Especially in darkness, this can be extremely helpful.

With a little bit of planning, it should normally be possible to arrange for sail changes, reefing or lowering of the spinnaker to occur when the watch is changing and four people are on deck anyway. This avoids dragging the last watch from their berths. But, of course, it cannot always be arranged this way, so then there is nothing else for it and they have to get back into their wet gear.

With the beginning of the special watch routine, I would also start using *hot berths*. The bunks up forward will be uninhabitable during a storm. This is why everyone should use berths amidships or aft, that are also screened off a bit from activities in the saloon or the navigation area. These are prepared in such a way that everyone can use them with their own sleeping bags or bed linen or, if things get really bad, simply in oilskins.

Navigation

Not long ago navigation in bad weather relied heavily on dead reckoning. In the age of GPS this is less often the case, though most forms of radio navigation are adversely affected by heavy weather. There is also the increased risk of electronic equipment failure in a gale, with the result that you may be thrown back on dead reckoning at any time.

So it is important to check and record your position regularly, using whatever means are at your disposal, even when your instruments are working. In this way, you will have a reasonably recent fix at which to begin your dead reckoning, should the need arise, and an idea of leeway, surface drift, course made good, etc. Armed with this knowledge, your dead reckoning is more likely to be accurate.

While conditions are still relatively calm the chart table should be cleared and organized. Everything that cannot be secured has to go. Equally, everything that must remain dry has to be stowed away. Once people start to navigate in dripping wet oilskins nothing in this vicinity will remain dry.

An elastic strop can be fixed across the navigation table to keep the chart in place. Charts not needed are stowed away. The chart in use and the adjoining ones are placed in an ordered pile. Also a piece of paper, or better still card, to log positions, etc. The times and frequencies of forecasts are noted down and an alarm clock set accordingly. The required course is pencilled onto the small scale chart to help with strategic planning.

Below decks

Any seagoing yacht should, in general, be well suited for rough conditions below decks. What we are now concerned with are the small things that need be considered.

First of all, everyone should stow away their belongings and perhaps put them into plastic rubbish bags to keep them dry. Only kit needed during the gale should be left out. This could include several towels, dry, warm clothes, sleeping-bag and toothbrush, ideally placed in a separate plastic bag and tied up (this, by the way, might be where all those missing sailties end up).

Depending on how much the deck or topsides are leaking, it may be wise to wrap up the bunk cushions in plastic bags. They will remain dry this way for a time. If the heavy weather persists, the plastic bags will give the sleeper some protection from the sodden mattress.

All loose items should be stowed away, and hanging lamps or other things should be secured. Carpets, if there are any, should be rolled up and stowed away. Wrap fragile items in clothes and put them in lockers with secure fastenings. Make use of all large compartments, like in the bilges or beneath the fo'c'sle berths for stowage. Seacocks and the transducers for log and echo sounder should be kept accessible and can be easily protected from being harmed by loosely stowed gear.

The bilges should be checked for rubbish that could end up blocking the pumps. It can do no harm to inspect and clear the strum boxes. The pumps may be needed urgently later on.

Loose heavy items, such as tool boxes, jerry-cans and so on, must be lashed down securely. All hatches, opening ports, openings to the engine compartment and the companionway ladder should be checked and, if necessary, secured. If possible, the forepart of the boat should be lightened by stowing the anchor amidships or emptying forward water tanks.

The galley

Before the galley is switched to storm-mode, a hearty meal should be prepared, in sufficient quantities that it can be warmed up again later. Such a meal is a good occasion for the crew briefing.

Somebody should prepare a number of sandwiches and other cold snacks. Later nobody will want to cook. Hot soups and tea in vacuum flasks will be in strong demand. Some tinned food should also be set aside to be warmed up later. Nobody will want to rummage through the bilges looking for food later on.

The provisions for the duration of the gale should be stowed in an easily accessible locker that can be opened when the boat is heeled without the contents cascading out. Other items in the galley are wedged in place with soft cloths and lockers, drawers and doors are secured. This is especially important in the case of heavy pots and pans. Once they start to fly, damage can be serious.

The cook needs to be able to secure himself in the galley. The hip strap that holds him in place should be tested and adjusted. Grease should be cleaned off the floor (something that is often neglected). Otherwise, not only is it slippery in the galley, but the grease gets on to the soles of shoes making them slippery wherever you go.

Nearly all cookers are gimballed, but that does not solve all problems. Depending on the centre of gravity, saucepans can be catapulted off cookers. Even fiddle rails around the burners do not always help. It may be necessary to trim the cooker, by putting extra weight in the oven to harmonize the motion of the cooker with that of the boat. I can recommend bags of potatoes for this purpose as they will do no harm if the oven door opens and they shoot out.

The usual fiddle rails to hold pans in place are not very effective. Unless they are of a heavy duty type, it may be necessary to tie the pots down with wire.

Paraffin cookers should be filled and the spirit for pre-heating should be in a small flask.

On deck

It should be possible to see at a glance what has to be done here. Everything that might get swept away has to go. This begins with the dinghy and ends with the Dorade ventilators. Even the ensign has to go, together with the staff. During a gale, national identity is not of prime importance. (This, by the way, is not only practical, but also conforms to international yacht etiquette.)

If the dinghy is on deck or in davits, the cover and the lashings have to be checked. The boat should be ready to be cut away. The necessary tools should be on hand.

Safety equipment should be made ready and checked. This includes jackstays on both sides from the cockpit to the foredeck or to the mast. A lifebuoy attached to a floating line should be ready to be thrown overboard at the stern, along with the danbuoy. Another good idea is a buoyant orange smoke signal, stowed near the helmsman ready to use. In a case of man overboard the smoke signal is more visible than the danbuoy.

The lashings of the liferaft and its painter must be checked. More than one liferaft has gone overboard when the boat was heeled. The average raft weighs between 30 and 50 k (65 to 110 lb). When the boat is heeled, they can pull at their lashings with a force of several times their own weight.

As long as the boat is reasonably steady it is time to check the rigging once more. This can be done with binoculars, looking up at the mast from both fore and aft. All fittings and bolts should be examined carefully. Most masts come down in heavy weather due to some failure of the rigging. It can do no harm to check shroud tension. Lee shrouds that are excessively loose flap about and can cause trouble.

Sails should be stowed tidily in the sail locker. Nothing is more frustrating than having to haul several sail bags on deck before the storm jib finally appears. Only one thing is worse: having the sail in the wrong bag. This really can lead to frayed tempers. Don't forget about night-time. Lights should be tested and a safe place found for the torch.

Gale checklist

No two yachts are the same. I advise every skipper to draw up a checklist for his or her own boat (Fig 13.1). In the event of bad weather it ensures that nothing is forgotten. When compiling this list the skipper should give it some systematic thought. Good ideas arise from cool reflection rather than in the heat of the moment.

I would prepare the list with columns for the names of the crew so that, in the preparations for heavy weather, each item can be ticked off with a name. I would not leave the briefing until the actual approach of a storm, but give one in the early stages of a cruise. Then, everybody knows what is expected of him or her in the event of a gale and can get used to the idea.

The skipper should not be included in the allocation of tasks. He or she should be free to co-ordinate matters and deal with those unforeseen events which always complicate life in these situations.

When to reef

The right moment to reef can only really be judged in retrospect. The traditional advice to reef in good time is not always easy to follow. The skipper has to decide on a certain moment to reef. To avoid being undercanvassed for too long this decision has to be carefully considered. Early reefing is no substitute for a degree of experience in judging the weather.

I think the important thing is that everything is prepared for reefing. This also includes the crew having been briefed and knowing what to do and how to do it, and the fact that the whole process will be properly co-ordinated. If everyone is prepared, the whole operation will take no more than a minute or two.

GALE CHECKLIST	Tom	Charlie	Liz	Ann	Phil	Sue
Crew						
Organize watches	✓					
Two hands on deck routine	✓					
Below decks						
Stow away belongings	✓	✓	✓	✓	✓	✓
Prepare personal kits	✓	✓	✓	✓	✓	✓
Prepare hot berths		✓	✓	✓	✓	
Secure lockers, starboard		✓				
Secure lockers, port			✓			
Secure bilge stores				✓		
Check bilge pumps and bilges					✓	
Secure tool box					✓	
Hatches, covers, companionway						✓
Seacocks				✓		
Empty forward tanks			✓			
Galley						
Prepare food		✓				
Trim cooker		✓				
Secure stores		✓				
Clean floor		✓				
Navigation						
Fix position						✓
Plan route						✓
Clear up chart table						✓
On deck						
Fit jackstays			✓			
Check safety equipment				✓		
Stow anchor amidships					✓	
Secure dinghy					✓	
Check rigging				✓		
Clear up lockers			✓			
Stow sailbags			✓			
Test lights				✓		
Torch					✓	

Fig 13.1.

Reefing the mainsail

Fortunately, these days most yachts are equipped for jiffy reefing. It can do no harm to describe the procedure for this most effective way of reefing at this point. Quite often I have seen clumsy and dangerous ways of reefing even practised by old hands.

To reef the main you sail close-hauled. The luff is let down by easing the halyard. The tack is hooked on and the luff tensioned up again with the halyard. Time: 10 seconds. Break. Then release the mainsheet. Haul in the leech pendant and tighten up on the winch. Haul in the mainsheet. Time: another 20 seconds. Three further points:

1 The topping-lift is set up in such a way that when the sail comes down, the boom drops a bit without hitting anything. The topping-lift can be marked off at this point.
2 The gate in the mast track is opened in advance so that the slides come out by themselves as the sail is lowered. If you want to take in the third reef straight away, the first and second reefs are completed first. Otherwise a lot of sail would be flapping about.
3 The reef points are only there to furl the reefed part of the sail. They should never pull at the remaining part of sail. I only use them for the sake of appearances and only if they can be tied without too much trouble. If the first reefs are tied to the boom, there is not too much sail flapping about once you are down to the third reef. Don't forget to undo the reef points before shaking out the reefs!

The fact that the entire process of reefing only takes a couple of

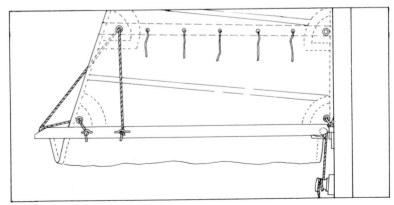

Fig 13.2 Reef pendant and points.

Morwena of Burton makes good, steady progress on a well-reefed mainsail. *Photo: PPL.*

seconds is intended to help free oneself from unnecessary risks. Working at the mast is never without danger. You may not be washed overboard, but to be thrown hard on to the deck can be quite unpleasant and result in serious injury.

A last tip about the mainsail: if you always use the hook on the windward side of the boom, spray will not be caught in the fold of sail.

The jib

As far as the jib is concerned, there are a couple of points to be borne in mind. Headsails should be unfurled with the sheets completely free. When unfurling the sail, the furling line has to be handled with some care and let out bit by bit. In strong winds the force on a sail can be considerable even when it is flapping and, if you are caught unawares, the sail can unfurl itself in one rush imposing a jarring shock on the luff.

If the furling line breaks or is accidentally released while you are sailing, the sail will come unfurled, but this time with the full weight of the wind in it. This is normally more than the sail can bear in a strong wind.

Conventional headsails have to change if the area is to be reduced. Working on the foredeck is easier while the sail is down, so you do not hank-on one sail with the other still up. You are not in a race.

The sail is dropped to the deck while the boat is head-to-wind for a moment, perhaps when tacking. Someone wedges himself in the pulpit in front of the forestay and pulls like mad at the luff if it does not come down by itself. The halyard is unshackled immediately and attached to the pulpit, so that it can be tightened again quickly to stop it becoming entangled in the rigging.

The helmsman then steers a slow reaching course, while the sheets are detached and the sail is pulled tight along the foot and flaked down on the leeward side of the foredeck. The person in the pulpit helps by pressing the sail down. It is then rolled up from the clew forward and, once you get to the forestay, the bag is pulled over it. Only then is the sail unhanked from the stay and the tack unshackled. With this method the sail can be kept under control.

The sailbag is closed and taken aft. The new sail is taken forward and the whole procedure is repeated in reverse. The tack is shackled on and the sail hanked on to the forestay while the main bulk is still inside the bag. Then the sail is rolled out aft along the deck. Sheets are bent on. The halyard is shackled on and up goes the sail.

On most yachts two people are enough for this operation. They have to work as a team and not mind getting wet.

It is not a good idea to have sails hanked-on and lashed to the lifelines. The effort saved is only small unless you are constantly changing up and down between two sails, and the seas will probably sooner or later tear the sail loose, so that someone has to go forward again anyway to tie it down again. If for some reason the sail has to be lashed to the lifelines, it is better secured to the upper one, so that the seas can wash underneath it without being trapped in the sail.

If the yacht has a foil forestay, it is a bit more difficult to take the foresail down straight into the bag. There are no hanks to hold the sail to the stay while it is put in the bag. In this case, the bag may not be a real bag, but a kind of wrapper that opens outwards to allow the sail to be hoisted directly from it. However, when it is lowered, as soon as the sail slips from the profile it will certainly have to be held down with hands and feet to prevent it from being blown away.

Should the boat be equipped with a detachable inner forestay, I would set this up at an early stage, even while the larger headsail is still set or unfurled. The smaller heavy weather sail can then be hanked on in readiness, but must be lashed down securely or kept inside the bag.

14 The crew

In heavy weather it is not just the helm and the sails that matter. Too many times situations have got out of control because secondary things were regarded as unimportant. It is a fact that during the Fastnet Race disaster people died of exhaustion because they had not observed the need for crew rest. This chapter deals with the basic rules of behaviour during a gale, what to do, how to do it and what it is better not to do.

Rest

It is natural that when things get exciting everyone wants to be involved. It actually takes some self-discipline to leave the exhilarating action to those on watch and keep out of it. At the beginning the skipper can hardly find a use for all the enthusiasm of the crew. But after 10 or 15 hours everybody gets tired at about the same time. It then gets lonely in the cockpit.

Those off watch have to be organized and have clear duties. The first is, above all else, to be fit and fresh again for the next watch. Getting the necessary amount of sleep cannot be left to chance. It is a serious task.

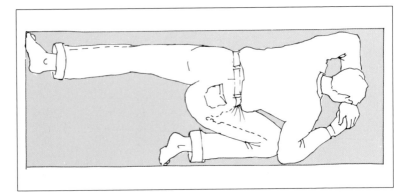

Fig 14.1 Secure sleeping position.

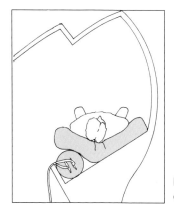

Fig 14.2 Fender wedged under bunk cushion.

Sleeping in a rocking berth is sometimes not at all easy, but it is possible and, after the third turn on watch, sleeping gets easier. You have to wedge yourself in so that your body cannot roll sideways. Rolled-up blankets or special cushion arrangements, with sailbags or similar things stuffed underneath, help (Fig 14.2). It is also helpful to lie on one's stomach, pull one knee up almost underneath the armpit and wedge oneself in against the side of the berth (Fig 14.1). Shoulders and hips are steady in this position and the body does not roll about. Try it and see.

The best places to sleep are of course the leeward berths. The berths on the windward side have to be fitted with solid bunk boards or lee cloths. The latter have to be pulled really tight as they always stretch a little. If they are loose you might as well forget about the bunk and use the lee cloth as a hammock. I always put the lashings through the eyelets twice, like a small pulley, and can then haul them tight when lying in the berth, without assistance.

If at all possible, you should take off wet clothes and crawl into the sleeping-bag. Time for sleep is short and you should make the most of it. And this is best done in a warm sleeping-bag. By the way, if you are about to buy one don't get one of the very narrow type, apparently made for mountaineers. You must have room in the sleeping-bag to pull one knee upwards and brace it against the side of the bunk.

At some stage or other, you will be so exhausted or be called on deck such a short time before you are due to go on watch that nothing seems to matter anymore. So you will stay in your wet gear. But try and keep the mess to a minimum. This is why it is a good idea to put the cushion into a plastic bag, so that it is protected and the sleeping-bag can be stowed away in a dry place.

97

Foul weather gear

Getting in and out of wet gear can be quite laborious at the best of times. Still, everyone should make a point of getting out of oilskins immediately after coming off watch, and perhaps putting on non-slip shoes and a woolly hat. The latter is very useful as protection against banging one's head down below in rough weather.

Wet oilskins are put away in the wet locker or, if this is not available, the heads compartment. They are hung buttoned up, so that the inside remains dry if possible.

As long as it is practicable, the principle of the 'wet lock' (like an air lock) should be kept up. This is a zone just inside of the companionway which cannot be kept dry anyway. Those on watch can move about here in their wet oilskins, for example, to navigate, fetch something from the galley or use the heads. This is also the place where wet gear is removed. Beyond this zone, oilskins are not allowed, for as long as you can keep it up, at least. There are times when the crew is past caring about little things like this.

Use the heads

I do not have any statistics, but reports suggest that a high proportion of man overboard incidents happen when men are peeing over the side. So men should make a habit of using the heads for this purpose, in a sitting position for stability. The only problem tends to be the weakness of the toilet seat. With the heavy forces at work in a pitching boat, they give way even under a body of normal weight. This is not something you need worry about, but perhaps you will be able to make some improvements before the next trip.

If you are seasick, you should also use the heads. It is true that you feel even more sick in this confined space, but once it is over and done with most people feel a lot better.

Seasickness

This can happen at any time and to nearly everybody. Someone on every yacht is almost bound to get *mal de mer*, especially in a gale. The motion of the boat is more violent and even some of those who have not been seasick before may now succumb. There really is nothing much that you can do about it. We are all part-time sailors, and real sea legs only develop when you are at sea continuously. Only a few people are lucky enough to have been born with the gift of never becoming seriously seasick.

If the sickness is not too serious, the casualty should carry on with his watches. Helming, especially, is one of the best medicines. But beware: helming during a gale should not be treated as a means of recovery for seasick crew members. Only those who can still concentrate and are fit enough despite seasickness should take the helm. Others can be kept busy as lookouts and sheet-trimmers.

Those off watch should not stay in the cockpit because they feel queasy. They cannot get their much needed rest there. Mild attacks of queasiness are best slept away in a warm berth. However, avoid reading or chartwork.

Severe cases of seasickness are excused of their watchkeeping duties. It may be necessary to change the entire watch system. The casualties disappear to their berths, with a bucket lashed nearby. (In days gone by the convention was to lash the sick persons themselves into their berths.)

Food

It is a great boon if the galley can be kept going during heavy weather. Even if someone can only manage to brew up the simplest of warm meals. A tinned stew heated up in the can, powdered soup or sandwiches with warm milk are the kind of dishes that can be attempted even under severe conditions. A steady supply of chocolate, biscuits or similar is useful for keeping the inner batteries charged.

It is also a good idea to have vacuum flasks refilled with warm drinks from time to time. The best are medium strength coffee or tea. Be careful about adding alcohol to beverages. Alcohol slows reactions which are all the more necessary in these gale-force conditions.

The cooker is dangerous in a gale. Bad burns occur if a pot flies off the stove and the hot contents are spilled over arms or legs. It should therefore be the rule to cook only in oilskins.

Whether the preparation of food is the responsibility of those on or those off watch, it has to be organized. With a small crew, the watch on deck should take care of it, to enable the others to get their much-needed rest. If two people are on watch, one can nip below from time to time and see to the food.

Morale

Sustenance is needed not only for the body, but also for the soul. Everyone on board is aware of the pressures. For the average

Sitting it out on board *Flyer* in the Southern Ocean during a Whitbread Round the World Race. *Photo: Onne Van der Wal/PPL.*

yachtsman, a gale is an extreme situation which goes well beyond normal experience. Everyone has their own way of trying to cope with the situation. The ability to face reality without giving in to wishful thinking, on one hand, or hopelessness, on the other, comes more easily to some than to others. For some it is a profound experience.

The influence of crew members on each other is of great importance. If one feels that it's the same for others, it is easier to accept the situation. So open and frank conversation is important, with nobody excluded. Extremes of temperament should be reined in. Excessive heartiness is just as dangerous as too much pessimism.

Keeping in touch

I do not know a satisfactory answer to this problem. On most yachts that do not have a full-time navigator, the VHF is turned down low or switched off when people are sleeping below. This is reasonable, but dangerous as contact with the outer world is cut off. Urgent gale warnings are missed, and one cannot respond to a Mayday call.

Some yachts have a cockpit speaker. This can solve the problem in principle. But in a gale you cannot hear anything from the helm position. The speaker would have to be attached to the wheel pedestal. I have yet to see this on any yacht.

Apart from receiving weather reports and Mayday calls, it is quite a good idea to know who else is around and where. It is encouraging to know that you are not alone out there and that there is someone else battling against the storm. So it can do no harm to call your neighbours on Channel 16 at low power. If you are in luck, someone will respond. You then change to an inter-ship channel and stay there. You can exchange tips and tactics, and there is the knowledge, just in case, that you can also ask for help.

Navigation

Working at the chart table during a gale is no easy task. Because the navigation tends to be less precise than normal, people tend to neglect it altogether.

Please don't neglect it, not even in the middle of the ocean, because in a case of distress you will suddenly need your exact position. And it is not only you who may be in trouble. When responding to a distress call, you have to know where you are in order to sail to the other position. And in confined waters it may be a question of whether to bear off a little or whether to tack or not. A change in the wind direction may raise the problem of a lee shore, and an alternative course may have to be thought of. All of these decisions depend on knowing one's exact position and having a record of your progress so far.

Of course, the time spent at the chart table will be limited. Basically, at each change of watch, the position should be entered both on the chart and in the log, even if it is only based on dead reckoning. The next watch can take this for their starting point. It also means that the helmsman has to keep track of the courses steered and determine the average over a period of time. After each major change of course, the second person goes below with the course steered and log reading to carry on the dead reckoning. The correction for leeway should be generous. Double the allowance for normal sailing conditions is about right. Accurately plotting the course is a job requiring patience and a bit of luck, but you'll manage somehow.

If the yacht is fitted with electronic navigation aids like Loran, Decca, Satnav or GPS, I would, of course, take the positions from them, but only in parallel to the dead reckoning. The differences in position will tell you about leeway and steering accuracy. Moreover, the two systems in parallel provide an invaluable check on one another.

Next to navigating, keeping track of the weather is almost equally important. Listen to the shipping forecasts and make a note of them, in order to follow the movement of the depression. By comparing actual wind direction, wind speed and barometric pressure with the forecast, you can determine how far the low has come and how far it still has to go.

In the cockpit

Wet gear must be roomy and watertight at the same time. This can be achieved if you take care when buying new foul weather gear. The clothes must be loose enough for air to circulate inside them when you move. If you undo them a bit in front from time to time and move about a little, the air inside will be exchanged and there will be less condensation. The garment should be watertight at the collar and cuffs. With modern wet gear this should be no problem.

I prefer the traditional sou'wester to a hood. Worn properly with the strap beneath the chin it gives perfect protection, and you can turn your head freely. Hoods are like blinkers.

It goes without saying that lifejackets and harnesses should be worn, with the latter clipped on. The ever present danger in rough weather is that someone will be washed overboard. Clipping on takes some practice. I have seen people that got so entangled in their lanyards that, trying to free themselves, they very nearly went over the side. Try to find the best possible points for clipping on. Some kinds of clip can open by themselves, usually if they get twisted round and then put under load.

For the person at the wheel a hip belt which can be hooked to both sides of the cockpit is ideal. It gives good support and you feel as if you are riding the boat.

The second person in the watch should find a place in the cockpit where he or she can complement the helmsman's field of vision. This can be uncomfortable, as people always prefer to sit with their back to wind and spray. But it is very helpful if they can point out the next breaking sea to the helmsman. But the second person should not stay on deck continuously, only when the helmsman needs them. It can be important for him or her to warm up down below in order to prepare themselves to take the next spell on the helm. Besides, there are always plenty of things to do below.

Working on deck

One basic rule should be that nobody leaves the cockpit without good reason, without telling others about it, without being clipped on and without being watched.

If you have to go forward, clip yourself on to the jackstay. The way forward is along the windward side of the deck. Crawl forward holding on to lifelines and grab rails. Once you get to the mast or foredeck, it may be necessary to hook on to another point as the jackstay may not allow enough freedom of movement. While clipping on somewhere else it is vital to have a secure hold, so that you are not caught off balance. Double lanyards and clips, so that you are always clipped on somewhere, are somewhat impractical. You spend ages clipping and unclipping yourself, and it seems safer instead to have a secure handhold while you are moving the clip and get the job done and yourself back into the cockpit quickly.

The progress of work on deck is monitored from the cockpit. If a big sea is coming that looks as though it may break over the boat, the people up forward are warned, using the fog-horn if necessary. Shouting may not be loud enough to carry forward against the wind. For those at the mast or further forward, this is the signal to cling on with all their strength. The most secure hold is to wrap one arm around the mast, shrouds, pulpit or even a lifeline and then hold on to your wrist with the other hand.

When a sea breaks over the deck your legs are swept from under you. You are pushed to leeward with incredible force. If you hold on tightly, you'll probably end up flat on the deck and soaked to the skin. In the Capetown to Rio Race, one unfortunate crew member ended up in the crosstrees. He had held on to the shrouds, when the yacht suffered a knock-down. He was swept up the shrouds, not realizing what was happening. He grabbed hold of the first thing that came his way, which happened to be the crosstrees, just before the yacht righted herself. Not that this is a very typical case.

Darkness

Everything is more difficult at night. It should be made clear to everyone that a person overboard at night is as good as lost. Not being clipped on at night poses a real threat to one's life. It should be emphasised as strongly as that.

It is important not to blind the person on the helm or on watch who has to try and see the seas approaching in the darkness. A brightly lit companionway, a torch flashed without thinking or too much light around the chart table can spoil the night vision of those on deck for several minutes.

Stormy nights are often pitch black. The helmsman has to steer by the instruments, which in breaking seas is only possible off the wind. Compass and wind direction are the main aids to keeping one's bearings. Trying to illuminate the sea with a searchlight is useless. The beam of light is far too narrow to be of any help. You can hear seas breaking at the last minute, still in time to whip the stern around and keep the boat on an even keel.

If someone needs to go forward at night you should think twice about it. It is dangerous. It is all too easy to be caught unawares by a big sea and end up being towed along by your harness. If you really have to go, take a torch with you, not only for working on deck, but because, in the event of going overboard, there is a better chance of being seen.

It seems natural to switch on the deck lighting for work on the foredeck. The drawback is that the helmsman cannot see the approaching seas and accordingly cannot warn those up forward. There is no ideal solution to the problem.

15 Active and passive storm tactics

How do you bring a sailing yacht through a gale? Which is the best way of avoiding unnecessary strain on crew and boat?

In fact, there is no single answer. The situation in every storm is different, as are the qualities of each boat and her crew. The multiplicity of differing recommendations from experienced sailors reflects this.

In this chapter we will try and identify the basic lessons to be learnt from individual experiences. These will concentrate on ways of coping with heavy weather which can be easily applied to modern cruising yachts and which have found the acceptance and approval of experts. Interestingly, this advice accords well with the physical properties of waves described in earlier chapters, so it has the benefit of a logical basis.

Not all big seas terrify. Clearly, these two crew and the helmsman are enjoying their experience. *Photo: Dr J Fuller/PPL.*

Helming in rough seas

In a force 8, which is gale force on the Beaufort scale, sailing in the open sea can still be quite enjoyable. The waves can be as high as 5 to 8 m (16 to 26 ft), but in the open they will be so long that an easy motion is still possible. Heavy breaking seas do not normally occur.

In this situation an experienced helmsman can easily cope with the waves by meeting them in the right way. Even in shallower coastal waters, where the seas are less majestic, the same method of steering through the waves can be applied, with the only difference that the course adjustments have to be quicker and more frequent in keeping with the shorter period of the waves.

When steering through waves the main objective is to keep boat speed under control. With large waves, speed is not determined by the wind alone, but additionally, and sometimes to the greater extent, by the uphill and downhill slope of the waves. A modern yacht will probably surf when sailing down a large wave and hit astronomical speeds, while the same boat can come to a virtual standstill when going up the wave. Boat speed has to be maintained at such a level that the yacht always remains manoeuvrable. Going too fast, the loads on the rudder become excessive. The yacht is difficult to control, even with a strong hand on the helm. Going too slow, the power of the rudder will decrease up to a point where it becomes totally ineffective. Side forces are then able to push bow or stern off course.

An acceptable speed range for a normal cruising yacht would be 4 to 9 knots. For certain manoeuvres to be carried out in heavier seas, speed must be controlled more precisely. For example, if you need enough momentum to shoot through a breaking wave crest. We'll come to that later.

Speed is controlled by slight changes of course. By steering rather more parallel to the seas, you can gain speed when climbing up a wave or lose speed when running down one. An alteration of 20° to 30° will normally be sufficient, but you can check this on the log and feel it on the helm.

Sailing close-hauled at, say, 60° to the wind, the sequence would be as follows. In the trough, the yacht sails on her normal course at 6 knots (Fig 15.1, 1). The next wave approaches and speed drops so the yacht bears off to maintain speed at 5 knots (2). The yacht now apparently climbs up the wave sideways, but in reality it slides past underneath. On the back of the wave (3) the yacht luffs up again as much as possible. Speed will increase dramatically going downhill, which can be used to work up to

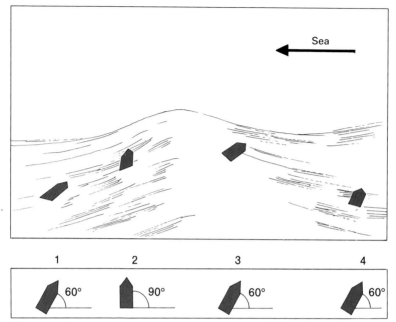

Fig 15.1 Sailing to windward in a heavy sea.

windward. If the yacht started to go too fast, it would be necessary to bear off towards the back slope of the wave (this reduces speed more efficiently than shooting up into the wind and surfing straight down the back of the wave). In the trough, the normal course is steered again (4). In short, when sailing upwind, bear off going up a wave.

On a reach (Fig 15.2) the waves will approach beam-on and create no uphill or downhill effect in relation to the yacht's course. This is why, in principle, no course corrections are needed to control boat speed. The option still remains open should an errant wave make it necessary.

On a broad reach uphill and downhill phases occur again. In the trough the normal course is steered (Fig 15.3, 1). The next wave approaches on the starboard quarter. It picks up the stern and speed increases which can now be reduced as required by steering closer to the wind (2). This could be necessary with some boats due to their underwater configurations which would place an excessive load on the rudder. With the majority of modern boats, however, crews would rather keep the yacht surfing along on her normal course. On the back of the wave (3), after the crest has gone by, the

How to cope with storms

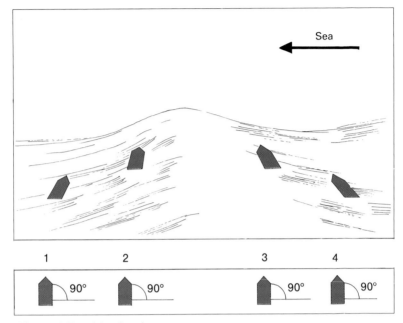

Fig 15.2 Reaching in a heavy sea.

yacht is sailing uphill. She can now use a little help, so again she heads up a little, sailing more across the wave. It would be advisable to trim the sails a bit tighter than normal for the whole sequence (on a broad reach sail trim is not as critical, anyway). In the trough, the normal course is resumed (4). In short, when sailing on a broad reach, luff up a little as soon as the wave has passed.

The cycle from one wave to the next can be very short. Roughly 15 seconds on a run and 10 seconds on a beam reach. Even allowing for the waves to not all have the same period, there will just be enough time for the helmsman to change course with short sharp movements of the rudder. There is no question of altering the trim of the sheets. Sailing upwind, sheets are simply kept tight, even when bearing off. On a broad reach they are trimmed in a bit more than would be necessary in normal conditions.

Whatever happens, flapping of the sails should be avoided. In heavy weather a sail can quickly flap itself to shreds.

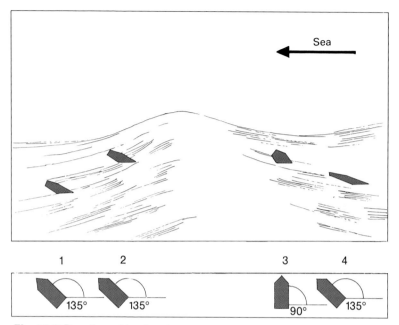

Fig 15.3 Broad reaching in a heavy sea.

How much sail?

The right amount of sail is critical. For a typical modern cruising yacht on a reach, three reefs in the main and a storm jib would be about the norm. Sail area is just about right if the lee rail is not quite in the water amidships. If this happened in a light displacement yacht, I would take the main down altogether, even though it would mean sailing about 10° to 20° farther off the wind. (In the heat of the moment, many crews overlook that the storm jib then has to be sheeted a bit freer, as even storm sails should be trimmed correctly.)

On a reach or running downwind, perhaps even a small working jib could be set as long as there is not too much weather helm. Sailing dead downwind, the sails have to be secured against gybes. The boom should be held downwards and forwards. The normal foreguy only pulls forwards and not downwards enough. So you have to use the kicking-strap. Or you can use the kicking-strap alone and shackle the end to the chain plates.

The jib has to be boomed out on the other side. To do this, the spinnaker boom is rigged up with topping-lift and downhaul and the weather sheet is led through the outboard end, while the jib itself is still on the leeward side. Then the yacht bears off on to a dead run as the leeward sheet is slowly eased and the windward sheet hardened in. In this way, the sail can be brought across to windward in a very controlled and easy way, even when it is blowing hard.

Storm jibs can be set at more than one height on the forestay. An oft repeated mistake is to shackle the tack of the sail directly on to the bow fitting. It is much better to have a strop between the deck and the tack of the sail, so that any seas coming over the bows can run off freely below the sail. Moreover, it will set better a bit higher up and out of the lee of the waves. It will, it is true, exert a bit more heeling moment, but it also offers more stability against rolling. The same applies to trysails.

Course considerations

When steering the boat in seas as described earlier, you will soon find that you can manage quite well, as long as there are no breaking seas around (for those there are special tactics). You will also find that your point of sailing will affect the ease with which you can cope with the seas. Sailing close-hauled, you will get a concentrated dose of the seas, while they appear to calm down or lengthen when you bear off on to a reach or a run. In typical conditions in a force 8 the waves appear to be 200 m long, rather than their actual 140 m, when running downwind at 8 knots. So everything is less hectic and the helmsman has more time to react to the waves. Moreover, the faces of the waves seem less steep and the course changes to counteract them can be less pronounced or may be unnecessary altogether.

The amount of sea room to leeward will dictate whether you can afford to run before a gale. Other things being equal, one would very probably prefer the easier motion downwind. This course also enables you to keep up a much higher average speed, which may help you to escape from bad weather or reach your destination sooner. Daily runs of 200 miles are frequently achieved by cruising yachts running downwind in heavy weather.

If you are not fortunate enough to have sea room you will have to sail upwind. You will find that when steering the boat in heavy seas you will not gain as much ground to windward as under normal sailing conditions. Your course relative to the wind is adversely affected by the need to negotiate the seas and by the amount of leeway. If you are obliged to sail closer to the wind, the engine should

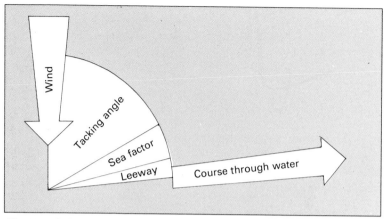

Fig 15.4 In heavy seas the course of a yacht sailing to windward is determind by three components. In addition to the tacking angle, there is a component for having to negotiate seas and for leeway.

be used to help. When the yacht is climbing up a wave, you will then not be forced to bear off.

Breaking seas

Individual waves will really start to break in the open sea from force 9 upwards, and in disturbed areas, such as close inshore or around headlands or in straits as soon as the wind reaches force 8. The waves have a height of between 4 and 10 m (13 to 33 ft) with lengths of 70 to 200 m (230 to 660 ft). Roughly 5 per cent of the waves break, so that a yacht would, on average, be caught by a breaker every 2 to 5 minutes. In coastal waters this frequency can develop with smaller waves and less spectacular breakers.

In general, the yacht is still steered in the same manner. But the waves are now higher and steeper and one has to keep a weather eye open (an ear at night) for an approaching breaker. And then ...?

Dodging seas

Of course one tries to avoid these breaking seas, but it is not easy. It takes some experience to tell from a distance whether a breaker will hit the yacht or pass harmlessly by. The bearing, relative to the yacht's head, of waves that are on a collision course is constant and

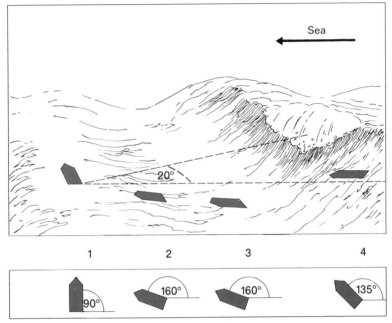

Fig 15.5 Dodging a breaking sea on a beam reach. The bearing to watch for dangerous seas on a beam reach or close-hauled is about 20° forward of the beam.

it is in this direction that the helmsman or lookout should concentrate their attention at the moment when the yacht is on the crest of a wave and the view is unobstructed.

Sailing close-hauled or reaching more or less parallel to the waves, the bearing to watch is about 20° to 25° forward of the beam (Fig 15.5). When the breaker is the next wave but one, about 7 to 10 seconds are left in which to react. No time to think! Put the helm hard up to turn away from the breaker on to nearly a dead run (2). The yacht will now be 'parked' on the back of the wave, bows pointing up the back of the preceding wave and with not much way on. No change to sail trim. Stay in this position for a few seconds and let the breaker pass down the side. When it is abeam you luff up carefully and sail over the crest behind the breaker (4). After a time you will acquire the necessary eye and practice at this.

I do not recommend trying to luff up past the sea. In order to retain some steerage way, you would only be able to luff up to 60° off the wind, which would not be very far off a collision course.

On a broad reach, the direction to look is nearly dead upwind,

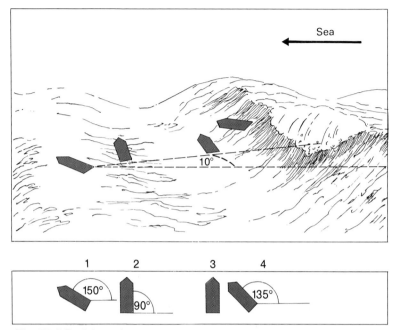

Fig 15.6 Dodging a breaking sea on a broad reach. The bearing to watch is about 10° forward of dead upwind.

only a few degrees ahead. You will have a bit more time and two options: either to luff up and cross in front of the breaker at increased speed (Fig 15.6), or to bear off to the parked position described above.

From a dead run, you can only escape by luffing, if you want to avoid a gybe. This can be a tricky situation if the breaker is approaching on your weather quarter. Then you can only try and cross in front of it or stay on course, hoping. Both options are quite unpleasant.

Taking breaking seas

You have to be very alert while dodging breaking seas for one not to catch up with you in the end. If this happens, always try to take it on bow or stern, *never* broadside-on. At the critical moment just before the wave strikes, the rudder is put hard over to point either bow or stern, whichever is quicker, into the sea (Fig 15.7).

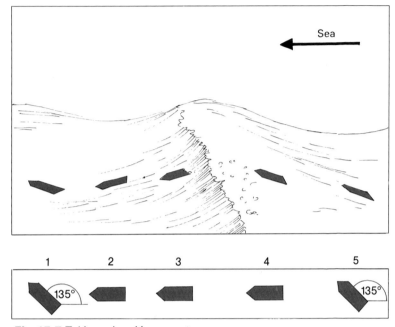

Fig 15.7 Taking a breaking sea stern-on.

Be careful not to overshoot. This can happen quite easily at first, as all attention is on the breaking sea and your sense of direction may be temporarily lost. The helmsman has to try to keep an overall view of the horizon, even (and especially) when things become critical.

In order to be able to turn quickly, boat speed must be right. Sailing at 9 knots, you cannot turn any yacht quickly enough. Nor at 2 knots. An experienced helmsman always keeps an eye on boat speed, even while dodging seas, especially when things start to look as if they could go wrong. It is then vital to have manoeuvrability.

Stern-on method

Taking a breaking sea on the stern is easier than taking it on the bow, as you will be making good speed down the forward slope of the wave. Yachts may even be able to surf out of reach of the breaking crest, but in a cruising boat I would not rely on this. More often the breaker will catch up with you (Fig 15.7, 3), but surprisingly slowly owing to the speed of the yacht. With luck, the end result is just a bit of water in the cockpit that gurgles away harmlessly down the cockpit drains.

The comparatively high speed of the yacht which reduces the impact of the water is all important. You can increase this effect by bearing away sooner, thus picking up more speed.

Head-on method

Taking the breaking sea on the bow is more difficult to carry out, but it has its advantages over the stern-on option. One loses very little ground to windward and gets surprisingly little water into the cockpit. The manoeuvre requires an agile yacht that responds promptly to the helm. Modern cruising boats will have few problems here, but the heavy long-keeled type will not be able to luff up quickly enough.

For this manoeuvre it is vital to choose the right moment to luff up and to have enough speed once this point is reached. To achieve

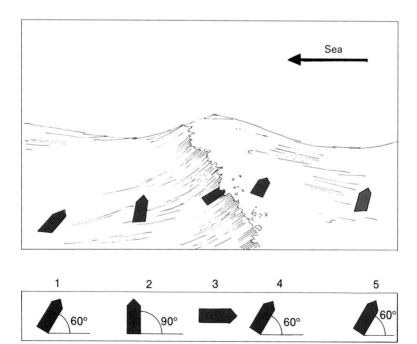

Fig 15.8 Meeting a breaking sea head-on.

this, it may be necessary to gain a bit of speed by reaching (Fig 15.8, 2). Shooting up into the wind has to be done at the last possible second to guarantee enough momentum to carry the yacht through. If you start luffing too early, you will stop dead before you have reached the crest. If you try to play it too safe by bearing off quite far to pick up speed, this speed will soon be lost again in the course of the long turn to windward that has to follow. Inexperienced helmsmen should try this manoeuvre at 6 or 7 knots, starting at a distance of around 30 or 40 m from the wave. The turn should be swift but not too tight, stopping when the sails start to flap. As soon as the bow dives into the breaker (3), the helm is put down again. The yacht should then not fall bow first into the trough behind, but emerge on a normal close-hauled course down the back of the wave (4).

The impact of the breaker is heavy, but it is met head-on, so it should not harm the boat too much. The lateral forces are small. Normally the water flows past on both sides and only some spray arrives in the cockpit.

On the crest, rudder efficiency is surprisingly high. This is due to the strong flow of water from the breaking crest, which momentarily increases the boat's speed through the water.

At the moment of breaking through the yacht has to be steered accurately. The storm jib is a good indicator of how far the yacht has luffed up into the wind. Overshooting has to be avoided at all costs. Once the storm jib is aback, an involuntary tack could follow. This could leave you at the mercy of the next breaking sea.

Bearing off on the crest, as the bows start to emerge from the water, has to be executed swiftly. If this is not done determinedly enough or too late, the yacht tends to shoot off the wave bow first and crash heavily into the trough. Some modern yachts, especially, with flat U-sections in the bows do not appreciate this treatment at all.

If you hit it right, the manoeuvre can be accomplished with the ease of a dance step. After a while, the helmsman will develop a feeling for it and slip into the rhythm easily. The yacht will cut almost effortlessly through the threatening seas and the danger could be that you will lose your respect for them. This is abruptly restored if the helmsman loses his timing! In very high seas it can be difficult to gain enough momentum. In this case, or if the helmsman is inexperienced, I would use the engine to help. It will help the boat to climb the wave and may give it the critical extra push through the crest. It is also reassuring to know that you can always increase steering control at the push of the throttle.

Passive heavy weather tactics

Steering through the waves, dodging the breaking ones or swinging bow or stern around to meet them are active heavy weather tactics. The helmsman keeps the initiative and counters the assaults of the waves.

Passive tactics, on the other hand, mean committing the yacht to an attitude designed to enable it to withstand whatever the sea throws at it, rather than taking the seas individually. These tactics can therefore be applied in very heavy seas, where reacting to them individually might not be possible anymore, or at night when there is not enough light. The price to pay is that the range of courses available with the active tactics is reduced to a very small downwind selection.

This is why you will normally try the active tactics first. Meeting seas head-on can become difficult when the waves become so high that you cannot gain enough momentum. In that case, the option of turning stern-on is still available. The more frequently the seas break and the more heavily they do so, the less the helmsman will be able to luff up on to the original course. In the end, as long as there is sufficient sea room, the yacht will just be running downwind. This is where passive tactics start.

Running downwind

The helmsman will keep a careful eye on the waves coming up astern on both sides and will keep the boat running before the seas by energetic use of the rudder. Only if this is achieved and the yacht is running dead before the wind, is she safe from breaking crests and from yawing to one side, should the bows bury themselves in the back of a wave. Lateral forces are kept to a minimum, so that even momentary loss of rudder efficiency can be safely coped with. Of course, the option of controlling speed by luffing into the sea is now gone. It now has to be done by reducing sail area and, if necessary, by towing warps.

The aim is to keep the boat at a controllable speed, both up the waves and down them. So when the yacht is sailing up the back of a wave, speed should not drop to below 4 knots and when shooting down the face it should not exceed a manageable level. What is manageable depends partly on the type of yacht and, to a greater extent, on the skill of the helmsman. As long as the yacht can be kept pointed straight down the wave, she can go like a train with the rudder firmly amidships. But, if course adjustments have to be made, speed has to be kept within sensible limits, though not too low. High speeds when running with the seas increase their apparent length and reduce their steepness. And when a breaking sea comes up astern, a higher speed reduces the impact. 10 to 14 knots when surfing down a wave is quite acceptable on a 12-metre yacht, just to give some idea.

Sail plans

There are two basic schools of thought concerning the right sail plan for running in heavy weather. One school believes in taking down main (and mizzen) at an early stage and sailing under jib alone. This, the theory goes, has the advantage that a wider range of courses can be steered without the threat of an accidental gybe and that concentrating sail area forward helps with directional stability. The other school believes in keeping a symmetrical sail plan for as long as possible, by having a boomed-out foresail on one side and the reefed main on the other. Both opinions have their strong points, otherwise they would not be as widespread as they are. It probably comes down to the individual characteristics of yachts when running downwind. If a yacht is unfamiliar, the crew should try both systems and decide which makes the yacht more manageable downwind.

Even running under jib alone, the sail should still be boomed out. Accidental gybes occur all too easily in heavy seas, and a gybe can damage a foresail as well as a main. If you have heard the incredible bang when a storm jib is caught aback in a force 10 you will appreciate this. But if the clew of the jib is hard up against the boom, the yacht can veer off course up to 40° or 50° on either side without danger.

Furling the main, even if it is only the bit left after the third reef, is always a struggle – a struggle to overcome one's own laziness as well as the wind in the sail. But this job has to be done properly, as a half-hearted attempt will inevitably not hold out against the wind, and the job then has to be done again.

The sail has to be furled tightly along the boom to offer minimum wind resistance and lashed with plenty of sail ties. I would not, as sometimes proposed, lower the boom on to the deck and lash it there. Even lowering the boom can cause severe damage on deck. The boom is better held on the topping-lift, secured sideways by guys. In this case, the connection between mainsheet and topping-lift is kept intact which is a back-up for the backstay. You never know....

The next step down is to run under bare poles. For the vast majority of modern cruising boats, there are very few occasions when this step is either necessary or advisable. It is only required in extreme gales which are thankfully very seldom encountered. I would probably hesitate to send someone to the foredeck in these extreme conditions to take down the storm jib. Keeping the storm jib would have the added advantage that, if speed on the back of a wave should drop too much, you can always accelerate by luffing on to a reach. Under bare poles this would not be possible.

Towing warps

Warps streamed astern were more common in the past than in current practice. Most modern yachts are quite manageable at 10 or even 15 knots, but traditional boats can be difficult to steer once speed exceeds 8 knots. The need for them to tow warps astern to help slow the boat down is understandable. Don't just tie the end to a cleat and then throw the whole lot overboard. This would impose an extreme shock on the cleat and probably pull it out of the deck. It is better to pay the line out gradually around the genoa winch, which can also be used to pull it back on board again. The most satisfactory way to tow a warp is in a bight made fast at either quarter.

Towing warps can be very useful sometimes on modern yachts, too. They help to stabilize the stern against the oncoming seas and so take some strain off the helmsman. The yacht will, of course, still have to be steered, but she will ride a lot easier before the seas. As a helming aid, the warp need not be quite as long, but should still measure at least half the length of the waves.

On smaller boats, towing the mainsail still attached to the boom has been used successfully to slow the boat down. The head of the sail was attached to a relatively short line of about twice the length of the boat. The effect of this was remarkable in calming down seas approaching from astern. Medium-sized seas were reported to have collapsed over the sail.

Keeping the warp down in the water by adding weight, such as an anchor, is less effective. This only serves to pull the stern of the yacht down and thus hinder it from rising to the oncoming waves. The result will be a constantly swamped cockpit. A sea anchor should never be towed astern to slow the yacht. The boat would come to a near standstill and every breaker would hit the stern with its full force. The value of the sea anchor is in maintaining an offing, a tactic which we will discuss a little further on.

Here you can see the warps towed by *Carmargue* during the disastrous
storm which hit the 1979 Fastnet Race. *Photo: Barry Pickthall/PPL.*

Heaving-to

A yacht hove-to drifts nearly beam-on to the wind with the jib aback and the main free, with the helm to windward. This is a very stable attitude in which the boat is nearly stationary. If a sea pushes the bow to leeward, the jib becomes less effective and the main starts to draw, so that the yacht picks up enough way for the rudder to bite and bring her bows back up to the wind.

It is important to understand the way in which a yacht moves when hove-to, in order to see the possibilities, variations and also limitations of this tactic. A wide range of sails can be set, as long as the yacht will always head back into the wind. This could be achieved with storm jib and trysail, storm jib alone, trysail alone, jib and mizzen, and so on, or even under engine alone without any sails at all.

The latter expedient is rather unusual and we shall therefore take a quick look at it. The yacht is kept on a course of roughly 45° off the wind with the engine just ticking over and helm lashed to windward. The engine should be run just fast enough to make the rudder work and hold the boat up to the wind, but no further. The amount of throttle required depends on the wind speed. If a wave pushes the bow down to leeward, speed picks up due to the reduction in windage and the rudder gains effect and turns the bow back up to windward. If the boat points up too much, windage increases and speed decreases, with it the effect of the rudder, so the boat is blown back on to the 45° course.

Depending on the circumstances, different methods of heaving-to differ in effectiveness. In very heavy seas it can happen that the yacht is swept helpless around, until it even gybes. You have to experiment with your yacht to find the best way of heaving-to. In any case, all sails and gear should be secured against the possibility of accidental gybes, although sometimes, curiously enough, the boat ends up back on the original heading after having performed an involuntary gybe.

One point in favour of lying hove-to in heavy weather is the calming effect the drift has on the waves. The area of turbulence that the yacht leaves to windward when drifting damps the waves and sometimes even makes breakers collapse. The effect is most pronounced with heavy long-keeled yachts that have a lot of underwater resistance.

The course of the drift is critical for this effect. The boat has to drift sideways in order to produce the area of disturbed water to windward. Most fin-keeled boats, however, do not drift sideways, but nearly always make headway to leeward, no matter how much you try playing around with the sail trim. These boats are not really suitable for heaving-to as a way to weather a storm. If you spend too long experimenting in severe weather, you run an acute danger of being swamped by a breaking sea or falling off the face of a big wave, because lying beam-on to the waves without the damping effect to windward water puts one in a rather vulnerable position.

Yachts of traditional design, however, have reported excellent results when lying hove-to. A watch on deck was not needed any more, and life below decks was tolerable. The yachts drifted at 2 to 3 knots about 150° off the wind so that warps trailing astern were still effective in producing a zone of calmer water to windward.

The loss of around 60 miles per day to leeward is only a third of what you would lose when running before the weather. For sailing boats whose design is suited to heaving-to, this is an excellent way of weathering a gale if it is no longer possible to sail to windward.

Lying to a sea anchor

Some skippers have never even seen a drogue or sea anchor. It is a funnel-shaped device, held in shape by hoops, not unlike a small wind sock. The bridle is attached to roughly 50 m of warp, with a lighter tripping line at the other end to get the contraption back on board again.

In pictures, though never in real life, have I also seen a sort of cable railway leading to the drogue which was supposed to transport little containers of oil. If you know how easily anything being towed, no matter of what nature, gets hopelessly tangled, you won't take the idea too seriously.

The holding power of a drogue or sea anchor increases with the square of the drift speed. Deployed when under way at full speed, it would tear off any cleat. So the boat is luffed up, when an opportunity presents itself, almost head to wind, and the sea anchor is let go at the moment when way has been lost. The warp is led through a fairlead at the bows and paid out gradually. This is the only way to avoid excessive snatching when the boat is checked by the anchor.

I would pay out a warp of a quarter of the wave length. Often half the wave length is recommended, but, should the sea anchor remain near the surface, at that distance it would be exposed to a surface current running exactly counter to that under the yacht. The result would be an alternate snatching and slackening of the warp which cannot be desirable. Instead, the anchor should hold the yacht as steadily as possible.

Once the sea anchor is deployed, the yacht may lie bow to the seas fairly comfortably. But this is only achieved after much experimenting with the length of the warp. Most of the time the yacht will yaw wildly to and fro, while the rudder will crash from one side to the other if it has not been secured amidships immediately. This instability has to be controlled quickly, otherwise the yacht could be caught beam-on by a breaking sea, while yawing off to one side. So the warp is paid out slowly round the winch, in stages every time the yacht starts to ride forwards again. In this way, the length of the warp can be found out at which the yawing will be minimal. This is specific to each design of boat and each pattern of waves.

If the yawing cannot be controlled by this method, another trick can be tried. A spring is tied to the warp with a rolling hitch just outboard of the fairlead and led aft outside the shrouds to the genoa winch. Now the warp is paid out a further 2 to 3 m and the boat should lie at an angle to the waves. This damps the yawing motion of most yachts, and the spring can be trimmed to achieve the best result.

When the yacht is finally lying satisfactorily to the sea anchor she will drift astern at around 2 knots. The rudder has to be lashed securely amidships. The boat seems to be making headway against the waves, but that is an illusion.

Almost stationary, the yacht now has to bear the full brunt of the seas. The impact is consequently severe, but the blows are aimed at the forepart of the boat, which is designed and built to withstand such shocks. Rest assured that the hull will stand up to it, even if the noise is terrible.

What are the advantages of a sea anchor and under what circumstances would you choose to use one? First of all, the yacht involved must be of a certain size, simply to be able to carry such a bulky item on board. Second, it would be a yacht not suited to lying hove-to, which is easier on the boat and, lastly, one which cannot be motored into the seas safely (another method, which will be discussed later).

Lying a-hull

This is a tactic often used by the singlehanders, which I would not recommend to anyone else, except those unfortunate skippers who have involuntarily become singlehanded due to a general epidemic of seasickness on board.

This method relies on the fact that a floating object will tend to lie beam-on on to the waves. An untended yacht left to her own devices will do the same. No sails, no headway, no helmsman. Everything lashed down on deck and all hatches closed.

Under these circumstances, leeway is extremely slight, even less than when hove-to, due to the lack of sails. On the other hand, the area of turbulence to windward that smooths the waves is also missing. The yacht lying a-hull is left to the mercy of the seas. This tactic relies entirely on strength of construction and the endurance of the crew. No wonder that some purpose-built singlehanded yachts look extremely strong, almost armour-plated. Likewise, many incidences of capsize and falling off waves involve singlehanders.

Use of oil

The use of oil could be combined with lying a-hull as this is the only way available to improve matters.

Just about every form of liquid oil can be used. It can be pumped out in small amounts through the heads. On account of the slow rate of drift, the oil slick should stay to windward of the boat for quite a while.

When lying hove-to, the problem is that the oil slick has to be to windward in order to be effective. Even if this is the case, the yacht's wake should be sufficient to create the previously mentioned area of turbulence that smooths the seas. The use of oil would then normally not be necessary.

When lying to a sea anchor, however, the use of oil seems appropriate, as the yacht is drifting dead to leeward and the oil slick would be in just the right place to be most effective.

It is a widespread belief that oil released to windward will be washed back on deck with the next wave and leave a slippery mess. Practical experience does not bear this out. Theoretically, it should never happen, as normal waves do not carry water from windward; only breaking seas would. And they should not occur when oil is used.

Use of engine

Motoring during heavy weather is often regarded as unseamanlike and it may not be popular to recommend this as a standard method of weathering a gale. But I do it nevertheless, as it is a question of safety, especially in two situations. First, if there is a serious need to make an offing. Second, if a crew caught out in heavy weather, due to lack of experience, do not wish or are not confident enough to sail through it.

One requirement is, of course, a powerful engine. This would be, on a modern 12 m (39 ft) yacht, about 50 hp, with a correspondingly large propeller. The power of a typical engine designed as an auxiliary for calm weather will only suffice to improve steering control and help gain ground to windward while sailing.

Weathering a storm under engine, without sails, is possible on all courses, though tactics differ.

On a course parallel to the waves the way to tackle breaking seas is the same as when sailing, bearing off before them to minimize their impact. But it is not as critical as when sailing to meet the sea exactly stern-to, as the danger of broaching is far less pronounced. The rudder is more effective due to the force of the propeller, which is constant no matter what is happening on the surface. Turning downwind also helps to increase speed in order to reduce the impact of the sea. Speed, of course, can now be controlled at a touch of the throttle, while the boat can be slowed down if required by heading into the wave.

Running downwind, a distinct safety factor when motoring would be the ability to keep up steerage way when going up the back of a sea. To drive the boat down the waves the windage of the rig would probably be enough on its own.

But in most cases, the engine will be used in an effort to gain sea room. The most comfortable course upwind lies around 50° to 60° off the wind. At this angle you can work steadily upwind without any complicated manoeuvres. Motoring more into the wind, the boat would slow down climbing a wave and shoot down it on the other side. More off the wind, you gain less ground to windward and it is more difficult to luff up into breaking seas.

In more detail, assuming an average course of 50° to 60° off the wind, one maintains a speed up the waves that never drops below 4 knots. This is the minimum needed to turn quickly into an oncoming sea. Breaking seas are never tackled at more than 30° off the wind, otherwise engine power would be useless and the bows will be pushed aside. On the crest, the original course is resumed and, with less throttle, the yacht is steered diagonally down the back of the wave. Overshooting the crest results in a jarring shock as the bows crash into the next trough. Motoring down the wave, speed has to be reduced, either by throttle or by steering more parallel to the seas, so that the bows will not be buried in the trough.

The distinct advantages of this system of weathering a storm under engine without sails are the simplicity of helming and the reduced risk for a less experienced crew. The yacht will forgive many an error on the helm and there is always the chance to correct the course with the aid of the throttle if it starts to go wrong. On the other hand the stabilizing effect of the sails is lost, so the yacht will roll much more in the heavy seas.

Going upwind under engine is an excellent way of making an offing and more effective even than sailing to windward and meeting the seas head-on. There is only one method that is more effective, the combination of both. This means motoring upwind with storm jib set. The storm jib will provide extra drive at 50° to 60° off the wind and requires no special handling. When it was really critical to make an offing, I would prefer this method over all others. And it can be employed in surprisingly high seas.

Confused seas

In the discussion of heavy weather tactics in this chapter we have tended to treat waves as more regular than they really are. In reality waves seldom follow a regular pattern in size or shape. The basic structure can be seen, but individual waves always differ from the norm, sometimes approaching sideways, sometimes exceptionally large, sometimes not there at all. Sometimes an alarmingly big wave rears up, but its small, rather inconspicuous neighbour is the one that suddenly breaks heavily.

Cross-seas are present in nearly all conditions. In heavy weather all sorts of interference effects occur. Analyzing them does not help you very much to helm the boat. You just have to deal with whatever comes along, however unexpected. The main focus of your attention has to be the area along the line of approaching seas, up to a distance of about two wave lengths, and a few degrees on either side because surprise attacks can come from there. Once you are familiar with the general run of waves, it is easier to spot dangerous ones.

However, your attention should not be exclusively confined to the immediate area. Keeping an eye on the overall scene, including the sky and the horizon, is also important for the safe conduct of the vessel.

16 Planning ahead

Sailing in heavy weather is not simply a question of picking a course and sticking to it until things get too bad. With this approach, it would be all too easy to get into a really difficult situation that could have been avoided with a little foresight. Planning is the key. As in a game of chess, you have to see a few moves ahead and consider what you would do in different situations.

Hopefully armed with a thorough analysis of the weather situation, the skipper will study the chart. He knows his yacht and which tactics are available to him, what course can be sailed and how much sea room is needed for passive tactics. Some typical figures for a modern family yacht are given as a guide.

Table 16.1 Typical rates of progress per hour using different tactics.

Tactic	Course relative to wind	Progress per hour	
		to leeward (nm)	to windward (nm)
Close-hauled taking seas bow-on	80°–90°	–	0–1
Running	150°–180°	6–9	–
Running towing warps	180°	4–7	–
Heaving-to	150°	2–3	–
Lying to sea anchor	180°	1–2	–
Lying a-hull	180°	1–2	–
Motoring upwind	60°	–	1–2
Motoring downwind	60°–180°	6–9	–

Weather routeing

If the yacht is out on the ocean with virtually unlimited sea room available on all sides, the only consideration when choosing a course to sail during heavy weather is how to minimize strain on gear and crew.

Using the available weather information, one's own observations (of wind and barometric pressure) and textbook knowledge of the behaviour of typical gales (see Chapters 4 to 7), the skipper should

127

be able to draw a rough outline of the weather system on the chart. A good trick is to draw it on a piece of tracing paper if conditions on board permit. The sketch can then be positioned at different points on the chart representing different points of time along the expected track of the depression. Wind speed and direction can be read off for each point.

The yacht's proposed course can now be considered in relation to this information. Can it still be maintained or will it have to be changed? It is also possible to see whether the yacht is in the path of the gale and what can be done to avoid it.

Admittedly, this process is a bit theoretical and also relies on having the time and space to use it. If these requirements are not met, one simply falls back on more basic rules of thumb, for example, using a vector diagram like the one used for tropical cyclones in Chapter 7.

The simplest rule of all relates to the structure of cyclones: to avoid a storm in the northern hemisphere, stay on starboard tack, except directly in its path when you should sail downwind.

Sea room

In coastal waters leeway is a prime consideration. Avoiding a lee shore is often the central aim of your navigational strategy.

Room to leeward is like an insurance policy during heavy weather. Wind and waves in the open sea usually do little harm to a sensibly handled yacht. But near the coast a multitude of dangers lie in wait – lack of sea room, breakers, shoals, not to mention lee shores with the risk of grounding and shipwreck.

The limit of sea room is not the shoreline itself, but the danger zones to seaward of the coast. Using basic knowledge about waves (see Chapter 8), the skipper can recognize these on the chart, near shoals and headlands, under steep cliffs, off islands or in channels.

Safety always requires enough room to leeward for one to be able to lie before a sea until the wind moderates enough to make sail again.

How many miles of sea room to leeward you should have can be calculated from the anticipated duration of storm in hours multiplied by the leeway in knots, plus a safety margin of 20 per cent.

Assuming that the gale will moderate in 12 hours time and that the yacht could lie hove-to drifting at 3 knots to leeward, the offing should be at least 43 nautical miles, calculated as follows:

$$12 \text{ hr x } 3 \text{ kn} = 36 \text{ nm}$$
$$36 \text{ nm x } 20\% = 43 \text{ nm}$$

I would mark a no-go area on the chart on the basis of this calculation, around lee shores and their associated dangers, as well as the best that can be made to windward. These parameters define the available scope for manoeuvres, within which you can select a course in the light of your heavy weather tactics, the port that you are aiming for and any of the special circumstances dealt with below.

Of course it is possible that the yacht's position is already inside the no-go area. This information is of prime importance for planning. The first concern should be to gain sea room at all costs. But, armed with the knowledge of how much sea room is needed, you will at least know when you have enough.

Changing tactics

If there is plenty of sea room, you can afford the luxury of laying a course on the basis of short-term considerations. Hence, in difficult circumstances you might lay a course that sacrificed sea room for more comfort. The lost sea room can then be won back later (or has been won earlier) by sailing close-hauled. A typical example is night and day. During the hours of darkness, active tactics are much more difficult to employ due to the limited visibility, so during the night a less demanding tactic is preferable. To make up for it, the best possible course to windward has to be sailed by day. Similar strategy can also be applied in tidal waters. As long as the tide is with the wind, you make as much ground to windward as possible. As soon as the tide changes and sea conditions deteriorate, you can draw on the capital you have made and bear off. Even the composition of different watches might be a factor, if one watch was much better at sailing upwind in heavy weather than the other.

It is advisable to plan these changes of tactic in advance by plotting them on the chart. This will dispel the illusion that six hours of bashing into the wind makes up for six hours of easy downwind work. Courses and distances should be plotted for each phase. This is the only way to ensure that you stay clear of the no-go area.

Some people may sneer at this detailed planning and prefer to gain as much sea room as possible, regardless of circumstances. They would grab every opportunity to gain to windward and build up a big reserve of sea room, for safety, as they see it. But consider the price to pay in terms of unnecessary punishment to windward, in terms of tired crew and material stress, perhaps even physical damage. There is no safety in this. I hope that everybody can see the sense in making this small effort to think and plan ahead. This should be the basis for any strategy for heavy weather.

17 Running for shelter

Old-time sailors are reputed to have felt safer at sea than in harbour in bad weather and perhaps this should be borne in mind when taking a decision to run inshore for shelter.

Don't be misled by the comforting sound of the word 'shelter'. Anyone who knows the sea will think more than twice before committing themselves to sailing shorewards during a gale.

The real problem is the reduction in sea room close to the shore. You lose room to manoeuvre. The lie of the coastline and harbour approach dictate your course. It is advisable to check in advance whether the approach is feasible at all in the present and expected weather conditions.

Approaching on a beam reach

Inshore in an onshore gale the beam reach has to be regarded as the farthest course to windward which is realistically possible. It would be wishful thinking to believe that you could sail closer to the wind in an emergency. On the contrary, you must always consider the possibility of increasing wind and sea and that you end up even further to leeward than anticipated. Moreover, the wind can always head you inshore and force you to bear off further. The wind often shifts close inshore and sometimes follows the coastline, but this cannot be relied upon.

If there is no margin for error to leeward, I would not consider approaching on a beam reach, unless perhaps it would be possible to gain extra distance to windward beforehand, maybe using the engine to help. In that case the decision to risk the approach can be delayed a bit. But if the safety margin is used up you will have no choice but to turn back, which should not be a problem if your approach was on a beam reach.

In talking of a beam reach, when planning the course, I mean the real wind, not the apparent wind that the burgee at the masthead shows. When the burgee shows a beam reach the real wind will be more aft. If the approach is on this point of sailing, there is much less possibility of turning back.

Approaching to windward

Under a weather shore, where the gale is offshore, it is safe to beat up to windward. The big difference in sea conditions is the absence of waves. As there is no fetch only a small choppy sea will develop. This will cause a lot of spray on deck, but is otherwise harmless. There is no need to dodge breaking seas here.

On the other hand, the wind can blow even harder inshore than out at sea. Funnelling and strong katabatic winds are an added hazard.

Apart from sensible boat handling and the right choice of sails, you will just need a little patience. Sooner or later you will gain your objective to windward. Note that, under these conditions, drag increases on storm sails, greatly if you luff up too much. The optimum course to windward is, therefore, with sheets eased slightly, angled between 60° and 50° off the wind, depending on the type of boat.

One should not be tempted to luff up more. As soon as speed drops off a little, all distance made good to windward is eaten up by the increased leeway. Don't hesitate to use the engine to help, unless you are competing in a race or the angle of heel exceeds the operating limits of the engine.

You may be able to make better progress to windward by motoring straight into the wind. Depending on the type of engine and propeller, this could work. However, you may not make any headway at all.

There are other alternatives. Beating to windward, you can always give up the attempt, but who would want to give up everything gained so far? Two better options are available if the attempt does not work out:

1 Anchoring. Under a weather shore in relatively calm water is not the worst place to anchor, even if the wind is howling. One can use heavy ground tackle to cope with the conditions. The wind is bound to drop at some stage and then it is only a short hop into harbour.

2 Waiting. It is less stressful under a weather shore in relatively calm water, than out at sea exposed to the full force of the waves. Although a navigation problem could arise under the shore if night falls. I once experienced real problems sailing up and down in a pitch black bay at night. The echo sounder was invaluable on this occasion.

Closing a lee shore

This is fraught with danger. The 'Bay of Misery' on Jutland's north-west coast takes its name from the many unfortunate fishermen who have been shipwrecked here, on their home territory that is often a lee shore. And they knew the area!

An approach to leeward is a one-way street. Everything has to be right. There is no turning back. It starts with the problem of navigation. In bad weather, visibility is often bad. Landmarks can often only be seen from half a mile out. A reliable GPS or Decca Navigator is a priceless asset. Radar shows little of a low-lying coastline. Depending on visibility, the approach may be especially difficult during the day, with the absence of lights. Often one needs to go far too close inshore in order to distinguish landmarks. To avoid the hazards of a lee shore the approach should be abandoned in good time, in favour of cruising up and down the coast at a safe distance until visibility improves or a conspicuous landmark emerges from the murk.

I would only risk such an approach on the basis of a reliable starting position. When everybody on board is tired and exhausted, one tends towards wishful thinking. All too often, the unidentified headland, tower or village dimly visible ahead is assumed to be the right one, with disastrous consequences.

In order to be able to luff up, the right sails have to be set. If you can turn the bows into the wind under engine, no problem. If the engine does not start, which can happen in rough conditions, the mainsail has to be hoisted in a series of improvised luffs into the wind. This will cost precious distance to leeward. The trick is to start the engine in time, while still sailing downwind, so that you still have enough room to leeward should it be on strike.

Assuming that the entrance to the harbour is straightforward, you only have to worry about the decreasing depth and the resulting short steep seas, which are not too uncomfortable as they come from astern. But then the first breakers appear. The yacht begins to surf and becomes difficult to steer. One has to try and take these seas dead on the stern. They will then foam past parallel to the boat.

A strong tidal stream often sets into and out of estuaries and channels between islands. If the tide is ebbing you will encounter a tremendous sea. If it is flooding it will draw you into the channel at breakneck speed and you may have difficulty scraping round the corner once inside.

Often approaches are not straightforward. In areas like the southern North Sea entrances often have bars and twisting channels leading through that change frequently. These entrances should not be attempted in an onshore gale. The complicated navigation, involving counting off marks and withies, is an enormous risk in the likely bad visibility. Breakers and strong tidal streams make handling the boat difficult. Often the channel is not wide enough to take the seas stern-on. The risks are just too high. If you go aground, the breakers will pound the yacht to pieces.

If there is no other choice, the most important thing is to keep a clear and cool head. It is all or nothing. Experience has shown that in these extreme situations, everybody in the crew tends to try to do everything at the same time and so become totally ineffective. So a clear distribution of tasks is vital. The most important job, navigation, should be delegated to two very reliable crew members. The helmsman should then concentrate wholly on steering, trusting the navigators blindly, and not be distracted by counting withies. He or she must concentrate exclusively on the seas and the channel. The skipper should think about the problems ahead and be ready to help in any unforeseen situation. The rest of the crew are advised to keep their opinions and observations to themselves, unless it is really important. Everyone feels the tension on board, and everyone wants to help in every way they can. This is understandable, but dangerous. Lack of a command structure is a sure way to make fatal mistakes.

18 Manoeuvres in harbour

Even if the harbour entrance is in sight, your problems may not be entirely over. There are still difficulties to overcome because, don't forget, there is still a gale blowing even inside the harbour. Perhaps not quite as hard, but perhaps even harder if topographical effects come into play. In any case, it will be similar.

Manoeuvring in harbour in a gale is an art in itself. Misjudgements in a gale are expensive, because impacts tend to be severe. Collisions will always cause damage under these conditions.

Preparing to enter

The process starts with lowering the sails, which should be done in a sheltered spot outside the harbour. Even though you may feel exhausted, time and energy must be found to furl the sails properly, because if a sudden gust catches the jib while it is lying on deck during a manoeuvre you may lose control. In this, we are not considering the appearance of the yacht, but simply safety. Also important is to have warps and fenders ready and whatever else you might need in harbour.

The anchor should be ready to be let go, even if anchoring is not actually planned. It can come in handy as an emergency brake in case things go wrong. Plenty of warps should be on deck, as well as one or two heaving lines. And in addition to the normal fenders, two emergency fenders should be ready on deck, again in case anything should go wrong.

Regarding water depth, you should consider not only the normal tidal range plus whatever difference the strong wind may make, but also wave height. I would always treat wave height as the full height of the waves, to be on the safe side if you find yourself at the bottom of a particularly deep trough, even if, theoretically, half the wave height should be sufficient. The variation in depth due to the wind depends on the duration of the gale and the length of the inlet. Especially in the case of long inlets or estuaries parallel to the wind direction, the variation in depth can be anything up to a metre. Not only is low water dangerous, but also higher than usual tides that may go over piers or breakwaters. It is rather difficult to moor your boat to an underwater pier.

Some harbourmasters can be contacted on VHF. If so, I would ask about depths and mooring arrangements. I would also ask about lines across the harbour or any other obstacles likely to be encountered. Surprises of this kind can ruin the best planned manoeuvre. If the harbourmaster cannot be reached on VHF, a general call on channel 16 to 'anybody in such-and-such harbour' sometimes gets a surprisingly good response.

Manoeuvring under power

The entrance has to be negotiated quickly, in case of local strong currents. Speed is also necessary to cope with breaking seas in the entrance. If you are pushed off course just outside or in the entrance, you may easily wreck the boat.

Once inside the breakwater, speed has, of course, to be reduced, but adequate steerage way must be maintained. Keeping up steerage way in a confined harbour is a key problem. One would love to stop the boat and have a quick look around, but that is not easy to do.

It is hard to keep the boat's head into the wind. The keel, especially of the modern fin-keeler, is ineffective at low speeds. Once you are stopped it will slip sideways through the water. The rudder has no effect, even if the propeller is pushing water past it, if the keel is ineffective as well. The bows just will not head up into the wind. Instead, the boat slides to leeward.

You can easily stop the boat head to wind if you keep the bow exactly into the wind with the help of the engine. But beware of the bows paying off on either side. The boat will then fall off quickly and you need room to turn the boat upwind again with a good burst of the engine. If you are too cautious with the engine, you may not get back exactly head to wind and the boat will crab sideways. This, on the other hand, may be your intention. You can move the boat into any corner of the harbour in this fashion, sideways, backwards or forwards, as long as the bows are kept into the wind.

Downwind, the only boats that can be held stationary are those that have virtually no propeller effect (the tendency of the propeller to 'walk' the stern to one side, especially when going astern). They can be held stern to wind by going astern on the engine. If the boat veers to one side, you can correct matters with a good kick ahead, which has to be countered immediately by going astern again.

With propeller effect, the stern will always be drawn to one side,

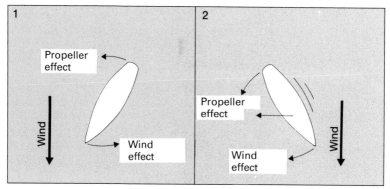

Fig 18.1 Propeller effect prevents a yacht from being held stern to the wind by going astern.

no matter how the boat is lying (Fig 18.1). Once she falls off, the wind will push the boat to that side (Fig 18.1, 2). The boat will thus start to progress sideways. Even with frequent bursts ahead the boat cannot be controlled, as the stern will start to swing again as soon as the engine is put into reverse.

These are the two basic preconditions to being able to cope with situations in harbour: either keep steerage way on the boat or stop head to wind. Head to wind, the boat can be manoeuvred ahead, sideways or astern on to any course without having to pick up speed and steerage way.

Turning in a confined space (Fig 18.2) is accomplished by stopping head to wind, making space in the process to complete the manoeuvre. Be careful not to let her pay off too far before regaining sufficient steerage way.

One exception to this rule is the yacht with a strong propeller

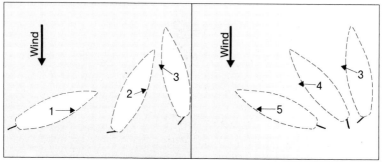

Fig 18.2 Turning in a confined space.

effect. In this case, it may be helpful (if you are turning the right way) to go astern as you come up into the wind to help the boat round. Otherwise it may not be possible to turn through the wind in the space available and the bow may fall back on the original side.

If you are unable to turn in time you could end up in the worst possible situation, broadside on to the wind in some leeward corner of the harbour with no room for manoeuvre and the only remaining resource being a set of good fenders. Short bursts of the engine ahead or astern can improve the angle of impact; contact is then made with the boat moving very slowly and without scraping along the side of a moored yacht or anything else.

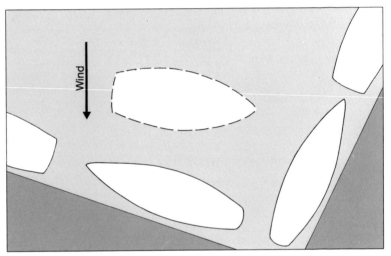

Fig 18.3 Trapped in a leeward corner.

Coming alongside with an onshore wind

You approach at a shallow angle, in terms of the course over the ground. In reality, the bows are turned to windward all the time, more so as speed is reduced (Fig 18.4). The aim is to maintain a straight track over the ground. A touch of throttle helps you to keep to windward. Be careful that the stern, which is to leeward, stays clear of the adjacent yacht (2). Once abeam of the berth, the boat is stopped, if necessary with a good kick astern (3). The wind will now blow the yacht sideways into the berth and all you have to do is make fore-and-aft adjustments. To ensure that bow and stern

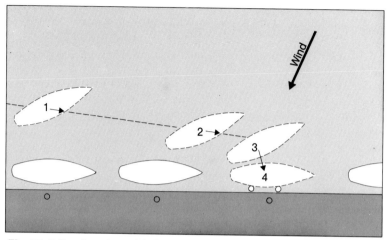

Fig 18.4 Coming alongside in a strong onshore wind.

approach the jetty simultaneously, the heading is corrected with little bursts ahead with the rudder hard over. The rest is done by the fenders.

Coming alongside with an offshore wind

You approach upwind and aim the bows at the forward end of the berth (Fig 18.5). Motoring into the wind, the boat can be kept under perfect control throughout. Someone in the bows signals the number of metres left to the jetty by holding up the corresponding number of fingers. Once within reach, someone takes the lines ashore. The bow line, forward spring and a stern line led forward are made fast ashore. Now motor slowly ahead with the rudder hard over to push the stern towards the jetty. Again, someone should signal the distance off at the bows. Simultaneously, the stern line can be hauled in and the stern pulled towards the jetty. Once alongside the jetty with all lines made fast, this is the ideal berth.

Mooring stern-to

Before motoring stern-first into a berth, the anchor is let go, hopefully in a position where it will not foul one of the neighbouring anchors. The rest is a question of manoeuvring astern, which is not easy with some boats at the best of times and, in a strong sidewind,

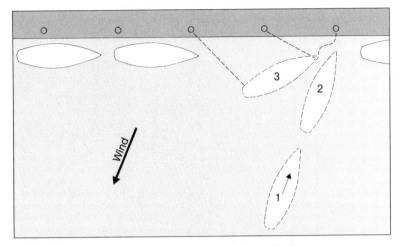

Fig 18.5 Coming alongside in a strong offshore wind.

can be very difficult. Anyone who still wants to try it should at least remember the following tips.

Dropping the anchor a bit to windward is a good idea only if the anchor warps of the neighbouring boats are lying across one another, anyway. If they are lying as they should, nicely parallel, it is far better to avoid messing things up and drop anchor in the middle of the free space between the others. By doing so you will avoid much trouble if, in increasing winds, the neighbouring yachts are forced to up-anchor and raise your anchor in the process.

When going astern, the yacht tends to sheer off as the bow falls off to leeward and the effect of the rudder is minimal. Thus, speed has to be fairly high, which is exciting for both the skipper and the onlookers. The stern has to point to windward, so that the desired course over ground is achieved (Fig 18.6, 1). At the right distance from the berth, the anchor is dropped (2), while maintaining speed astern. Courage! Only when you are closing with the bows of the adjacent yacht should the speed be reduced (3), to soothe the nerves of everybody around. From this point onwards, with help from the neighbouring yachts, the boat can be slowly and carefully manoeuvred stern-first into the berth, disregarding any propeller effect (4).

If you slow down too early, the yacht will sheer off to one side and your propeller will come into the vicinity of the neighbouring anchor cables. The only remedy now is to put the engine out of gear and raise the anchor. The yacht has to be pulled clear of the others by means of her own anchor warp. Then you up-anchor and start

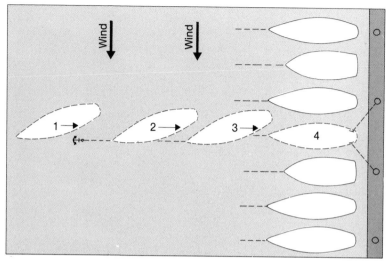

Fig 18.6 Mooring stern-to in a side wind.

anew. Some crews, who obviously have had practice at this, can do the whole thing with the anchor down by dragging the chain across the bottom. Difficult, but possible.

Using the anchor cable as a brake when going astern can help greatly with the steering if a slight pull is always maintained on the cable. The cable has a stabilizing effect on the course if the angle from the vertical is between 30° to 45°. To counteract the wind, the bow points slightly to leeward and the cable correspondingly to windward. Easing the cable will let the bow swing to leeward; tightening it will pull the bow round to windward. But it takes practice to assist with steering from the bows in this way. Oversteering is all too easy and this will cause trouble with the helmsman!

Mooring chains

Mooring chains are like anchor chains laid across the bottom of the harbour at right-angles to the quay. Yachts moor stern-to and you grab the mooring chain where it comes out of the water at the quay and then pass it to the bow where it is made fast to the boat with a short warp.

Easily said. With a strong cross wind, this is not easy. For a start, motoring stern-first into the berth is more difficult, as we

141

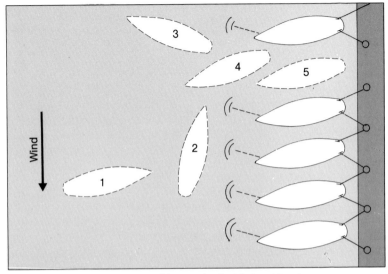

Fig 18.7 Berthing stern-to with a yacht that is hard to steer.

now have no stabilizing effect of an anchor at the bows. To use the anchor where mooring chains are laid in a harbour is unwise, as it is apt to get caught under the heavy ground chains. You will then need the services of a diver, who will probably be lying in wait for customers in harbours thus equipped. A good trick is to unshackle the anchor and use only the chain. Dragging over the bottom, this develops enough friction to help with the steering.

Modern yachts which are responsive to the helm can approach the berth stern-first if they have enough steerage way, but some older long-keeled boats are less easily handled. With these, you will have to approach the berth going ahead (Fig 18.7, 1) and turn through the wind just outside the berth (2), so that you end up slightly to windward of it (3). The wind will then push the bows round as you bring the boat into the berth in reverse gear.

During the last part of the manoeuvre the yacht has to be aimed between the adjacent yachts as just described. To prevent the bow from swinging to leeward while the crew are grabbing the mooring chain, the stern line on the windward quarter is quickly secured ashore and led directly to the windward genoa winch. As soon as this is tight you motor forward very gently and the bow will swing back to where it belongs. If the rudder is turned to one side or the other, another benefit is unveiled: the stern can be moved from one side to the other at will. Fore-and-aft control is achieved, mean-

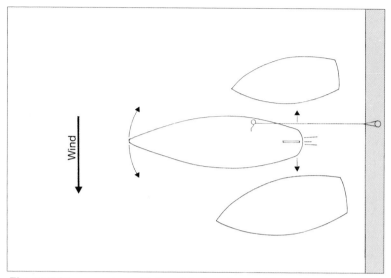

Fig 18.8 Manoeuvring with the aid of engine, rudder and stern line.

while, by adjustment of the stern line. It is surprising how easily the boat can be controlled by one man from the cockpit in this way. The throttle moves the bows; the rudder moves the stern; the genoa winch moves the boat fore and aft (Fig 18.8).

The bow line must be made fast to the mooring chain well ahead. To achieve this, the boat, still motoring against the stern line, is eased forward by 3 m. The bow line is then attached to the chain and the boat finally winched back into the berth. The chain should now be as tight as necessary for the strong wind and your neighbours should be envying your skilful manoeuvre.

Anchoring in an emergency

During the more complicated manoeuvres the anchor should always be ready for use. You will need it, for example, if the engine or controls fail. The only remedy then is to turn head to wind quickly and let go the anchor. It is a matter of nerve and judgement to let out as much chain as the space (probably very restricted) will allow. Every additional foot of chain that is paid out could decide whether the anchor holds or not.

Anchoring as an aid to manoeuvring

With an experienced crew member tending the anchor winch, the anchor can also be used as an aid to manoeuvring into a berth when the approach is downwind (Fig 18.9). The anchor is dropped while the yacht motors slowly ahead and the cable is paid out freely so that the bows are not damaged. As you turn into the wind, the chain is checked then made fast to bring her head to wind. When mooring alongside, the cable can be made to act like a bow thruster, by paying it out or hauling it in.

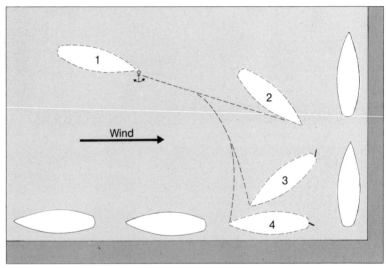

Fig 18.9 Using the anchor as an aid to coming alongside.

Unsuitable propeller shaft arrangements

After all this information about manoeuvres under power (a subject about which a lot more could be said), one major precondition has to be mentioned. Nearly all the manoeuvres described rely on the rudder being directly in the flow of the propeller. Unfortunately, there are many yachts where this is not the case. Some have Z-drives protruding out of the hull a fair distance away from the rudder and some older long-keeled yachts have conventional shaft-drives that are offset to one side of the centreline. The former, in particular, can only be manoeuvred under power with a good amount of steerage way. Turning on one spot is not possible in a controlled manner. I would not enter a crowded harbour with such a yacht in a gale.

Anchoring in shelter

Often, a sheltered bay is the better alternative, as there you do not have to cope with complicated manoeuvres. Instead, one question occupies the mind: will the anchor hold? The answer is that you can never be 100 per cent sure.

We do not want to go over the fundamentals of anchoring here, but let us look at ground tackle. In extreme conditions, this is the most important consideration.

Two anchors are better than one. However, they are a hassle and you should use them to the best advantage. This is not the case if the two anchors are laid out in a 'V' on separate cables. This arrangement only serves to spread the weight of the wind if the anchors are not too far apart and if the wind direction remains

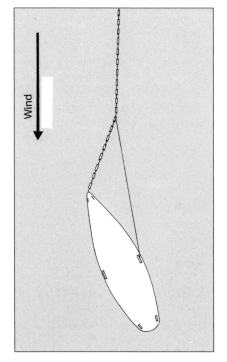

Fig 18.10 Using a spring to reduce sheering at anchor.

constant. Otherwise, only one anchor at a time will bear the full strain.

The better system of ground tackle for gales consists of two anchors in tandem. They should be shackled to the anchor chain at a distance of around 3 m from one another. The chain itself is then let out to its full length. This arrangement uses the full holding power of both anchors all the time, and one will help the other to dig in. Moreover, the friction and damping effect of the full chain is always there.

Anchor winches have sometimes been pulled right out of the deck, especially if the bolts were fairly old. I would therefore always secure the chain with a short strop to some other strong point on deck.

Sheering to and fro when lying at anchor is not only uncomfortable, but it also imposes severe strain on the sternhead fitting. This can be greatly reduced by a spring attached to the anchor chain 5 m from the bows and then led to a cleat amidships. The yacht can then be made to lie at a slight angle to the wind direction and, once the right angle is found, the sheering will stop.

19 Emergencies

Most of us prefer not to think about emergencies as the probability of their occurring is so small. And if it does happen it always happens to someone else. Anyone who thinks like this should think again. Safety equipment is not always expensive and safety drills can even be fun. Someone who devotes some time and thought to possible emergencies will be better able to handle them psychologically and have a better chance of survival in the event of a real emergency.

I would recommend practicing some emergency procedures. One exercise could be trying to enter the liferaft in a wave-pool, or trying to cut through an old piece of shroud-wire, or manoeuvring a yacht out of shallows into deeper water (at first only in calm weather). Man overboard drill can be practised in higher waves with a fender. This is the only way to gain experience.

The distress situations dealt with in this chapter are only those that typically arise in heavy weather, or that will take a significantly different course if they occur in gale force winds. Again, we will not be concerned with basic seamanship.

Man overboard attached by a harness

Man overboard is the most common and critical of all distress situations. In bad weather the threat to life is immediate and the chance of rescue not always high.

First the easiest case: somebody is in the water alongside the boat, but still attached by their harness. The method of getting this person back on board makes use of the fact that to leeward the water comes quite close to the deck. The person in the water will accordingly be lifted up to deck height from time to time and with a little luck and a little skill can pull himself aboard the boat, rolling on to the deck underneath the lifelines. Someone on deck can help by grabbing his clothes and pulling. The whole thing needs to be done rather quickly, as being dragged through the water at 6 knots is nobody's idea of fun. The harness bites into you; you are half-submerged and it is difficult to get air into the lungs.

If the person in the water is not strong enough to manage by himself, someone grabs the lanyard and pulls him out of the water. The legs will be swept upwards by the force of the water. He can then be rolled on to the deck, if necessary using the boathook for further assistance. The boathook will get a hold on a person's clothing if it is twisted.

If the casualty is on the windward side, the yacht is put about without touching the jibsheet. Then the boat will be hove-to on the new tack and again heeling towards the person in the water. You can then pull him on board in much the same way. As the water will not be streaming past as fast, his legs will not be swept upwards. The boathook can help again when hooked into a trouser leg.

If a long line led aft from the mast is used as an attachment point for harnesses, it should be of such a length that anyone who falls overboard will be alongside the cockpit.

Man overboard separated from the boat

The usual manoeuvre is useless in gale conditions, as you would have to sail too far to leeward and would have great difficulty in getting back to the casualty to windward. The main thing is to stay close and keep up to windward.

Fig 19.1 Man overboard. Tacking immediately to a hove-to position.

You must make sure that the casualty is kept in view all the time. In as little as 10 seconds or less, the person could have vanished behind a wave. This is why reactions have to be automatic and quick. The helmsman must throw the yacht hard about on to the other tack, riding hove-to with the jib aback, while shouting 'Man overboard' as loudly as possible. If a fog horn or some other sound signalling device is to hand, this too can be used to raise the alarm.

Tacking immediately to a hove-to position is the best way to keep in contact with the person in the water (Fig 19.1). If alone, the helmsman now throws the danbuoy overboard, but does not touch any other gear. At short intervals he takes bearings of the casualty using the steering compass, to help find him again should he be hidden behind a wave.

As long as he is alone on deck, the helmsman should avoid everything that makes him take his eye off the person in the water. Whether he can start the engine or not depends on the boat. On some yachts you have to go below to start the engine, or dive into some deep locker. In that case it is better to leave the engine alone and keep on watching the casualty. On the other hand, if you can start the engine, the boat could be driven straight to windward without losing any more ground.

Under no circumstances would I try to manoeuvre the boat singlehanded under sail. This could be quite dangerous for the person in the water.

Ideally the yacht will be hove-to within throwing distance of the man overboard, but this can only be achieved if the helmsman's reaction is instantaneous and the boat is either on a beam reach or

Fig 19.2 Man overboard. An ideal situation where the boat is hove-to within throwing distance.

149

sailing to windward. If this is the case, obviously the helmsman will throw a line to the casualty. If alone on deck, the helmsman has to throw the line once the boat is hove-to.

When the rest of the crew emerge on deck they can be organized into a rescue team. If it has not been done already, the engine should be started and the boat headed flat out towards the person in the water, not forgetting to check first for any lines trailing over the side.

In this hectic situation, a clear division of labour is vitally important. One crew should be responsible for watching the casualty, one to help in the cockpit and someone should be in overall command.

Working to windward against wind and sea can be extremely difficult. Of course, the sheet of the jib which has been aback will be freed, but the engine may still only be powerful enough to stop the boat going backwards, and maybe not even that. If you cannot make progress under engine alone, the boat has to be sailed to windward, possible now that all hands are on deck. If tacks are necessary, they should be kept very short. Sight of the person in the water must never be lost.

The textbook manoeuvre of shooting straight up into the wind next to the casualty will probably not succeed in these conditions. Even worse, the yacht could fall off a wave backwards and damage the rudder. Instead, the yacht has to be manoeuvred into a position hove-to to windward of the casualty.

The engine is used in conjunction with heaving-to to position the yacht correctly. In an emergency like this, the engine is used even in the near vicinity of the person in the water, but obviously with great caution. The helmsman keeps a constant watch on the casualty and will knock the engine out of gear whenever necessary.

The jib is kept sheeted in during the manoeuvre, so that the yacht will heel towards the person in the water. I would try to roll him on to the deck in the manner already described above. It might be easier to use a boarding ladder at the stern, but the yacht will probably be pitching so violently that the chances of being injured are higher than those of being able to use the ladder. In either case, a line is first thrown to the person or, even better, two or three lines, so that he can be sure of reaching at least one and tie himself to it. By the way it is a mistake to throw a light floating line in a gale. It will just be blown away. A good heavy sheet or warp is much better, even if it will not float.

If the casualty is already running out of strength, a second crew member must get into the water, securely tied to the boat of course, and tie the victim on with his line. To get him back on board, the spinnaker halyard or a block and tackle attached to the shrouds can be used.

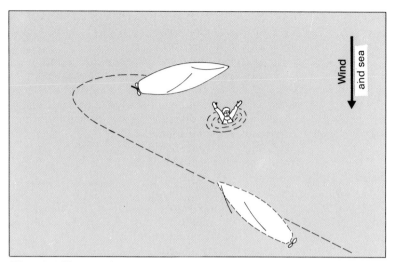

Fig 19.3 Man overboard. Heaving-to to windward.

The use of rescue equipment in rough conditions is not always straightforward. With the possible exception of the danbuoy, there is not even time to deploy items ready for use on the pushpit at the instant when the accident happens. During a gale the helmsman would lose sight of the casualty in the water while he was untying the lifebuoy and heaving line. And untie he has to, as most of the standard quick-release fastenings are useless in gales and the equipment often has to be secured by extra lashings.

The opportunity to sort out the rescue equipment will come as you approach the person in the water. By then all hands are on deck and someone can actually release all the necessary items. But even then there are snags. Use of the heaving line is only sensible if you plan to pass very close to the person, as in Fig 19.3. As you pass him and heave-to to windward, the line is pulled around him in a semicircle. This is ideal, but if the yacht were head to wind next to him, the line would just stream out astern. And if the swimmer did manage to grab the line after a misjudged attempt to luff into the wind, he would soon have to let go as the yacht bore off automatically and gathered way again. So use of the heaving line can be recommended only when heaving-to.

The lifebuoy can only be thrown a very small distance without being carried off by the wind.

The manoeuvre described here is generally suitable for the average modern cruising yacht, but it is not the only alternative. For other types of yacht and larger or smaller crews, variations may be necessary. But the basic rule remains the same: stay close and keep in sight of the person in the water.

I recommend every skipper to find out the best way of rescuing someone in the water for his individual boat and then practise the manoeuvre with his crew. Explaining the procedure to the crew should be part of the normal safety briefing or, as I personally prefer, the topic of a relaxed discussion during the first quiet night watch or the first coffee break at the start of a cruise.

Search patterns

It is easy to imagine what kind of stress attends a real man overboard situation. The object of recovery is not just an old lifejacket used for practice, but a human being. And not just anyone; it's Chris or Susan!

If, in spite of everything, the person is lost from view, then things really get bad. Fear and panic easily set in. Ill-considered reactions are likely, and dangerous. Steering blindly towards the point where the casualty is wrongly believed to have been seen last or random searching to and fro only costs precious time. It can also cost an unrealized amount of leeway, which could be fatal.

Using the bearing taken on the steering compass, you look hard in that direction and try to pick him out again. If you have not seen anything after three waves have passed, every other manoeuvre has to be abandoned immediately and the boat headed, as long as it is not already too far off, along the direction of that bearing. Time and log reading are recorded so that someone can keep track of your position by dead reckoning and work out a rough ETA at the person in the water. If this estimated position is reached without finding him, a clear search pattern has to be instituted at once. One tends towards wishful thinking in these situations and hanging about in the estimated position for too long, which could, after all, be wrong anyway.

Obviously, it is wrong if you cannot find the casualty. So you must widen your search area, without missing out any of it. There are several possible search patterns. The following one is best suited for our purposes as it stays close to the position of the accident and does not require much navigation.

The search begins about 50 or 100 m to windward of the estimated position of the person. With the help of the engine you will get there with one or two tacks of one minute duration. The starting point is marked with a buoy. If the danbuoy is already in the

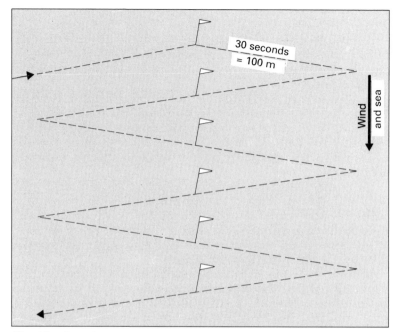

30 seconds = 100 m

Wind and sea

Fig 19.4 Search pattern. Marker buoy drifts steadily to leeward.

water, you can use fenders, cushions or buoyancy-aids, with a warp attached to act as a sea anchor. It is best to deploy two or three of these marks, so that you can at least find one of them again later.

From this point, the yacht sails off on a course which corresponds roughly to 100° off the wind over the ground (the burgee will be showing a beam reach). The seconds are counted off from the point of departure. After 30 seconds, which is 100 m at 6 knots, the yacht is tacked back towards the marker buoy, sailed beyond it for a further 30 seconds, and then tacked again. The boat sails to and fro in this way slowly getting further to leeward with the drift of the buoy. The drift of the buoy moves the search continuously to leeward. If the buoy drifts to leeward at 1 knot, the legs of the search are 35 m apart in the middle and 70 m at the extremes. This is as much as it should be and the yacht should not be sailed on one tack longer in an effort to try to enlarge the area covered.

Of prime importance for the success of this search is, again, a clear division of labour. The helmsman is responsible for the accuracy of the search pattern, and so he or she watches the course, keeps an eye on the marker buoy, counts the seconds and tacks the yacht. The rest of the crew scan individual sectors of the water.

After six legs a square of roughly 200 by 200 m has been covered, centred on estimated position of the accident. (This position, incidentally, has no set to leeward, as the drift of a person in the water is next to nothing.)

If the search pattern has not led to finding the person, it has to be repeated in an adjacent sector. Obviously, the search will start where, on the available evidence, the probability of success is highest. I would not widen the search pattern too quickly, as the mesh gets wider and the risk of missing the person increases accordingly.

To repeat the search pattern, the estimated position of the accident has to be reached by very precise dead reckoning. This position is most important. Then the marker buoy is deployed and the search begun again. At the start of the second search pattern, at the latest, a navigator should be appointed to plot courses and the whole search pattern on the chart.

Modern electronic navigation systems, such as Decca or GPS, have a special man overboard (MOB) facility that can be activated easily, often by pressing a single button. If the boat has such a system the crew should be briefed on how to activate it and thus fix the exact position of the accident. In the event of a real shout of 'Man overboard', the first person who passes the set hits the MOB button. The display will continuously show the bearing and distance of the casualty.

Even better are sets that have a plotting mode which allows the course of the search to be displayed on screen. The point at which the button is pressed is also shown, so the search can be accurately controlled.

Lastly, a word on outside help. Other boats, planes or rescue craft are not likely to be involved in the initial search pattern. But should it prove necessary to abandon this in favour of a wider search, outside help becomes vitally important. So no time should be wasted in contacting the relevant search and rescue organization so they can assess the situation and start the appropriate action.

It is important to maintain radio contact in order to co-ordinate the yacht's own search with measures taken by others. In some cases it may be best for the yacht to stay at the estimated position of the accident to act as a beacon for approaching planes and rescue vessels.

Leaks

Water ingress is another emergency that is particularly relevant to
a book about heavy weather for two reasons. First, at times of bad
weather you are more likely to encounter dangerous floating
objects that have been lost overboard from the deck of ships, that
can easily hole your boat. Second, water inside the boat develops
totally exceptional characteristics in rough seas. A sea will develop
inside the boat. You will have breakers below decks. By the time
the water is high enough to float the floor boards, all hell will have
broken loose down below!

As soon as rising bilge water is discovered emergency measures
must be taken. In this case, all available crew members are sent to
different corners of the boat to check seacocks and search for the
leak. All through-hull fittings, not only those with seacocks, should
be checked, as well as pipes and hoses leading away from them, like
cockpit drains, exhaust pipe, transducers, and the outlets for the
bilge pumps. Due to the violent motion of the boat, something can
easily come undone or break. Bear in mind that extreme angles of
heel can put skin fittings that are normally above the waterline,
like pump outlets, under water. After pumping, the water can then
flow back into the boat through the pump. This happens frequently
with pumps without a non-return valve.

Things are really serious if the leak is not detected soon enough.
In the 1970s a beautiful large classic yacht was lost in the
Skagerrak for this reason. The water was only discovered after a
maelstrom had already become established below decks. Nobody
could have gone below without being injured by floating fittings
and furniture. There was no chance of finding the leak, even less of
repairing it. The crew were taken off and the boat sank.

With incidents like this in mind, there can be no doubting the
necessity to check the bilges frequently during heavy weather. The
bilge check should be included in the normal watch routine.
Automatic bilge pumps are activated once the water has risen to a
certain level, but it would be safer if an alarm was also sounded.

What if, in spite of everything, a large amount of water is found
sloshing about in the cabin? There is only one thing to do: pump as
fast as possible, and use buckets as well. The people bailing should
stand in the water, if necessary harnessed to the companionway. As
long as your head is above water you can bail out more water with
a bucket than any pump. So don't hesitate to get down into it.

If the leak is in the bows a sail can be pulled underneath the hull
from on deck. I recommend that you practise it first at 6 knots in a
moderate sea! But it works. I once used a No 2 jib, with the tack

attached by a short length of rope to the bow fitting. Two men, one on either side, kept hold of the head and clew respectively. The jib was thrown into the water ahead of the bow and was pulled beneath the boat by the flow of water. The two people holding on to head and clew were then able to position the sail in the right place.

With flooding, you also have to be prepared for the batteries to be flat and the VHF to be dead. For this reason it is advisable to send out a preliminary message stating the situation and the measures taken, even if things do not look too dramatic at the time, not forgetting to give your position. At short intervals you can then confirm that everything is under control and finally cancel the distress message once the emergency is over. Should the VHF fail, on the other hand, the alarm will then be raised and a rescue operation started.

Most rescue craft can provide submersible pumps of very large capacity. If you can keep the yacht afloat until the arrival of this kind of help, you have basically won. These pumps are connected by a long cable to the electricity supply of the rescue vessel. All you have to do is put them into the water.

Abandoning ship

The decision to abandon ship and take to the liferaft or have the crew taken off should only be taken in a case of extreme necessity. Two fundamental mistakes are often made. One is to abandon the yacht prematurely (19 of the 24 yachts abandoned in the 1979 Fastnet Race were later found afloat) and the other is to alert the rescue services too late. The latter would happen less often if certain yachtsmen rid themselves of the misconception that you do not put out a distress call until you are ready to abandon ship.

An initial PAN PAN call if you are beginning to get into trouble is justifiable and incurs no cost. On the contrary, it helps the rescue services to get organized and be at the scene in double-quick time should a real emergency arise. Should the need not arise after all, so much the better.

Early VHF contact has further advantages. The crews of the rescue vessels are experts and know the area intimately. They can give valuable advice on where to head for shelter in the prevailing conditions and which areas should be avoided. You can have your progress monitored and even arrange a rendezvous.

If the rescue service knows in advance where and who the potential casualties are, everything can be better co-ordinated and planned. The lifeboat might even go to a central position if several boats were in danger and then dash to whoever hit serious trouble first.

Again, VHF contact is important. If it is made at an early stage, the stress factor is reduced and it is easier to describe the situation calmly and precisely. Do not hesitate to use channel 16. It is there to be used, even if, hopefully, you have no MAYDAY to transmit. Sometimes contact is lost when changing to another channel. More important, the direction-finding apparatus of some stations ashore, as well as rescue vessels, only operates on channel 16.

Once contact is established with the rescue services, your situation might not seem quite as bleak. The decision to abandon ship may not be so imminent anymore. It may still be considered as an option, but now less precipitately. More important now are the possibilities of assistance from the rescue service – monitoring your position, escorting you, providing pumps, towing, or taking off sick or injured, to name only a few.

Launching the liferaft

Only when all else fails is it time to launch the liferaft. Normally, this is only for one of two reasons: either the boat is on fire or it is sinking.

Bear in mind that, on a yacht prepared for a gale, the liferaft is not generally ready for instant deployment. It is usually securely lashed down or stowed away. A typical raft weighs between 30 and 40 kg, so you should not ask the smallest person on board to fetch it. It is placed in the cockpit so that it does not get washed overboard by a wave. The crew don warm clothes, oilskins and lifejackets. A signalling torch and all available distress flares should be taken, and, as it can take some time for you to be rescued, food and fresh water.

Meanwhile, someone transmits a MAYDAY call. I would suggest having the boat's position checked by a second person. At a time of extreme stress it is easy to make mistakes. This one could prove fatal.

The raft should be launched to leeward. If it inflates to windward the wind will blow it into the yacht and it could be damaged before you have even got into it. When boarding the raft keep it well clear of the stanchions. It is easiest to jump face down on to the canopy of the raft, even if it may be painful for those already inside. Secure yourself by a line first, otherwise it is all too easy to miss the raft in a heaving sea. Practise this in a swimming pool.

Rescue by lifeboat

While the lifeboat is on its way maintain constant VHF communication, covering the position, drift and condition of the yacht, as well as her distinguishing features, the number of persons on board and details of any injured. The lifeboat should be told everything. The situation is discussed in detail and preparations made, such as making ready to secure a tow rope or streaming a sea anchor to steady the boat during the final approach of the lifeboat. You may be asked to fire a flare or smoke signal.

Once the lifeboat is on the scene, the coxswain will assess the situation and suggest suitable actions. The skipper of the yacht is normally well advised to follow these suggestions, but not obliged to do so.

Whatever happens, the lifeboat will probably try and pass a line. This will be needed for towing or taking people off. To pass the line, the lifeboat will probably manoeuvre close astern of the yacht. Should the crew of the yacht be depleted by injury or exhaustion, the lifeboat's inflatable dinghy will be used to put one of the lifeboat's crew on board. Only as a very last resort would the lifeboat itself try to come alongside the yacht. In heavy seas the two boats would inevitably collide, causing great damage.

A tow rope line will always be handed over by the lifeboat, attached to a heaving line by which the crew of the yacht can pull it on board. The lifeboat will probably stay clear and astern of the yacht during this procedure. Only when the tow rope has been taken forward on the yacht and made fast will the lifeboat move ahead of the yacht and take up the tow.

Should individual crew members or even the entire crew have to be taken on board the lifeboat, this will usually be done in the following manner. The lifeboat stands a short distance off while the line is passed from its bows to the yacht. The crew should be ready to leave the yacht, meaning that they are wearing warm clothing and lifejackets and have everything with them that they need. The first person is now attached to the line and jumps into the water. This short ducking cannot be avoided unless the boats are allowed to collide. The lifeboat crew will pull you on board almost before you know it. Once you are on deck, the line is passed to the yacht again and it is the next person's turn.

Only if injured or exhausted people have to be taken off will the lifeboat vessel use its inflatable. It can be launched in any weather, but not necessarily retrieved again. In that case the dinghy will follow in the wake of the mother vessel until some sheltered spot is reached.

The dinghy can come alongside the yacht more safely, although the impact can still be severe. Crossing from one boat to the other is consequently difficult and dangerous. It may still be easier to be pulled across in the water, rather than risk being squashed between the boats.

Rescue by ship

If a ship has agreed to take the yacht's crew on board, the task is much more difficult. One of the problems is that big ships cannot manoeuvre easily in heavy seas. Whether they can handle beam-seas or not depends on their state of loading. Some ships roll heavily in beam-seas, worst of all when they are stopped. This rolling is dangerous for the cargo and the crew. On the other hand, heavily laden supertankers lie nearly still in all sea conditions. These are ideal for giving shelter in their lee.

One can imagine how difficult it is to manoeuvre a big ship alongside a small yacht in reduced visibility. Ships are not designed for this kind of work at close quarters, even without the problem of poor visibility. Stopping a large vessel in the open sea with any precision is often impossible. Crews of ships may not be practised at such manoeuvres.

Rescue equipment normally may not be ready to hand and has probably not been used for a very long time. Passing a line to the yacht is not easy under these circumstances. It is hard to launch a ship's lifeboat in a heavy sea, and even more difficult to retrieve it again. Inflatable dinghies are normally not carried on cargo ships (though they are more frequently on warships, which are generally better equipped for dealing with emergencies).

If a ship does succeed in coming alongside a yacht, you have to expect the yacht to be smashed against the ship's side in the heavy seas. As both vessels are rolling and pitching, the collisions will be extremely violent. Even though the yacht may be regarded as a total loss anyway, it creates a highly dangerous situation for her crew. Climbing straight up a boarding ladder from the yacht's deck may well be impossible. The yacht will be rising and falling several metres and only someone extremely fit and strong could grab the ladder at the moment when the yacht is at the top of a swell and scramble clear before the yacht comes up the next time. And even then he would still be in danger, as the mast would be constantly smashing into the ship's side, seriously endangering anyone hanging there. Someone once told me that the only thing to do in these circumstances is to wait below deck until the mast has come down, which does not take very long. I don't think he was joking.

What is the answer? VHF contact is again vital so that the options can be discussed, but not many are available. The ship will probably try and approach at an angle of 30° to the wind and stop abeam of the yacht between 10 and 50 m to windward. Lines will be thrown, probably by several crew members simultaneously.

The crew of the yacht, in the meantime, should have prepared themselves for being taken aboard the freighter. As, in the circumstances, it will probably not be possible to have one line each for every crew member, I would tell my crew to tie themselves together by their harnesses.

Once the attempt to catch a line from the ship has been successful, quick action is needed. The crew, now securely tied together, attach themselves to the line and jump into the water. The group can then be hauled aboard the ship or can board via a ladder or nets.

If the yacht drifts against the ship's side during the manoeuvre, the crew will have to be picked up from the foredeck or the cockpit in such a way that nobody can get caught in the shrouds. You will have to hold on to the yacht with all your strength, as the impacts against the side of the ship will be violent. The ship's crew must then pull the whole group of you clear of the yacht. Make sure that you are not pulled directly upwards toward the ship's deck, as you could be caught by the mast still smashing against the ship's side. It is vital to signal clearly to the men above to pull you clear of the yacht, either astern from the cockpit or ahead from the foredeck. Just make sure you get well clear of the yacht!

An alternative would be to use the liferaft. You should ask the master of the ship whether he would prefer this method. Once in sight of the ship, the crew abandon the yacht and board the liferaft. The freighter will now head for the liferaft and lines are thrown again. The advantage is that you cannot be crushed by your own boat, but the disadvantage is just as obvious: passing a line to the small liferaft is even more difficult than getting it to the much bigger yacht. Moreover, there is no turning back once the yacht has been abandoned. You cannot paddle the raft upwind towards the freighter, as the wind will always blow it to leeward and, due to the pockets under water that stabilize it against capsize, it has a lot of water resistance.

If a line cannot be passed across to the yacht, the chances of rescue are very slim. At this stage the ship may attempt to come even closer to the yacht, even at the risk of a collision. If you are within range of air-sea rescue services, the master may decide to ask for the assistance of a helicopter.

To abandon the yacht when no line has been passed and to try and reach the ship by swimming should only be considered as a very last resort. It would have to be with the crew tied together and swimming on their backs. With an inflated lifejacket, this is the only way you can swim, but you make little progress through the water.

Rescue by helicopter

A helicopter is the ideal rescue vehicle, provided it can reach the scene. It has a rather restricted range and is liable to icing. These are the only handicaps. A helicopter can take people off boats in any seas, often without even getting their feet wet.

The helicopter will lower a sling in which you can install yourself and then be winched upwards. This is the principle. In detail, the whole operation again begins with VHF contact to enable the helicopter to take RDF bearings of the yacht and to discuss subsequent events. Very probably, the helicopter pilot will give clear instructions on how things should be prepared and carried out. Generally, there is not much time. Hovering over the yacht, the helicopter uses as much fuel as when flying along. The crew should therefore be ready to be taken off and loose items on deck should be secured. Everyone should be wearing a lifejacket and have any few personal belongings inside his clothing. Do not forget the vessel's papers and logbook. These may be needed to sort things out later. The sequence of leaving the yacht has to be agreed. The first to leave the yacht should be somebody who is confident of being able to handle the situation. His or her example is important to help the others follow suit. The last to leave is the person organizing matters on the yacht.

The helicopter always approaches from leeward. The lifting strop will be touching the water. This prevents you from getting an electric shock off the cable. The winchman in the helicopter looks down and directs it over the yacht.

The cable is caught as soon as possible, perhaps using the boat-hook. Take care because the helicopter is stationary while the yacht is going up and down in the waves. For this reason the cable should be caught while the yacht is in a trough. The wire will inevitably slip through your hands a couple of times, so gloves are a good idea. When the sling is on board, the cable should be lying slack in the water.

It is essential to avoid getting the cable caught around any part of the boat or rigging. If the winchman starts to wave frantically, it

The Coastguard constantly practice helicopter rescues to keep skills honed to the precision needed for lifting survivors from stricken vessels in heaving seas. *Photo: HM Coastguard.*

probably means that you are about to do just this.

The sling is put on so that the cable is at the front. It lifts the body under the armpits. The elbows, therefore, have to be held down. The hands remain free, but you can cross them in front of your chest for further security. Sometimes the sling has another smaller loop attached at the front that can be pulled downwards as an extra safety measure.

Once you are in the sling, no time is wasted. The thumbs up sign is given and the ascent begins. Again care should be taken that the cable does not get caught anywhere while it is being winched in, for example, under a cleat or behind the wheel. Dangers lurk everywhere. The helicopter may pull you sideways, inevitably ducking you in the water. This may be necessary to clear the mast, stays or other parts of the boat. Imagine what would happen if you were to swing around the backstay and become entangled. The winchman will then have to use the emergency cable release which is devised for exactly this contingency.

Dangling in the air clear of the yacht, you will feel surprisingly secure in the sling. Experience shows that there is no fear or dizziness. You look upwards at the winchman who will pull you safely on board. The technique that he will use, because it is the easiest method, is to turn you so that you are facing outwards and pull you in backwards.

This is not the moment to say thank you. The winchman cannot hear a word through his helmet anyway and he will already be concentrating on getting the next person up off the yacht.

Stranding

This is a topic which is not much discussed in sailing circles. In an old heavy weather manual dating back to the turn of the century, the following advice is given: 'If stranding cannot be avoided any longer, do it thoroughly and with plenty of way on. Pick a spot without rocks, take the largest wave and head under full sail as far up the beach as possible, so that the next wave will not cause you any further harm.'

This is a summing up. The important thing is to keep calm, even in the dreadful situation where running ashore can no longer be avoided, and to try and minimize the damage. I know of several stranded yachts that were later pulled off the beach again, having suffered no serious damage apart from scratched topsides.

Stranding occurs when a yacht is driven on to a lee shore by some mishap. Before it happens, of course, every effort is made to try and get away from the shore. You sail to windward as accurately as possible, maintaining sufficient speed and keeping leeway to a minimum. The engine is run at full throttle to give assistance. You must cut through the breakers to avoid being driven shorewards by them. If you are towing a dinghy, cut it loose.

Without an engine or with impaired sailing ability, you must face the fact that you will probably not make it. You may have to consider anchoring. With a lot of luck, this could prevent stranding. Without drawing attention to it, you should already be watching the shore. Study rocks, beaches and cliffs while the yacht, in her fight to get clear, beats up and down the coast. The more immediate the danger becomes, the more you should keep a relatively hospitable piece of coastline to leeward and, if possible, one also affording good holding ground for the anchor.

The second anchor is shackled on to the chain above the main anchor and both are made ready for use. In this dire situation, two anchors are better than one.

Anchoring is the last chance to avoid stranding. That is why it has to be planned and executed carefully. Just letting go the anchor in the heat of the moment would be unwise. Many things have to be considered. Where is the best holding ground? What is the right depth of water? The water should not be so deep that there is not enough cable for the anchor to bite, but it should not be too shallow either. The damping effect of the chain is also needed. The best spot could be inshore of the first breakers. The sea there has lost some of its violence. But will it still be deep enough? At all events, don't anchor in the main area of breakers, but if possible further out. Bear in mind the advantage of having a clear area to leeward, free of rocks, in case the anchor does not hold.

Anchoring should be done carefully. The second anchor is let go first and the main anchor follows. The chain is paid out under control, with a slight check kept upon it so there is not too much of a snatch at the end. Otherwise the chain could easily jump off the winch. All the chain is paid out, the sails are lowered and you keep your fingers crossed.

But do not waste time just hoping! Now is the time to use all the tricks in the book to try and start the engine. Every skipper should know how to bleed the fuel system, change filters or take fuel directly from a can.

If the anchors do not hold, the moment of truth has come. A second attempt at anchoring will be futile, if the first has failed. It would be wiser to use the last remaining bit of sea room to control where you go ashore. The object now is to get the boat on to the shore in one piece and as high up as possible, so that it is out of reach of breaking waves. If she grounds too early, she will be pounded by the waves and seriously damaged.

Check the shore for a spot with the least surf. This is probably where the bottom will be cleanest. Hoist the jib, slip the anchor cable, and the boat will gather way towards the chosen spot. She should be moving quite fast when she hits the shore. Hold on tight before the crash. The impact with the bottom will be quite violent. Anyone who is not holding on tightly will be thrown forwards, hopefully not into anything.

Once the first shock is over, it is time to take stock. How is the yacht lying? On soft ground or is a rock grinding at her hull? As long as she is still being lifted by the incoming waves, she can be moved. Lines are taken ashore, tied to rocks, trees or whatever else is available and led back to the genoa winches and hauled in very tight. Every time a wave lifts her keel, the yacht will move in the direction of the warps.

The next concern is the tide. If you are stranded on a falling tide, you have a short interval in which to think things over. If the tide is rising the next decision has to be made. One possibility is to pull the yacht farther up the shore on the rising tide, and secure her on the beach with the kedge anchor. The other is to try and float her off again. The latter sounds tempting, but can only work if the surf decreases quickly and if strong ground tackle is available.

For detailed advice on refloating a beached yacht refer to *Running aground and getting afloat*, published by Adlard Coles Nautical.

Final thoughts

The book ends on a rather pessimistic note with distress, which is quite unintentional. A last word of encouragement seems appropriate.

We have looked at meteorology, heavy weather phenomena, technical considerations, preparing the boat, crewing, and handling the boat at sea, on the approach to land and in harbour. All aspects of heavy weather have been described, analyzed and discussed. Perhaps, for some readers, the subject has now lost some of its mystery.

The author's aim has been to increase understanding of what is going on in a gale. If you understand what is happening you are less likely to be taken by surprise. Surprise may lead to a wrong decision that, in turn, can lead to tragedy. However, with knowledge and the confidence it brings, almost any situation can be mastered.

Knowledge also helps one to assess one's own capabilities. Some may now look forward to the next spell of heavy weather with greater confidence; others, perhaps, with rather less enthusiasm than before. In either case, the book will have achieved something.

Sailing should not be the subject of too much dogma. Apart from the laws of science, which are unalterable, opinions differ on many points. It is good for these opinions to be exchanged, compared, tested and, from time to time, changed. This is a constructive process.

Anyway, in some way or other, hopefully, the reader will have profited from reading this book. Next time it blows, he will be ready for it!